Food Power

Food Power

The Rise and Fall of the Postwar

American Food System

BRYAN L. McDONALD

OXFORD
UNIVERSITY PRESS

OXFORD
UNIVERSITY PRESS

Oxford University Press is a department of the University of Oxford. It furthers
the University's objective of excellence in research, scholarship, and education
by publishing worldwide. Oxford is a registered trade mark of Oxford University
Press in the UK and certain other countries.

Published in the United States of America by Oxford University Press
198 Madison Avenue, New York, NY 10016, United States of America.

© Oxford University Press 2017

Library of Congress Cataloging-in-Publication Data
Names: McDonald, Bryan (Bryan L.), author.
Title: Food power : the rise and fall of the postwar American food system / Bryan L. McDonald.
Description: New York, NY : Oxford University Press, [2017] |
Includes bibliographical references and index.
Identifiers: LCCN 2016021508 (print) | LCCN 2016033628 (ebook) |
ISBN 9780190600686 (hardcover : alk. paper) | ISBN 9780190600693 (Updf) |
ISBN 9780190600709 (Epub)
Subjects: LCSH: Agriculture and state—United States—History—20th century. |
Agriculture—Economic aspects—United States—History—20th century. |
Agriculture and politics—United States—History—20th century. |
Food supply—United States—History—20th century. |
Food security—United States—History—20th century. | United States—Foreign relations.
Classification: LCC HD1761 .M26 2017 (print) | LCC HD1761 (ebook) |
DDC 338.1/97309045—dc23
LC record available at https://lccn.loc.gov/2016021508

9 8 7 6 5 4 3 2 1
Printed by Sheridan Books, Inc., United States of America

For my parents

CONTENTS

ACKNOWLEDGMENTS

This book was conceived and written at Penn State University and its nature and responsibilities as a land-grant institution—and my resulting ability to draw on colleagues from humanities, social sciences, and agricultural sciences—deeply informed my thinking as I wrote. In the Penn State history department, I want to thank William Blair, Gary Cross, Greg Eghigian, Lori Ginzberg, Amy Greenberg, Tony Kaye, Ari Kelman, and Michael Kulikowski. I am also grateful to other colleagues at Penn State who provided encouragement from a variety of perspectives and helped ensure the fidelity of my reading across disciplines, including Mia Bloom, Leland Glenna, John Horgan, Jonathan Marks, Anastasia Shcherbakova, Susan Squier, Donald Thompson, Nancy Tuana, and Steve Walton. I am especially grateful to Eric Novotny and the staff at the Penn State University Libraries for their assistance in locating sources and unearthing needed materials from the archives. I also appreciate the helpful advice and support from scholars outside Penn State and across diverse disciplines, including Kent Hughes Butts, Nick Cullather, Geoff Dabelko, Gregory Domber, Kristin Hoganson, Sheyda Jahanbani, Tim Luke, Richard Matthew, Char Miller, Adam Rome, and Ken Rutherford.

I received research support from a number of sources that greatly facilitated the completion of this book. I am particularly thankful for resources provided by an Early Career Professorship in the Rock Ethics Institute that was made possible by a generous gift from Douglas and Joyce Sherwin. I also received support from the Department of History at Penn State and the Haag Family Fund at Penn State. Important work on this manuscript was completed during a one semester residential fellowship from the Penn State's Institute for Arts and the Humanities and I am grateful for the support and community provided by the Institute.

I am grateful for helpful comments provided by anonymous reviewers from Oxford University Press. Their suggestions helped enormously in improving the final manuscript. Susan Ferber at Oxford University Press was an outstanding editor and I appreciate her diligence and assistance with the development of this book. I am also grateful to Maya Bringe from Newgen North America for her assistance in moving the book through the production process.

I also want to thank my family for their love and support during the writing of this book.

Food Power

Introduction

Food Power, the Food Network,
and American Security

In 1951, the Czekalinski family of Cleveland, Ohio, posed in a photo depicting all the food they might eat in a year. Gathered in the cold-storage locker of the West Ninth Street warehouse of the Great Atlantic and Pacific Tea Company, Steve, his wife Stephanie, and their sons Stephen and Henry wore coats against the cold and were surrounded by two and a half tons of food, including 698 quarts of milk, 578 pounds of meat, 131 dozen eggs, 56 pounds of butter, 72 pounds of shortening, 180 loaves of bread, more than 1,000 pounds of vegetables, and 400 pounds of fresh fruit, plus sugar, flour, cereal, coffee, and more. Steve, who worked in the shipping department of DuPont's Cleveland plant, earned $1.95 an hour, and the family spent about $25 a week, or $1,300 a year, on food.[1]

The photo and accompanying article, "Why We Eat Better," were conceived by public relations officials at DuPont for their internal magazine, *Better Living*, in order to show the bounty of foods available to an average American industrial worker with an average size family. The photo of the Czekalinski family was the centerpiece of the article, positioned on a two-page spread that also included insets showing the foods that were unavailable to the families of average workers in England, Belgium, Germany, Poland, and China.[2] The picture was subsequently printed in *Life* in 1951, reprinted or described in a number of newspapers in the early 1950s, used again by DuPont in 1975, and then selected in 1998 by Harold Evans, the editor of *U.S. News & World Report*, as the image of the century.[3] In addition to being compelling, this photo of an American family surrounded by food is also a clear reminder that food, beyond providing sustenance, can also have a role in politics, in this case, by demonstrating the superiority of the American way in providing a modern standard of living. The food in the photograph is not just a backdrop—it is an embodiment of the power of the United States in the years after World War II.

The use of food as an element of national power is often discussed under the concept of "food power." For Americans in the years after World War II, food power could be used as a demonstration of the good life that was enjoyed by a larger and larger number of people. As revealed by the enduring relevance of the 1951 photograph of the Czekalinski family and their food, the demonstration of abundance, prosperity, and stability through food was a powerful message, both to Americans at home and for people of many nations abroad. Food was an integral part of President Roosevelt's vision for a world that enjoyed "freedom from want," one of the four essential freedoms he identified as the framework for postwar lives of plenty and prosperity, which would ensure peace and security for all the world.[4]

Food power, of course, could also be used coercively. In 1974, Earl Butz, secretary of agriculture in the Nixon administration, described food as a weapon that could be used to achieve American national objectives.[5] A postwar agricultural revolution had filled the silos and storage facilities in America with food. Changes in agriculture and food production resulted in so much food that for most of the three decades after the end of the war, Americans grappled with food, not as an asset, but as a problem. A surplus of food—including staple crops like corn and wheat but also milk, butter, and meat—depressed farm prices and hurt rural prosperity while raising the costs of federal farm programs and food-storage efforts.

By the 1970s, Butz realized that this surplus food, far more than was needed to fulfill even America's growing needs, could be a valuable weapon in the arsenal of democracy at a time when the global need for food was rising. In 1976, Butz noted that he had heard a Communist counterpart say, "You have something more powerful than atom bombs. You have protein."[6] Communists weren't the only ones to recognize the importance of American food power. As Butz told a reporter with *Time*, his influence with both American and foreign diplomatic officials increased considerably during the 1970s because when he came "calling with wheat in my pocket, they pay attention."[7] Food was always valuable, but in the wake of a global food crisis from 1972 to 1974, there was renewed attention to the link between food and security. Food power, to many American policymakers, represented "the diplomatic influence that a food-exporting country exercises over the decisions and activities of other nations because of the control (either actual or perceived) that the exporting country has over a specific market or segment of a market, or as a concomitant to the ability of the food-exporting country to provide food aid to needy countries."[8] Food power could be deployed indirectly, in the form of trade or humanitarian assistance, or directly, in the form of giving or withholding food in times of crisis.

During the first three decades of the Cold War, Americans struggled to understand how food could best be used as an element of national power. Advocates of the food-as-a-weapon approach placed food alongside other desirable commodities, such as natural resources or military and industrial technology, seeing it as a vital substance that could be used to gain an advantage in foreign relations. During the world food crisis in the 1970s, the important and outsized role of the United States in global food export markets became clear. Some officials felt food gave the United States a powerful tool to use in forcing countries to adopt policy positions favored by the United States. Learning from the cavalier way the Organization of the Petroleum Exporting Countries (OPEC) had used oil as a weapon against supporters of Israel in the 1973 Yom Kippur War, one senior State Department official summarized the food-as-a-weapon approach with the blunt assessment that "we have the food, and the hell with the rest of the world."[9] Other officials confirmed that American policymakers had considered using a food embargo in response to the oil shutoff.[10] In this sense, food power was seen in a limited way, the ability to manipulate international transfers of food in order to accomplish diplomatic goals.[11]

But the opportunities to use food power in such an openly coercive way were limited. They required that the United States have large amounts of surplus food available for export. They required, further, that other sources of food were not available, something hard to guarantee during a time when Canada, Australia, and Argentina were also regularly producing bountiful surpluses. Coercion also clashed with view that access to food was something to which all people had a right. The status of food as a human right was affirmed in the 1948 Universal Declaration of Human Rights, which stated, "Everyone has the right to a standard of living adequate for the health and well-being of himself and of his family, including food."[12] Thus, though food could be conceptualized as a lever of coercive power, in practice, American leaders and policymakers found food to be more useful as a softer form of power, deployed through the avenues of trade or foreign assistance.[13] Power, in international relations, can be defined as the ability to influence the behavior of others in order to achieve a desired outcome. It is generally measured with reference to such criteria as the population size, geography, natural resources, economic strength, military force, and social stability of a given actor, typically a state.[14]

Debates during the postwar years about how food power could help the United States its achieve the goals of stability, prosperity, and security were part of a larger conversation about the role of food in the security of states, communities, and individuals. The absence of sufficient food was clearly recognized as a root cause of conflict and insecurity. For example, in 1962, Orville Freeman, President Kennedy's secretary of agriculture, wrote, "The history of mankind and the records of his wars clearly demonstrate that food is a prime weapon, a prime target, and the prime element of survival."[15] Freeman's attribution of the centrality of food to conflict is part of a long tradition recognizing that food, and the ability to control availability, access, utilization, and stability of food, could be vitally important to the legitimacy and security of states.[16]

In the mid-twentieth century, however, although food was recognized as a root cause of conflict and instability, it was not typically discussed primarily as an issue of national security. Instead, food was seen as a problem that could be solved through the careful application of government policy to try to balance supply and demand. Policymakers of the time were particularly concerned about the problem of agricultural surpluses. In the postwar period, American agriculture was booming. Farmers were producing much more food than American markets could absorb. So the government stored the excess. The costs of doing this worried officials, who thought that if they could reduce the surpluses, they could reduce the costs of the farm programs while also boosting the incomes of farmers.

A great deal of policy between the late 1940s and early 1970s revolved around efforts to reduce agricultural surpluses. What policymakers at the time did not seem to understand was that even though food was not seen as central to national and international security, the surpluses provided by America, along with allies such as Canada and Australia, helped under-gird a thirty-year period of relative stability in global food supplies and prices. From the end of the postwar period until the early 1970s, the huge agricultural surpluses generated by the United States helped to stave off a major global food crisis and provided a powerful tool that could be used in the event of localized need as a result of natural disasters or agricultural failures. Food, though primarily discussed in conversations and policy debates about domestic farm issues, was a critical element of American national power that helped provide stability in a volatile Cold War security environment.

Moreover, in their efforts to unload the surpluses, American officials created new avenues for dispensing food, including aid programs, such as Food for Peace; domestic nutrition-assistance programs; and fallout-shelter-provisioning programs. They aligned food disbursement with national security doctrines, such as containment, in an effort to shore up America's allies during the Cold War and prevent the spread of Soviet power. And they sought to help farmers, from Mexico to India, become more prosperous and productive through the scientific and technical assistance of the Green Revolution. For all of their problems, these programs meant that fewer people around the world went hungry. These efforts also demonstrated the ability to utilize food as a form of assistance to those in need while also establishing the success of the American way in the postwar years. The ability of the United States to dispense food to help those in need—even the Soviet Union—was something that government leaders would point to again and again as evidence that the American system was superior to communism. Abundance was the foundation of an international food system, and the United States was at its center.[17]

But that postwar system came to an end in the early 1970s. American policymakers had finally managed to eliminate surpluses—not realizing how critical they had become to the security and stability of the United States and the world. Then the world food crisis hit, between 1972 and 1974. The lack of American agricultural surpluses was not the sole cause of the crisis. The early 1970s saw a perfect storm of severe unexpected events, "shocks," which contributed to the food crisis. These shocks included harsh weather in key food-producing regions, a growing global population, and changing food-consumption patterns. Also important were policy decisions, such as President Nixon's agreement to sell massive quantities of American grain to the Soviet Union and his decision to take the United States out of the Bretton Woods system, ending of the direct convertibility of the United States dollar to gold. International politics, such as the 1973 Yom Kippur War and resulting OPEC oil embargo, played a hand as well. Yet, of all of these shocks, a key causal factor of the crisis was the fact that American surpluses were no longer available to cushion the blow. Without these surpluses, the postwar food system collapsed.[18]

This book tells the story of the rise and fall of the American food system from the end of World War II to the early 1970s. It argues that during this period food was central to national security. Although American policymakers were often focused on doing away with surpluses, they constructed a postwar global food system that depended on abundant food supplies that stabilized food prices and ensured food availability. This system was profoundly altered in the early 1970s by the elimination of those surpluses. The resulting conditions—with which we are still living today—are not the centralized system of the postwar period, in which a single actor (the United States) played an outsize role. Instead, it is a global food network, in which no single actor or entity can definitively alter or affect food markets or conditions. It is, as the UK government's Foresight Programme has noted, "not a single entity, but rather a partially self-organised collection of interacting parts."[19] This distinction between a system and network matters, because much of the thinking about how to solve contemporary world food problems rests on calls to dismantle or reorient today's "food system" to make it more effective in meeting nutritional, economic, social, and environmental goals.[20]

The new world food order that has existed since the 1970s, however, is not a system. It is a network that stretches from farms to forks around the world and includes many activities involved in producing, gathering, harvesting, processing, transporting, preparing, and consuming food. In the United States, for example, almost two-thirds of fruits and vegetables and 80 percent of seafood—in total between 10 percent and 15 percent of all food consumed by American households—is imported.[21] This intertwining has created a network of local, regional, and national food systems that has reshaped the global food landscape. This network emerged in fits and starts, in response to the efforts of a broad range of actors, policies, and events at home and abroad.

The world food network depends on sometimes tenuous connections between far-flung participants and rests on a shared agreement that food is central to the security and prosperity of human societies (even though its constituents vary, sometimes widely, in how and why they envision that to be true). In contrast to the relatively stable, American-driven postwar food system, the contemporary world food network is a complex and ever shifting landscape where states, companies, international organizations, nongovernmental groups, individuals, and communities advance and contest visions of ideal food relationships. Why are food problems, from malnutrition to the sustainability of food production to contamination of the food supply, so challenging to solve, and why are critics' calls for change so hard to implement? In part, it is because the "food network" is, in comparison to a "food system," less responsive to straightforward policy or market-based solutions. Whether food relations are a *system* or a *network* is much more than a question of terminology. It is directly relevant to understanding and addressing food problems and the landscape of solutions.

The concept of a "system" is used in reference to food in two primary ways: first, as a way to trace energy flows, and second, in regard to the role of food in modern political and economic arrangements. The idea of tracing food-energy flows has its origins in the early twentieth-century ideas of Charles Elton. In his 1927 book *Animal Ecology* (1927), Elton described the workings of natural communities in order to enable the more effective management of plant and animal industries. He used the term "food chain," to describe the the flow of energy from plants, which convert sunlight into food, to herbivores and then to the predators that feed on herbivores. Together, all the food chains in an ecological system made up a "food web."[22] Notions of food chains and food webs underlie the understanding of a food system as a series of linked processes through which "raw materials and inputs are turned into edible food products that are consumed by end-users."[23] A "food system" is thus "the entire set of activities and relationships that make up the various food pathways from seed to table and influence 'the how and why and what we eat.' "[24]

A second use of the term "food system" comes from systems theory. Systems theory emerged in the mid-twentieth century as a way to understand complex patterns of interaction in modern political, economic, and technological systems.[25] These ideas were taken up in the 1950s and 1960s by scholars of international relations to refer to "an arrangement of the actors of international politics in which interactions are patterned and identifiable."[26] Terms like *food system, food order*, and *food regime* all refer to just such a "system," in this case the processes and activities that link the production and consumption of food in regular and traceable ways.[27]

Examinations of food systems can occur on multiple scales, from local areas to agro-ecological regions to nations or even to the entire world. The similar emphasis on production and consumption in both ways of describing a food system is not terribly surprising, given that early ecologists leaned heavily on the same set of ideas that saw nature through "the forms, processes, and values of the modern economic order as shaped by technology."[28] Both views of the food system were not only strongly shaped by their reliance on economic order as a critical lens, but also by the sense that agriculture and food production were sets of hierarchical activities (which can be defined either by energy level or political level) that could be managed by humans in order to produce a desired outcome.[29] The food system, though, is not a single, unified system but rather is a network.

Networks are interconnected systems that allow sharing between systems and contain regularized interactions between nodes of activity. Emerging in the late twentieth century, network theory responds to the sense among scholars that human social, political, economic, and technological systems were changing faster and at greater magnitudes than ever before. The speed of change, and its unprecedented scale, results, at least in part, from the increased interconnectedness of the modern world and the recognition that the "dominant functions and processes in the Information Age are increasingly organized around networks."[30] Theorists have identified the importance of networks in everything from travel to energy to food. Networks are a series of interconnected nodes, and the distance is shorter between two nodes that belong to the same network. The form a node takes may vary depending on the network in question, for example, airports or port facilities in a transportation network or a large-scale farm or major retail distribution centers in the food network. Larger airports or distribution centers represent *hubs* (high-traffic nodes), while smaller airports or individual stores can be understood as *nodes*. Networks thus are patterns of relations that collapse distances and that allow something—be it information, energy, airplanes, or food—to travel rapidly and regularly along the links of the network. Networks, along with an associated set of changes related to globalization and the rise of information technology, have helped to dramatically increase the speed and scale of global interactions.[31]

That speed and scale are part of what makes it difficult to fully comprehend the flows and shifts of the contemporary global food network. Understanding patterns of food relations as a network that exists within and between nations illuminates links that exist between key nodes and hubs. However, it does little good—when understanding the network is the goal—to try and assign a simple hierarchical order to rationalize the increasing speed and scale of global interactions around food. Instead, the complexity, contingency, and co-involvement of conditions and events at multiple scales of nodes and hubs must be appreciated. To suggest that contemporary food relations are more properly conceptualized as a network than a system does not, however, mean that food problems cannot be addressed and managed. Rather, the complex, interactive structure of the contemporary world food network highlights the fact that management and control, especially by one hub—be it a state, international organization, or company—will be very difficult.

This book seeks to offer an explanation for why the contemporary food network arose in the mid-1970s. It looks back at the system that existed prior to the 1970s, investigating the aims that motivated the American policymaking efforts responsible for its development. In tracing the rise and fall of this postwar system, the book also helps explain contemporary challenges related to ensuring food security, at a time when we are still grappling with the expectations and goals of the postwar food system, even if we are no longer living and working within its parameters. The American focus of this book is not to suggest that actions outside of the United States were not relevant to the postwar food system but is instead an assertion that American actions were central, and often generative, to efforts to bring people and places together through food.

It is also worth noting that although the focus of this book is on the period of roughly 1945 to 1975, the landscape of contemporary food challenges has a number of critical antecedents in the great transformations in food since the end of World War II. Nineteenth-century improvements in transportation, such as the bulding of canal and railroad systems, linked new markets and reduced the time and cost of transporting goods. The rise of large food processors created regional and national food companies, such as Quaker Oats, the National Biscuit Company, W. K. Kellogg, H. J. Heinz Company. The development of the science of nutrition, and changes to farming as it became industrialized also led to major shifts.[32] However, the government's utilization of food as a form of deployable national power to advance national security and national interests deepened in the postwar period. This development was concurrent with, and in many ways enabled by, a range of scientific and technological developments that allowed for greater productivity and the increasing integration of local, regional, and national food systems with global markets.

One result of these changes is that the importance of food to national and human security has, over the past thirty years, become more widely apparent and more widely discussed. Food-security challenges are, of course, among the oldest problems faced by states; but they took on a distinctive character in the late twentieth century. A further consequence of the intensification and mechanization of agriculture and food production is the increasing interconnection between food, water, and energy systems, an interactivity recognized by the US National Intelligence Council as one of the key megatrends that will shape the world in coming decades.[33] Through the great acceleration in the speed and scale of global interactions around food in the twentieth century, food became more than just a source of calories or a signifier of cultural identity; it served as a critical nexus in the relationship between humans and nature, in which efficiency and productivity were increasingly prioritized.[34]

In response to the negative unintended consequences of agricultural intensification—as well as to concerns about reductions in productivity and rising demands for food—a number of scholars, scientists, activists, and policymakers have identified the impact of agriculture and food production on the environment while also recognizing the need to amplify the positive benefits of intensified agricultural production and to minimize its negative environmental effects.[35] Amid the swirl of problems confronting contemporary world leaders and policymakers, food has emerged as a critical component of the security and prosperity of nations and individuals. But contemporary leaders are not the first to confront needs and wants for food, or to consider that food can be a vital tool in ensuring the stability and flourishing of human societies.

In exploring the use of American food power to promote American national security and national interests, this book investigates a series of roughly chronological moments in the rise and fall of the postwar food system. Chapter 1 examines the plans developed in response to unexpectedly severe and widespread postwar reconstruction and humanitarian crises. Food was central to the both the military effort abroad and on the home front during the war. and it emerged as a core issue after the war as well, when America was the only country in the world producing more food at the end of the war than at its start. Initial plans for post-war reconstruction in Europe ranged from proposals to deindustrialize Germany and return it to a pastoral state to efforts to provide food and needed material through the continuation of wartime programs and voluntary aid to friendly nations. Only as the Cold War began to take shape did America settle on the Marshall Plan as a way to use American agricultural abundance to both promote postwar reconstruction and serve as a bulwark against communism. More than a quarter of the more than $13 billion that the United States provided for European reconstruction between 1948 and 1953 was either provided in the form of food or was earmarked to aid in rebuilding Europe's agricultural capacity. Widely supported by the American people, the Marshall Plan thus established several trends that would continue through the next several decades: first, American abundance could be used to aid allies, especially (though this was just beginning to be clear in the early 1950s) to stymie the expanding influence of the Soviets; and second, American abundance was increasingly not only an expectation at home, when ending wartime rationing, even amid widespread global hunger, was necessary to boost morale of its citizens, but also a critical element of the American image abroad.

Chapter 2 assesses the "food problem" that arose in the 1950s as Americans faced an unlikely challenge: rising food prices but lower farm incomes. As Americans became more affluent, they spent more rather than less of their income on food, defying the existing economic dogma. In part, this was a result of the increased costs to food companies of food-processing technologies and advertising, which were passed along to consumers, and meant that Americans were paying more for foods having so-called built-in services, such as cake mixes and instant coffee. At the same time, this increased spending on food did not trickle down to farmers, who were earning less of every food dollar, causing concern among policymakers about falling rural prosperity. Above all, *abundance* emerged as a watchword for American prosperity and security in a dangerous Cold War world. The central role of food and the American consumer society was most dramatically demonstrated in the 1959 Kitchen Debate between American vice president Richard Nixon and Soviet premier Nikita Krushchev, which took place at the American National Exhibition in Moscow. There, more than forty cakes a day were prepared by General Mills employees in official Betty Crocker Kitchens in front of eager Russian audiences, some of whom (contravening the exhibition's regulations) nabbed samples off plates the bakers had put within easy reach.

Even as abundance became emblematic of American agriculture and food at home and abroad, the "farm problem" continued to bedevil policymakers, who worried about the status and votes of American farmers. Chapter 3 considers the efforts to shape farm policy to preserve small-scale farming and eliminate surpluses even as the the modern agricultural revolution was beginning to produce historic and ever-increasing harvests. This abundance presented policymakers with a new problem in world affairs: the challenge of what to do with too much food. President Dwight Eisenhower and his secretary of agriculture Ezra Taft Benson sought to solve the "farm problem" and address surpluses of food production by dismantling Depression-era government farm programs and restoring a free market in agriculture and food production. When those reform efforts were unsuccessful, they tried next to reduce surpluses by deploying them abroad as food aid, a strategy that led to the passage of the 1954 Agricultural Trade Development and Assistance Act, which established the first permanent American organization designed to provide food aid to foreign nations. Their creativity in attempting to reduce the costs of agricultural surplus storage generated the most effective use of "food power" to date—a new system in which America was providing extensive food aid and assistance abroad and, in doing so, inadvertently stabilizing global food markets.

This offensive use of agricultural abundance abroad had a counterpart in the defensive use of food at home. Policymakers in the 1950s also considered ways to utilize American abundance by stockpiling food in preparation for atomic attack. Chapter 4 explores the shelters, foods, and plans that were developed to protect Americans, farms, and livestock from nuclear war. The high cost of shelter construction and stockpiling programs led the government to pursue an advisory strategy that encouraged Americans to undertake "do-it yourself" efforts to build shelters and fill their shelves. As this chapter shows, even this advisory role required government experts and civil defense planners to consider what sorts of food were best suited for use in shelter environments. But as Americans began to better comprehend the dangers of radioactive fallout and the enormous destructive potential of thermonuclear weapons in the 1950s and early 1960s, enthusiasm for shelters waned. Americans began to feel that the best way to prepare for nuclear war might be to use American abundance to help ensure that nuclear war never occurred at all.

Chapter 5 examines the central role of food in American efforts during the 1960s to promote peace and stability in global affairs. Food aid gained renewed attention and resources from the Kennedy administration, which added humanitarian assistance to goals of American assistance programs. President Lyndon Johnson also eagerly deployed American food power in efforts to promote American security, but chose a more involved approach than Kennedy, seeking to influence the behavior of nations key to American's foreign policy agenda, such as India and Vietnam—by tying the granting of aid to the willingness of their governments to support policies in their own countries that the United States desired. During both the Kennedy and Johnson administrations, a new way to utilize American abundance emerged: deploying not only food but also the knowledge and tools needed to produce food, through a range of technical assistance programs that involved combined efforts of the government, private foundations, and international organizations to promote a "Green Revolution" that sought to peacefully transform the lives of people around the world.

The end of the 1960s brought turbulence in American affairs at home and abroad, and sparked a set of changes that resulted in the first global food crisis since the end of World War II. Through the continued deployment of food as humanitarian assistance; increased export sales to allies, even the Soviet Union; and changes to domestic agricultural policy, the Nixon administration finally succeeded in eliminating agricultural surpluses at home. But the surpluses, long viewed as a problem at home, had been a stabilizing influence on world food supplies and food prices. In the early 1970s, just as domestic surpluses were being used up, a series of unexpected political, demographic, economic, and environmental shocks converged to plunge the world into the deepest food crisis in twenty-five years. Although American ideas and plans were central to the emergence of a postwar world food system, as chapter 6 examines, those ideas could not weather the convergence of so many trends into a new world food crisis. The crisis ended the postwar system and replaced it with a network that involved many more actors and priorities in world food relations.

In the three decades between the end of the Second World War and the world food crisis in the 1970s, food power, for American leaders, policymakers, and citizens, was much more than a tool that could be used narrowly to coerce states and people into doing what the United States wanted. Postwar efforts to incorporate food into security issues were part of larger efforts to expand the range of topics considered to be national security issues, as leaders, military officials, and scholars sought to map and understand a changing landscape of threats and vulnerabilities. Historians such as Edward Meade Earle had argued before World War II that changing global conditions were creating a new strategic environment in which the nature of the threats to the security of states would evolve and shift.[36] This sense of a continually evolving security landscape was endorsed by the National Security Act of 1947 (and its amendment in 1949), which did not define national security but created new governments departments and agencies, such as the Department of Defense, the National Security Council, and the Central Intelligence Agency, to identify and address threats and vulnerabilities.[37] Initially, national security was defined rather narrowly; for example, in the late 1940s military officials were wary of taking responsibility for civil defense, arguing that it was a civilian responsibility.[38] Yet, after 1950, narrow conceptualizations of national security were broadened to include challenges like food, health, and environmental change.

By early in the twenty-first century, food insecurity was recognized as threat to the security and stability of the United States and its allies and partners. This concern was expressed, for example, by United States' director of national intelligence, James Clapper, who in 2014 identified the competition for access to food as a growing security threat.[39] Attention to the relevance of food to security is driven by a set of contemporary trends, including record high global rates of malnutrition and obesity, far-ranging and high-profile food-safety episodes, outbreaks of violence and unrest fueled in part by high food prices and high price volatility, and concern about impact on food systems of changing trends in weather and climate.[40] The emergence of food as a topic relevant to national security was not just a reflection of contemporary events, however; rather, it was the result of a decades-long effort by military officials, policymakers, and security thinkers to broaden understanding of the events, trends, and processes that could challenge the national security of the United States and the human security of the American people. In order to address threats to its national security, the United States deployed food in multiple, sometimes contradictory, ways in order to meet a complex set of expectations at home and abroad. Food power provided aid and reconstruction assistance in the aftermath of conflict and during times of need. Food power promoted American prosperity and spread postwar material and nutritional abundance across the nation and around the world. Food power was central to understanding the evolving threat of nuclear weapons, and as leaders and citizens began to understand the true horror and devastation of a possible nuclear war, food was a central element to American efforts to promote peaceful international relations.

Debates over the status of food during the mid-twentieth century often turned on different visions of the role food would play in efforts to promote American security and prosperity. Was food a weapon, a commodity to be valued and exchanged through markets, or a substance to be provided to those in need? When we explore different visions of food power, it becomes clear that food was an essential part of America's postwar modernization strategy, its vision of what it meant to be a stable, secure, and technologically advanced nation.[41] The focus of American policymakers and experts on the overarching goals of containing communism, creating free markets for agriculture, or feeding the world led them to see the challenges facing them in stark, often apocalyptic terms. At the same time, they shared the modernist belief that scientific and technological progress would find the solutions to pressing problems, such as malnutrition, in order to improve human well-being but also to lessen hunger as both a cause and effect of conflict and instability. This focus on grand strategic questions and overconfidence in science and technology led to a privileging of efforts to increase agricultural productivity at home and abroad and to less sensitivity to the intended and unintended consequences of those efforts.

Concurrent with the efforts of policymakers and experts, a variety of groups challenged these technocratic visions of food and constructed alternative ideas about what food could be. Thus food also emerged as a critical component of alternative modernization strategies offered by groups such as farmers in the 1950s or the counterculture in the 1960s.[42] These groups argued for the need to create food pathways that ensured farmers a fair share of postwar prosperity or provided food in ways that strived to be "fair," "natural," or "local," but they were inextricably interwoven into the same elements of the global food network that resulted from the postwar planning, such as "big ag" or "big food." The coexistence—in some cases the codependence—of these contesting visions of the food network is part of what make its governance, management, and reform so challenging.

Tensions between these visions of food turned food politics into a battleground in the late twentieth century—one in which the interests of security and foreign policy experts, farmers, businesses, and politicians contended with a growing social movement whose adherents worried about the role of food in causing or contributing to conflict, inequality, and instability. These food activists called for the construction of food systems more sensitive to alternative goals, from protecting the livelihoods of family farmers to nurturing local food ways to reducing the unsustainable use of natural resources. Amid these calls to reform contemporary food systems, however, there are still insufficient understandings of the modern origins of the contemporary world food network.

Intensified global interactions around food result from a number of trends and drivers, from population growth to demographic and dietary change to readily available supplies of cheap energy and water to the changing nature of international trade and business to developments in science and technology. Among these many drivers, there remains a critically understudied nexus that helps to underline the direction and form of food problems in the late twentieth and early twenty-first century. The story of American understandings and uses of food power during the early decades of the Cold War helps shed new light on the debates and decisions of American leaders and policymakers as they sought to navigate an uncertain and rapidly shifting landscape of challenges to national security and prosperity. Efforts to understand both America's role in the world during the mid-twentieth century and to address contemporary food problems will be enhanced by a more complete understanding of the ways in which postwar American policymakers and experts sought to shape the politics of security and prosperity by linking people and places around the world by deploying food as an element of national power.

Freedom from Want

Creating a Postwar Food System

The 1947 communist takeover of America was swift, brutal, and decisive. At the core of the effort was a secret cabal that had worked quietly for years to infiltrate America's political, labor, media, and security institutions. Now, all that was required was a moment of crisis that would provide an opportunity to strike. An opening came in the form of an unusually hot, dry spring that brought drought and dust storms throughout the Midwest and with them, insect infestations that decimated crops. Prominent newspapers such as the *Daily Times* warned that Americans faced starvation. The communists sprang into action. They used the tensions between farmers and consumers to provoke food riots, manipulated the labor unions to strike, exploited racial tensions to incite urban riots, and activated sympathetic writers and editors to take over the media and further fan the flames of unrest. With the situation at a boil, the president and the vice president were assassinated and the secretly communist Speaker of the House was able to gain emergency powers and nationalize control over food supplies. The commanders of the armed forces were machine gunned down, Congress was held at gunpoint, and the new leaders made sure that only loyal party members got food, even going so far as bombing warehouses and burning food supplies to worsen the food shortages. What had begun with bad weather and a bad harvest soon ended with the communist takeover of America and, eventually, the world.[1]

This fictious warning about the way that a food crisis could lead to the eradication of freedom in America was described in colorful detail in *Is This Tomorrow: America Under Communism!*, a forty-eight-page comic book published in 1947 by the Catechetical Guild Educational Society of St. Paul, Minnesota. Its aim, in the words of the publisher, Father Louis Gales, was "to use every strength to expose the aims and purposes of the Soviet system."[2] The Guild published and distributed more than four million copies of *Is This Tomorrow* to highlight the dangers of religious intolerance (in the comic, Catholics are prominently featured as standing up for freedom against the communist forces). The comic urged readers to fight communism through the "ten commandments of citizenship," which included the advice to stay abreast of foreign problems; be tolerant of other races, religions, and nationalities; and to "be American first."[3] Based on the success of the American version, the comic was adapted for audiences in Australia, Quebec, and Turkey.[4]

Above all, food played a critical role in *Is This Tomorrow*. Reduced food production as a result of natural disasters precipitated the political crisis described in the comic. The fictional communist forces used food strategically, artificially exacerbating food shortages and rewarding loyalty to the new communist government with access to food (and withholding it as a punishment). *Is This Tomorrow* is a window into the anxiety some Americans felt about communism in the early days of the Cold War. But it can also be read as a reminder that food could be used strategically by states (or their agents) to manipulate political outcomes. *Is This Tomorrow* carried added resonance for publics in America and other parts of the world who were struggling with a food crisis in which as many as one of every four people on the planet was going hungry. In the immediate postwar period, food, and especially the ability to control food supplies, was emerging as a vitally important issue for the legitimacy, stability, and security of states. The danger that hunger and want would push people to support, or merely allow, the replacement of democratic governments with communist regimes motivated Americans' support for the Truman Doctrine and the Marshall Plan, which both, in part, sought to ensure that there were stable supplies of food worldwide.

Those fears pushed policymakers to find ways to restock the shelves of stores and pantries as quickly as possible. Getting food on the shelves in devastated nations such as Germany was a complicated process and engaged every sector of society. It meant resuscitating lagging economies, modernizing prewar agricultural sectors, boosting food production, ensuring efficient transportation, and putting money in the pockets of consumers. At home, American policymakers balanced a complex set of competing needs. Policymakers and economists worried that the rapid demobilization of military forces and the transition from wartime to civilian production could result in the return of the economic problems and high unemployment of the years following the First World War. Farmers recalled their interwar experiences and worried that the sudden end to the the Second World War would result in declines in prices and reduced demand for American goods. Americans also expected that, in addition to a return to a prosperous peacetime life, their pantries would benefit from victory, as food rationing would end and their food choices would increase.[5]

However, as the government struggled to come up with plans to meet all these needs at home and abroad, they found that there was no resuscitating the old ways. The prewar international food order was gone—because of not just the war but also the many economic and technological shifts that had profoundly altered farming around the world in the preceding decades. Instead, policymakers began to propose new systems for managing international food supplies. The American government put its weight behind proposals that privileged the American role in the food system. As the postwar food system took shape, America was at its core, using its sizeable food surpluses to further its strategic interests. Such efforts were motivated, above all, by the desire to avoid letting food crises lead to political and security crises like the one depicted in *Is This Tomorrow*. America's ability to avoid such a crisis lay in the plans and proposals of the late 1940s.

This chapter explores the way these plans laid the groundwork for a new vision of the offensive use of American food surpluses. This vision had its basis in the wartime years, when citizens were encouraged to think of food as a resource to be carefully husbanded and strategically deployed. While rationing eased in the immediate postwar years, many parts of the war-torn world were experiencing hunger. In response, both US and international bodies began to formulate visions for addressing global hunger. As Americans—with some of the largest agricultural surpluses in the world to dispense—began to take the lead on postwar planning, particularly in Europe, those proposals turned into plans of action. As they took shape, American policymakers became aware that food assistance could be a critical component of stabilizing allies and, as the Cold War heated up, helping stave off the warning of *Is This Tomorrow*, not just in the United States, but around the world.

THE WORLD FOOD SYSTEM BEFORE
AND DURING WORLD WAR II

Establishing a pattern of international relations around food—essentially creating a new global food system—emerged as a key element of postwar planning for reconstruction and global governance. The two world wars had not only ended the existing international order, but had also raised awareness of global interdependence in the production and consumption of food. Experiences with want and need in many nations during and between the wars brought food into a central position in many countries and made agricultural producers, consumers, and policymakers aware of the newly developed connections between the international food trade, prosperity, and security. The end of the former, relatively stable though not unproblematic food order in the 1920s sparked efforts around the world to navigate an uncertain global food landscape. In the United States, this uncertainty led decades of efforts by American policymakers to control farm production and boost farm income while stabilizing food prices in an effort to solve what came to be known as "the farm problem."

Postwar concerns about food stemmed in part from the breakup of the prewar international food order—and the international order more broadly. Between the 1870s and the 1920s, a relatively stable international food order had emerged around comparatively free-trade system based on the gold standard. National and international competition prompted farmers, fishers, and ranchers to seek comparative advantage through advancements in technology and productivity using early machinery such as steel plows and horse drawn threshers and reapers. In contrast to farmers' typical worries about producing enough food, by the early twentieth century, farmers were beginning to produce consistent surpluses. Between 1870 and the 1920s, the wheat production of the United States, Canada, Australia, and Argentina tripled, while their populations merely doubled, leaving plentiful surpluses that could be exported. Europe benefited from this situation, as its wheat imports increased by a factor of six. Greater reliance on imports allowed Europe to pursue economic specialization, increasing higher-value exports while also lowering food costs for workers.[6]

Though many people benefited from cheaper, more plentiful foodstuffs overall, during the late nineteenth and early twentieth century farmers around the world experienced significant dislocation. Greater focus on production efficiency tended to concentrate producers in certain areas. In the United States, for instance, growing reliance on exporting commodities like wheat helped to centralize agriculture in the Midwest, the West, and parts of the Pacific Northwest, such as eastern Oregon: large, flat areas with fertile soil that could be worked with horse-drawn and, later, fossil-fuel-powered machinery. Farmers in areas conducive to the large-scale production of wheat and other grain crops that were easily storable and transportable did particularly well in the new international markets. The emergence of a global food system, however, brought new worries. Improvements in transportation and communication technologies meant that farmers were no longer just fretting about how well their crops did in comparison to their neighbors but also about how well they did in comparison to competitors in other states and other countries. In some places, such as the United States, the Populist Movement was started by farmers seeking redress for their grievances.[7]

The productivity of agriculture and the prosperity problems of farmers were further boosted by the increasing industrialization of agriculture. By the early twentieth century, farmers, agricultural scientists, and businesses were increasingly confronted with greater capital requirements and the need to adopt efficiencies. They focused on efforts to apply industrial models to rationalize farm production and, in the words of one International Harvester advertising brochure, turn every farm into a factory.[8] Boosted outputs reduced food prices but also farm incomes. Trends toward greater productivity and lower farm incomes, combined with the boom and then rapid decline in farm prices following World War I, placed more pressure on farmers, especially small farmers, that led to economic crises in rural areas during the interwar years.[9]

Before World War II, a greater interest in food planning was already emerging as recognition of global problems in food and agriculture increased. One of the most successful areas of activity of the League of Nations was in development of linkages between nutritional institutes that resulted in nutritional surveys in nations around the world and the articulation of a global target dietary standard of 2,500 calories per day for a working adult. This standard was the first global nutrition target set by an international organization. A 1935 report from the League of Nations provided the first documented account of the extent of hunger and malnutrition in the world and proposed efforts to promote greater food production in areas of deficiency but also greater trade that would help nations overcome shortfalls.[10] Assessing the impact of the report, the *New York Times* said it was "the most important book of the year" because it revealed that the imbalance of food in the world "is the challenge underlying the disorders of this epoch, the pretext for modern wars."[11] This report can be seen as the beginning of efforts to develop a world food system based on improved food production, increased global cooperation, and less-restricted trade designed to address food deficiencies. This vision though, was not the only idea of a food system at play in the 1930s.[12]

Alongside the first links in a postwar global food system based on greater cooperation and coordination, an alternative idea arose based on greater national or regional autarky or self-sufficiency. As historian Nick Cullather has written, a "narrowing pattern of international exchange, evident by the mid-1920s, deeply worried US leaders. Protective tariffs imposed by Europe, Japan and the colonies, and the formation of currency blocs in response to the Depression, cordoned the world into closed spheres, a nightmare for American free traders."[13] While such efforts sought to promote greater self-sufficiency, they also promised greater tension and conflict among nations and regions over imbalances in the world food supply, precisely the sort of conflict and competition the League of Nations report sought to avoid. Food was certainly not the sole cause of the Second World War, but it was an important factor driving both Germany and Japan toward war because both countries faced the need to feed rising urban populations that desired more nutritious foods. Both nations sought to meet these needs not through greater trade, but by acquiring new land and resources for both food and industry.[14] The end of the prewar food system would also shape the wartime experiences of people around the world.[15]

Even before America's entry into World War II, government officials were confronted by food problems resulting from the widespread malnutrition during the Great Depression. One of the starkest examples of the problem came in September 1940, when 40 percent of the first million men called for induction were found to be medically unfit for military service, many because of tooth decay caused by poor nutrition.[16] Advances in nutritional science also altered food strategies during the war, as government food officials sought not just to maintain caloric targets but to also encourage Americans to eat a healthier diet containing more vitamins and minerals to promote physical and mental fitness. The length and magnitude of World War II meant that the experiences of Americans with food were different than in World War I. America's relatively brief participation in the previous conflict had required only voluntary conservation efforts and voluntary efforts to boost food production through strategies such as planting Liberty Gardens. World War II required much more formalized food conservation and rationing strategies.[17]

Facing a war on multiple fronts, American officials soon realized that voluntary conservation would not be sufficient to meet wartime food needs. Food rationing was put in place, starting with sugar in May 1942; coffee was added that November, followed, by early 1943, by a much wider range of foods, including meat, cheese, fats such as butter and lard, canned fish, and canned milk. Rationing was more often necessitated by shortages of critical materials, such as tin, glass, and rubber, used to package food or the unavailability of ships needed to transport foods, such as green (unroasted) coffee beans, rather than shortages of the foods themselves. Despite the inconvenience, rationing received broad popular support. Americans strongly disapproved of ration cheaters and those who purchased food on the black market. Seventy-four percent of respondents to a May 1945 Gallup poll reported that they felt buying at black market prices was never justified.[18]

Rationing changed diets and brought about a resurgence in home food production. A revival of the war gardening campaigns from World War I, this time called Victory Gardens, changed American eating habits. By 1943, more than twenty million Victory Gardens were producing more than 40 percent of the nation's produce, dramatically boosting the consumption of fresh fruits and vegetables. Wartime gardens were especially important during World War II, because fresh fruits and vegetables were not rationed, unlike canned varities, and because food produced by Americans did not cost them any money. Alongside efforts to boost home food production, there were also campaigns to promote home food preservation. In January 1944 a Gallup poll reported that 75 percent of American families were doing their own canning, producing an average of 165 cans or jars per year.[19] While rationing limited food choices, it resulted in dramatic improvements in Americans' diets, especially lower income Americans, who began eating more meat and poultry and foods rich in nutrients like calcium and iron. By 1948, differences in consumption of vital nutrients among low-, middle- and higher-income Americans had virtually disappeared.[20]

More food was going to directly to American military forces. The most basic difference that many soldiers and sailors noticed was abundance, including almost three times the amount of meat allocated to civilians. In 1942, the average American civilian male consumed 125 pound of meat, while the average soldier ate 360 pounds of meat, most of it beef.[21] Nonetheless, the armed forces still only used a small share of American food production. In 1942, for example, the military used 12.5 percent of beef, one-quarter of the canned vegetables produced, less than 5 percent of total dairy products, and 4 percent of eggs.[22] While military diets during previous conflicts had often incorporated locally available foods, by World War II the armed forces had moved toward a standardized food system. Army cookbooks that had once included Mexican- and Tex-Mex-style dishes that cooks would have prepared using locally sourced ingredients were replaced with manuals featuring recipes using standardized ingredients provided by military logistical systems that would ensure proper nutrition and at least 5,000 calories per soldier per day.[23]

There were other improvements to military food service as well, including field kitchens that provided hot meals to troops close to the fighting. Military field rations also improved. C-rations were meals contained in two cans, one a meat and vegetable mix and one containing coffee, sugar, and crackers. The variety of C-rations increased and by the end of the war, ten different main-course meat cans were available. The Army did not pretend that this greater variety meant that military food held up to the standard of home cooking, however. New foods, such as the Ration D survival chocolate bar produced by the Hershey Corporation, were designed to taste "just a little better than a boiled potato" to ensure that soldiers would eat it only in emergency situations.[24] Even so, while American military personnel often complained about food in their letters home, for many of them, military service meant a greater availability of food than in civilian life, especially of high-cost foods such as beef and packaged foods.[25]

Wartime experiences also made Americans familiar with arguments that victory in the war and peace afterward required a combination of healthy diets and plentiful agricultural production. This concept was most clearly enunciated in President Franklin D. Roosevelt's address to Congress of January 6, 1941, which introduced the Four Freedoms as foundations for a postwar world. The third freedom, freedom from want, was articulated as an economic system that would "secure to every nation a healthy peacetime life for its inhabitants—everywhere in the world."[26] The idea of a world free from fear and want was also incorporated into Principle 6 of the Atlantic Charter, a joint declaration of Allied war aims released by

Roosevelt and British prime minister Winston Churchill on August 14, 1941.[27] And while Americans were willing to make sacrifices during the war, they expected that victory would bring an end to wartime restrictions and rationing. Although experts had warned, correctly, of the possibility of a severe postwar food crisis, in November 1946, the United States government ended rationing on all goods except sugar; sugar rationing would continue until 1947.[28]

As the depths of the postwar food crisis in Europe and other parts of the world became apparent, American officials, including President Truman, were reluctant to reinstate rationing and instead encouraged Americans to undertake voluntary conservation measures. This led to some friction with allies, who believed that America could be sending more food.[29] While changes in food and food availability had been more widespread than at any previous time in American history, the wartime deprivation Americans experienced was far less severe than that faced by people in Europe and other parts of the world. In Britain, for example, victory brought an increase in rationing and austerity as new food controls were added to oversee the sale of potatoes and, for the first time, bread.[30] Although American citizens and policymakers were wary of returning to wartime food restrictions, they had been conditioned to see food as a critical component of national security efforts and to understand that security at home required deploying American abundance abroad.[31]

WANT AND FEAR IN THE POSTWAR YEARS

As Allied victory seemed increasingly probable, the United Nations again turned to the question of creating a international food system that could help alleviate hunger. Vice President Henry A. Wallace described the goal of the United States and its allies as creating a world in which it was "possible to see all of the people of the world get enough to eat."[32] Norris Dodd, the second director-general of the Food and Agriculture Organization (FAO) of the United Nations, talked about the need to ask, "How can international trading arrangements be improved so as to facilitate a larger and more regular flow of products at prices fair to producers and rea-sonable to consumers?"[33] Although there was agreement on the general direction , there remained a great deal of disagreement about the form the system should take. Nevertheless, eliminating world hunger was central to visions of a postwar world.[34]

John Boyd Orr advanced one of the most far-reaching proposals. Boyd Orr, a Scottish nutritionist who became the first director-general of FAO, envisioned the creating of a World Food Board that would be responsible for both short-term policies to manage emergencies and long-term struc-tural reforms to harmonize global production and consumption of food. Orr's proposal for a World Food Board was based on the Allies' successful experiences with the wartime Combined Food Board, established in 1942 by Roosevelt and Churchill to plan and coordinate the use of the food resources of the United States, Great Britain, and Canada (collectively referred to as the United Nations following the adoption of the Atlantic Charter in 1941).[35] Orr's proposal called for the centralized global man-agement of key commodities.[36]

The ambitious plan encountered stiff resistance from nations dubious about its ability to fully address the problems and, perhaps more impor-tantly, unwilling to fund or surrender control of their national food poli-cies to an international body. Speaking in Washington, DC, on October 28, 1948, Dodd, who at the time was the United States' under secretary of agriculture, noted, "Governments are not likely to place the large funds needed for financing such a plan in the hands of an international agency over whose operations and price policy they would have little or no con-trol."[37] Dodd and other policymakers turned to the idea of establishing the FAO with a mission to promote nutrition, improve the efficiency of agri-cultural production and distribution, improve conditions for rural people, and contribute to a growing world economy.[38] Instead of a World Food Board, Dodd and US secretary of state George Marshall began advocating that America act independently to structure a global food system, with itself as the central node, using America's bountiful agricultural surpluses as its foundation. As a result, plans for a centrally managed and controlled global food system did not come to pass. However, the debates over global food management in the postwar years provide insight into the origins of postwar food power.[39]

The first challenge facing the creation of a postwar food order was meeting the urgent need for food in nations around the world. The war had caused considerable disruption to food production and exchange, and this was followed by harsh weather and bad harvests in 1946–47, so that when the war ended, almost a quarter of the people in the world did not have sufficient food. American policymakers began the postwar period with poor information and incomplete reconstruction plans. Initially, American policymakers relied on a strategy for recovery that depended on existing institutions and limited additional programs of loans and aid to be made on a country-by-country basis. This ad hoc approach was insufficient given the magnitude of food crisis, and as the depth of the postwar humanitarian and economic crisis became clear, there was criticism, both at home and abroad, of what many saw as lack of preparedness. In fact, the scale and scope of European reconstruction was beyond the expectations of planners and policymakers.[40]

Millions of people in Europe and around the world faced immediate shortages of food and other basic survival needs. One of the critical challenges that the war laid bare was that the nature of agriculture and food production had fundamentally changed during the late nineteenth and early twentieth centuries with the development of the prewar food system. Farmers had become dependent on international markets—for inputs like fertilizer and machinery as well as for the sale of their agricultural products—and the disturbance of international trade flows caused by prewar economic criss and wartime disruptions resulted in the collapse of the prewar global food system. Though the end of the prewar system was not fully apparent to policymakers at the time, they did recognize the critical importance of restarting the production and exchange of food as a critical postwar task. The global disruption of agricultural production caused by the war was so severe that, according to a 1946 appraisal of global food supplies by the FAO, the United States was the only country producing more food after the war than before.[41] The severe weather in 1946, including cyclones and droughts, reduced wheat production in four of the world's major areas of wheat production (Africa, Australia, India, and Argentina). Wheat production in China and the Ukraine was reduced by war. In the years just after the war, shortages in fertilizer, feed for animals, and agricultural machinery reduced agricultural production in Europe. The 1946–47 winter in Europe was one of the harshest on record, further reducing harvests, while frozen canals and bad weather complicated the transportation of food supplies.[42]

The cumulative result of these factors was a dramatically reduced supply of food worldwide. The United Nations Relief and Recovery Administration (UNRRA) considered 2,500 calories per person per day to be a minimum required for basic nutrtion; at the time many Americans consumed an average of 3,300 calories a day. In the fall of 1945, the average German was eating 1,550 calories per day. By March of 1946, these numbers had dropped precipitously. Germans in the American zone were receiving 1,250 calories per person per day, but only 1,015 calories per day in the British zone and 940 calories per day in the French zone.[43] Estimates by the Emergency Economic Committee for Europe found that in 1946 more than 140 million people throughout Europe would have to live on a diet of 2,000 calories per day, while another 100 million would have to subsist on 1,500 calories per day.[44] Though American policymakers were chiefly focused on Europe, the food crisis was global and affected as many as a half million people around the world, including East and Southeast Asia and Africa. Assessing its potential impact, British under-secretary of state for foreign affairs Hector McNeil worried that famine might kill more people in 1946–47 than the fighting did during the worst years of the war.[45]

The problem of hunger was compounded by postwar plans that had not recognized the need to rebuild the systems of food production and distribution. Instead, initial postwar American planning emphasized relief, to be carried out by existing wartime organizations.[46] For instance, the United States provided food aid through the Governmental and Relief in Occupied Areas (GARIOA) program established in 1942 to provide relief to civilians in Austria, Germany, Japan, Korea, and other occupied areas. Of the total $2.9 billion in aid provided, nearly $1.2 billion of it was in the form of food and animal feed. Food aid was especially critical during the harsh 1946–47 winter, when the United States shipped more than 16.5 million tons of food, one-sixth of the American food supply, to Western Europe to forestall famine. Others agencies, for example, the UNRRA, established by forty-three nations in November 1943, continued to operate after the war. The UNRRA had been tasked with providing grants to support all areas of a recipient country's economy.[47] The United States contributed $2.9 billion to UNRRA, amounting to 73 percent of the operating budget, for postwar relief, with the largest share of funding going to Italy and Greece.[48]

The United States also helped establish new permanent international organizations to address postwar food and reconstruction needs. The FAO was the first of these, created even before the war ended, when representatives of seventy-seven nations gathered in 1943 at Hot Springs, Virginia.[49] A further set of institutions was established at the United Nations Monetary and Financial Conference held at Bretton Woods, New Hampshire, in July 1944. Forty-four nations gathered at the conference and agreed to create two organizations to address long-range reconstruction needs and provide stability to international trade and financial systems.[50] The International Monetary Fund (IMF) was established to stabilize currencies, and the International Bank for Reconstruction and Development (IBRD) was intended to provide support to countries devastated by the war. In addition to securing congressional approval for American membership in the Bretton Woods institutions, administration officials were also able to get the United States to contribute about one-quarter of the initial $8.8 billion in funding for the IMF and 35 percent of the initial $9.1 billion in funding for the IBRD.[51]

In addition to support for relief organizations, the United States continued to provide aid to European nations on an individual basis, though without any overarching strategy or program to guide such efforts. Food was often a critical component of relief programs. In addition to official government aid, which was extended to European countries mainly in the form of loans and credit, private individuals and relief organizations provided more than a half billion dollars in aid, and much of it was focused on daily survival needs. For example, the Oxford Committee for Famine Relief (OXFAM) began, in 1942, to send food to Greece, and the Cooperative for American Remittances to Europe (CARE) came together in 1945, as a joint effort by more than twenty private American relief organizations that sent millions of CARE packages with surplus military rations, canned meats, powdered milk, dried fruits, as well as sugar, chocolate, coffee, and cigarettes.[52] But the conditions in Europe and other parts of the world devastated by war were dire, and even these aid efforts were not sufficient to catalyze economic recovery.[53] In part, the slow start of postwar recovery efforts was the result of the rapid gains made by the Allied forces in 1944, which meant that combat in Europe ended sooner than planners expected. As a result, American officials had failed to agree on a strategy for postwar reconstruction prior to the end of hostilities.

The resulting deprivation led to an American focus on Germany's food supplies and food system. During the winter of 1946–47, the importance of revitalizing the German economy gained wider acceptance in America. President Truman appointed Herbert Hoover to head a commission to study the economic condition of Europe, including Germany, amid concerns about widespread starvation, disorder, and lack of progress in recovery. Although he was a Republican and had been unable to stem the America's economic crisis in the early 1930s, Hoover earned a place as one of Truman's trusted advisers on recovery issues because of his expertise in famine relief in postwar societies. Hoover had gained international acclaim for his role in food relief efforts in Belgium, Russia, and other parts of Europe at the end of World War I. He also brought his global business experience as a mining engineer and a willingness to travel in order to get a first-hand view of conditions on the ground. In 1946, as honorary chairman of the Famine Emergency Committee, he traveled around the world to assess the food situation and recommended to the president and his administration actions that could be taken to alleviate a famine that was, at the time, affecting as many as a half million people around the world.[54]

After visiting Germany and Austria in early 1947, Hoover produced three reports that were critical of the punitive American policies toward

both countries. Initial postwar recovery efforts were guided by a plan proposed by treasury secretary Henry Morgenthau, who advocated dismantling not only German military capabilities but German industrial life as a
whole. Beyond demilitarization, his plan called for dismantling factories,
flooding mines, relocating workers, and converting Germany into a pastoral nation.[55] Though the Morgenthau Plan was not implemented, its core
ideas influenced policies such as Joint Chiefs of Staff directive 1067 (JCS
1067), which took effect in May 1945 and instructed the military not to
economically rehabilitate Germany or strengthen the German economy.[56]
The directive guided German occupation activities for almost two years
and deepened the already difficult postwar humanitarian and recovery
situation.[57] About the policies then in place Hoover wrote, "There is the
illusion that the new Germany left after the annexations can be reduced
to a 'pastoral state,' " adding, "it cannot be done unless we exterminate
or move 25,000,000 people out of it."[58] Instead, he made an argument for
economic stability and recovery, grounded, above all, in steady supplies
of food. America, he wrote, would have to shoulder the costs of relief
"until the export industries of Germany can be sufficiently revived to pay
for their food. The first necessity for such revival is sufficient food upon
which to maintain vitality to work."[59] Thus not only food was central to
the recovery efforts but ensuring that Germany was self-sufficient in food
also increased security for America, which was otherwise saddled with
the responsibility of funneling supplies to an ailing Europe. Hoover's argument was well received, and increasingly, Americans began to support the
idea of helping Germans rather than punishing them.[60]

American policy as envisioned by Hoover needed to both ensure
the immediate survival needs of Germans and also provide the income
needed to restore trade between Germany's cities and rural areas and
between Germany and other nations. Hoover listed his reasons for incor-
porating Germany in the European recovery efforts, including ensuring
peace, preserving the health and safety of American military personnel in
Germany, and reducing the costs to Americans of relief efforts and maintaining an occupying army. He also appealed to the moral reasons to integrate and rehabilitate Germany, arguing, "After all, our flag flies over these

people. That flag means something besides military power."[61] His reports concluded that the economies of Germany and Europe were interlinked through the exchanges of raw materials and manufactured goods and that restoring the productivity of Europe would require also addressing conditions in Germany. This recognition encouraged the 1947 replacement of JCS 1067 with a new directive (JCS 1779) that argued for Germany's potential to play a critical role in an orderly and prosperous Europe.[62] This policy shift signaled the end of efforts to transform Germany into a deindustrialized, pastoral state toward one that envisioned a strong, industrialized Germany as a bulwark against Soviet aggression but one that was curbed by deep integration into a broader European community.[63]

By the start of 1947, immediate postwar concerns were giving way to the understanding that addressing the needs of devastated areas and developing a strategy for the emerging Cold War required a more comprehensive effort than existing policies. The problem was made more acute when UNRRA ended its operations in Europe on January 1, 1947, without any designated successor agency to take over its duties, and ceased operating completely in 1948.[64] For the United States, the need for postwar relief was becoming entangled in the need for an overarching grand strategy to guide its support for Europe. What emerged would come to be called the doctrine of containment. Facing a foe that was driven by internal dynamics to be hostile to the outside world, American policymakers followed the set of ideas laid out in George Kennan's "long telegram." Rather than attempt to roll back the Soviet Union's control over Eastern Europe, the United States would instead seek to halt the expansion of its sphere of influence by preventing friendly countries from falling to communism. Kennan challenged the United States to be willing to be deeply engaged in shaping the postwar order. In particular, he urged that the United States

> must formulate and put forward for other nations a much more positive and constructive picture of sort of world we would like to see than we have put forward in past. It is not enough to urge people to develop political processes similar to our own. Many foreign peoples, in Europe at least, are tired and frightened by experiences

of past, and are less interested in abstract freedom than in security. They are seeking guidance rather than responsibilities. We should be better able than Russians to give them this. And unless we do, Russians certainly will.[65]

Kennan's conviction that responding to the Soviet threat would require the United States to offer a "positive and constructive" picture of the world as an an alternative to that offered by the Soviet Union faced clear and immediate challenges given the conditions faced by millions of people in war-torn areas.[66]

A further impetus for American action came in early spring 1947, when Truman announced that the United States would end a long-standing tradition of peacetime noninvolvement in foreign military and political affairs and would step in to provide support to Greece and Turkey, since Britain was not able to continue doing so. In an address to Congress on March 12, 1947, Truman presented a set of ideas that came to be known as the Truman Doctrine. He spoke of America's need to continue supporting world peace and freedom, warned that failure to help Greece and Turkey could have grave consequences, and reminded Americans that deprivation abroad directly threatened American security, warning that "the seeds of totalitarian regimes are nurtured by misery and want."[67] The need to contain communism provided Truman with the core focus that would finally unify American policy and policymakers in the postwar period. If the United States were to truly assist free people in working out their destinies in their own ways, as Kennan urged and Truman promised, it must develop a clear and beneficial solution to the worry that cold, hungry, and unemployed Europeans would turn to communism for survival.[68]

THE MARSHALL PLAN AND THE BENEFITS
OF AMERICAN FRIENDSHIP

On June 5, 1947, secretary of state George C. Marshall attended Harvard's graduation ceremony to receive an honorary degree. Marshall, who caused a bit of a stir by wearing an ordinary suit and tie rather than the traditional cap and gown, was expected to make a few perfunctory remarks to the two thousand graduates and alumni in attendance.[69] Instead, he delivered an address that had, according to the *New York Times*, "world-wide significance."[70] Marshall argued that substantial American reconstruction assistance to Europe was needed if there were any hope of "breaking the vicious circle and restoring the confidence of the European people in the economic future of their own countries and of Europe as a whole."[71] He called for American foreign assistance, rather than a continuation of palliative measures, as a cure for the problem, asserting, "Our policy is directed not against any country or doctrine but against hunger, poverty, desperation and chaos."[72] The plan he proposed would constitute the largest granting of American food aid up to that point and would radically shift American expectations of the role they—and their food—could play in global affairs.

Recognition of the need for an initiative to shore up Western Europe had emerged in the spring of 1947. While attending the April 1947 Council of Foreign Ministers meeting in Moscow, Marshall was shaken by the seriousness and urgency of the problem facing Western Europe given the failure of economic recovery and the prospect of economic disintegration. In early May, Marshall recalled George Kennan early from a year of teaching and writing at the National War College and asked him to to establish a policy-planning unit modeled on the War Department's Division of Plans and Operations. He tasked the new group with developing a solution to the economic problems in Europe and gave Kennan only a few weeks to set it up.[73] Kennan delivered his group's recommendations to Marshall on May 23, and Marshall drew on these ideas—as well as those of the under secretary of state, Dean Acheson; the under secretary of state for economic affairs, William Clayton; and special assistant Charles Bohlen—for his speech at Harvard on June 5.[74]

The Marshall Plan enabled the United States to strengthen and support European governments that were friendly to the United States while also addressing a chief structural problem that was hampering European recovery. Europe needed immediate aid in the form of food, fuel, and

medicine, as well as assistance in rebuilding its economies and infrastructure. Europe needed to import a great deal of material, yet European countries had few exports with which to pay for such goods. US aid was thus
critical. But the assistance plan was also an opportunity to shape the future
structure of Europe. Rather than a system of self-sufficient countries, the
United States sought to develop an integrated Europe, united by a single
market that could benefit from economies of scale. Not incidentally, this
more stable and prosperous Europe would also, policymakers hoped, be
more secure against internal communist subversion and able to join the
United States in a mutually beneficial system of trade. The Marshall Plan,
along with the Truman Doctrine, indicated a dramatic shift in American
policy as policymakers, congressional leaders, and prominent private citizens accepted the new global responsibilities of the United States.[75]

Marshall's 1947 speech, however, did not articulate a detailed plan, but
instead called for European nations to cooperatively develop their own
reconstruction proposal. Marshall had argued, "There must be some
agreement among the countries of Europe as to the requirements of
the situation and the part those countries themselves will take in order
to give proper effect to whatever action would be undertaken by this
Government."[76] Representatives of sixteen European nations met in Paris
in July 1947 to develop their response to America's offer.[77] European officials did not, however, have a blank slate to work with, as American policymakers, including George Kennan and William Clayton, had devised a
set of principles to guide the recovery plan, which they felt must transcend
national boundaries; make maximum use of European materials, information, and resources; and factor in the reintegration of Germany.[78]

While aid was initially available to all countries, including the Soviet
Union and countries under its sphere of influence, the conditions set by
the Americans would have required the Soviets to relinquish the command management of their economy and open themselves up to obser-
vation and assessment. Understanding that Soviet participation would
not be possible unless they agreed to those terms, Soviet foreign minister
Vyacheslav Moltov withdrew from the conference. Stalin went even further. Concerned that Soviet satellite nations, such as Czechoslovakia and

Poland, would be tempted by the prospect of receiving American assistance, he forbade their leaders from accepting US aid—even flying them from Czechoslovakia to Moscow to inform them of his decision.[79] Far from dooming US efforts, however, the Soviet refusal to cooperate worked to the United States' advantage; for example, congressional support for the plan increased because of Soviet opposition to it.[80]

Convinced of the need to build American popular support for providing aid to Europe, the Truman administration launched a massive public relations effort. Truman, who was reluctant to restart food rationing, spoke the American people about the importance of voluntary conservation measures to free up food to be used as aid. On September 25, 1947, he held a press conference, asking all Americans to "waste less" and reduce their use of wheat so that more grain could be sent overseas.[81] He announced the creation of a Citizens Food Committee to develop plans and help carry out a food conservation effort. He asked that Americans to "conserve by being more selective in foods we buy, particularly livestock products whose production requires large quantities of grain."[82] Following the broadcast, the White House was besieged with letters from schoolchildren, who vowed to clean their plates at mealtimes, and from groups pledging to help, including farmers, bakers, and even distillers, who announced a voluntary sixty-day suspension of producing grain alcohol. By November, a Gallup poll that asked Americans if they planed to voluntarily save food by participating in strategies such as meatless Tuesdays found that 38 percent planned to do so and 22 percent were already doing it.[83] This popular support would fuel the image, at home and abroad, that America would share its bounty with the world—in exchange for defense of its values.[84]

Administration officials, including Truman and Marshall, as well as private groups, such as the Committee for the Marshall Plan, headed by former secretary of war Henry L. Stimson, undertook a range of activities to promote the plan.[85] While government officials and business leaders, farm organizations, and labor groups spoke out in favor of the plan, Marshall himself was the most visible and effective spokesperson. He traveled thousands of miles to speak to audiences around the country, recalling later, "I worked on that as hard as though I was running for the Senate or the presidency. It was just a struggle from start to finish."[86] In October, Marshall spoke in Boston to a gathering of six hundred delegates from the Congress of Industrial Organizations (CIO) about the urgent need to supply food and coal to Europe, receiving an ovation from the delegates and being hailed by the CIO president, Philip Murray, as "one of the world's greatest champions of peace."[87] The efforts by Marshall and others to sell the plan marked an important shift in American awareness of and need to respond to world hunger. These efforts were successful; a Gallup poll reported in December 1947 that in the five previous weeks, the number of Americans who viewed the plan favorably rose from 47 percent to 56 percent, and only 17 percent were opposed to it.[88]

To determine whether the United States could in fact bear the costs and impacts of an aid program estimated to cost $17 billion over a four-year period, the administration commissioned three studies. These included one by the Council of Economic Advisers that examined the potential impact on the domestic economy; one headed by secretary of the interior Julius Krug that considered the impact on America's natural resources; and an inquiry by the President's Committee on Foreign Aid chaired by the secretary of commerce, W. Averell Harriman, on the principles and policies that should guide American aid to Europe, which also examined the potential impact on domestic economy. All three studies concluded that the assistance goals could be met, but that it would require sacrifices, since many of the key products most needed by Europeans, such as wheat, coal, fertilizer, steel, and farm machinery, were also in high demand and short supply at home.[89]

The battle over the plan in Congress was complex. Republicans had taken control of both the House and the Senate in the 1946 midterm elections and the prospect of debating the plan during the 1948 election year weighed on the minds of Congress. Nevertheless, the plan enjoyed strong bipartisan support and was championed by Arthur Vandenberg, the influential Republican senator from Michigan who chaired the Senate Foreign Relations Committee. Vandenberg had been a leading isolationist in the 1930s but became a strong supporter of active American involvement in the world following the attack on Pearl Harbor. Also crucial to efforts by Vandenberg and Marshall to gain support for the plan were personal experiences and recollections of congressmen and senators who had traveled to Europe during the summer and fall of 1947 to witness first-hand the conditions on the ground. The Select Committee on Foreign Aid, chaired by Republican Congressman Christian Herter of Massachusetts, had divided up and sent its members to study in five sub-areas of Europe. Some of the members of Congress who returned and spoke of their commitment to an aid program were Republicans who, like Vandenberg, had once been staunch isolationists, including Congresswoman Frances Bolton of Ohio, Congressman Karl Mundt of South Dakota, and Congressman Everett Dirksen of Illinois. The administration's marketing of the plan, in which the sacrifices and efforts of the American people were presented as central to its success, carried over into the congressional debates. Some of the groups that the administration had won over during its public relations push played a role.[90]

Farmers' advocates and peace-minded women's groups were among the many groups the administration had cultivated over the previous months who publicly supported the plan—intertwining peace, foreign aid, and America's interest in providing sustenance to recovering Europe. Allan B. Kline, president of the American Farm Bureau Federation, testified to the House Committee on Foreign Affairs, "I along with millions of other farmers, share the deep conviction that our Nation must meet the responsibilities of world leadership" and further emphasized that among all the issues of concern facing America's farmers, the paramount question in their minds was "what can be done to attain an enduring peace?"[91] Mrs. J. L. Blair Buck, the president of the General Federation of Women's Clubs, echoed Kline's sentiments, indicating that her federation had "as a first interest the building and maintaining of peace in the wordl [sic]" and, in response to questions from committee members, stated her belief that the American housewife would be willing to make sacrifices to support recovery policies so long as "she feels they are being carried out in a way that will really build peace."[92] World events further emphasized the link between recovery assistance and peace and helped boost the plan's prospect in Congress. The February 1948 replacement of Czechoslovakia's democratically elected government with a dictatorship aligned with the Soviet Union galvanized fears that hunger and want would lead to further communist takeovers of democractic nations. The collective impact of bipartisan support, broad-based public involvement, and disturbing world events helped ensure the passage of the Economic Cooperation Act (ECA) of 1948, with the Senate voting for the bill 69 to 17 and the House voting 329 to 71. Senate and House members swiftly resolved their differences over the bill, and Truman signed the act on April 3, 1948.[93]

Under the Marshall Plan, European aid took many forms, including fuel, machinery, vehicles, raw materials, and semifinished products, such as cotton and lumber and even tobacco, but food and the vital precursors needed to produce food, such as fertilizers and animal feed, were the key components. The need for food was especially critical in the beginning to bridge the gap until European agricultural production could be restored. The lack of purchasing power of consumers in Europe's cities and towns, as well as the existence of price controls in occupied Germany, had reduced incentives for European farmers to produce food, and many fields lay fallow. Fertilizer and animal feed and products like tractors could help restart and modernize European agricultural production, but it would take time before this would begin to have a sizeable impact in European economies.[94]

In terms of what America's contributions should be, Allen W. Dulles argued, "In first line, it will be food, fuel and fertilizer, to keep body and soul together, so that there will be men and women in Europe with the strength and the will to work. And then they will be given some of the tools so that they can increase their own production of food, fuel and fertilizer."[95] The Krug report, one of the three reports commissioned by the Truman administration in 1947 to assess the viability of the Marshall Plan, identified wheat as the cheapest effective food source to help meet basic food deficiencies. The bumper wheat crop in 1947 of 1,407 million bushels (607 million bushels over the ten-year average of the harvests from 1936–45) meant that the United States was able to meet its export needs without significantly reducing its domestic use of grain.[96] American agricultural abundance was emerging as the strategic underpinning for an audacious foreign policy proposal.[97]

Even as Europe began recovering, however, its food needs remained critical, and food continued to constitute a significant portion of American aid. In the first nine months of the Marshall Plan, the slow pace of agricultural recovery in Europe and continued bad weather had made food a high-priority import, and $905 million of the first $2.1 billion of aid consisted food, feed, and fertilizers (though feed and fertilizers accounted for only $28 million of this amount).[98] Under the ECA, the United States provided a total of $14.1 billion of aid to Europe between April 3, 1948, and December 31, 1953, of which $3.6 billion was in the form of food, fertilizer, and feed, including $1.8 billion of bread grains, $138 million of meat, $118 million of dairy products, $59 million of feed and fodder, and $54 million of fertilizer.[99]

The Marshall Plan aid greatly facilitated the development and stabilization of democratic governments in Europe. A 1977 Congressional Research Service review concluded, "In addition to humanitarian considerations, it seems likely that without the $9 or $10 billion in agricultural commodities provided during this time, the political situation in Europe would not have evolved nearly as favorably for the continuation of democratic government."[100] In addition to direct food aid, other aid given under the Marshall Plan also supported food systems, as much of the fuel and machinery given under aid helped increase food production, and even more helped rebuild the infrastructure necessary to move food from farms to markets to consumers. As Marshall argued in his Harvard speech, restoring the food system also required restoring the broader economy so that workers in the cities had the goods and money to exchange with the farmers who had the food. The total value of support for food systems under the Marshall Plan would thus be higher than simply the total of $3.6 billion of food, fertilizer and feed. Nevertheless, even this amount represents more than a quarter (29 percent) of total American aid to Europe under the plan.[101]

American policymakers strategically utilized Marshall Plan funding to deploy food aid as one of the frontline responses to emerging communist

threats. In 1950, Congress approved $50 million of previously appropri-
ated funds to furnish emergency food assistance to Yugoslavia, taking
advantage of the tension between Yugoslavia and the Soviet Union. In
1951, amid concerns about a possible famine in India, Congress refused
Truman's request for a $190 million in aid for India; but it did allow the
president to lend India $190 million of Marshall Plan funds so that it
could purchase 2 million tons of US grain. International altruism was a
win-win for the United States, as the disbursments of food aid also made
good use of the crop surpluses that were beginning to accumulate in the
late 1940s. Provision of aid had a major impact on US agricultural exports.
American wheat exports increased dramatically in the postwar period,
from 56 million bushels of wheat and wheat products in 1945 to 505 million bushels in 1949. Beyond simply expanding American wheat exports,
government assistance also dramatically altered the sources of funding
food exports. In 1950, direct market purchases made up only a small percentage of American exports, as food aid financed 90 percent of the wheat
and flour and 87 percent of the feed grains exported by the United States.
These figures show that food was becoming a critical tool for American
policymakers to use in advancing American foreign policy goals.[102]

The Marshall Plan thus resulted in a profound shift in the American
food landscape, but in rather subtle ways. Though the plan was the result of
a highly visible public effort to rally citizens, policymakers, and representatives to the need to assist with European recovery, the "food aid" under
the ECA was not yet the established and strategic tool it would become
in later decades. The Marshall Plan was intended to be a temporary, one-
time effort to boost European recovery. Even that narrow goal, however,
was starting to drift toward a more global focus by the end of the program.
Nor was there a great deal of sophisticated popular consciousness—as
there would be in the 1960s and 1970s—about global hunger as a sys-
tematic and recurring problem and the importance of American capabilities in alleviating food needs. But the roots of both of those tendencies,
which would eventually guide, direct, and frame the strategic deployment
of American food as a tool of foreign relations, can be traced back to the
postwar period and to the plans and proposals that policymakers created

in order to stabilize regions, and particularly Europe, in which America had a strategic interest. As the most successful of these plans, the Marshall Plan demonstrated the diplomatic power of food and revealed to policymakers and to the American people the humanitarian and strategic value of the growing bounties of food that America was producing.

In formulating reconstruction and recovery plans, American policymakers began to draw connections between food and national security and, slowly, began to realize how America's surplus food could be deployed strategically around the globe. In the last years of the war and in the early postwar years, such connections were often murky and buried. Instead, recovery plans often, only incidentally, proposed the remaking of agricultural and food systems. However, as the Soviet threat began to loom large in American minds, a sensibility coalesced around what it was that America had to offer the world: the bounty that Americans themselves were eager to enjoy in the postwar years. While the offensive deployment of American food power was not without costs, its effectiveness was clear. Despite resistance and reluctance, American officials, including Truman, the universally well regarded and statesmanlike Marshall, and once-isolationist Republican senator Arthur Vandenberg were able to convince American policymakers and citizens that European stability and prosperity was vital to American interests and national security. The Marshall Plan, and the outward turn in American focus that it demonstrated, remains in many minds a clear example of America overcoming its isolationist instincts and taking its place on the world stage, launching what the booster Henry R. Luce foresaw as the American century.[103] The benefits of deeper American engagement with the world became apparent to American policymakers in the decades that followed its implementation.

Beyond offering America's allies in Europe material, financial, and moral assistance, George Kennan recalled that it also helped lay out a strategic and operational direction for the United States that "finally broke through the confusion of wartime pro-Sovietism, wishful thinking, anglophobia and self-righteous punitivism in which our occupational policies in Germany had thus far been enveloped, and placed us at long last on . . . a constructive and sensible path."[104] Kennan was not alone in his assessment of the Marshall Plan's importance. Historian Harry Bayard Price, tasked with compiling an official history of the Marshall Plan in 1951, judged that the great problem for the United States at the end of World War II was establishing "a secure and workable free world system" and argued that the Marshall Plan "went beyond any previous international effort in its attack on the economic aspect of the problem, and the results must be regarded in retrospect as the first steps on a long road."[105] There is ongoing debate among historians about its necessity or effectiveness, but the plan was successful and generated bipartisan support, and through the decades, it has frequently been invoked as model for other grand-scale plans, such as for African development, poverty reduction, and addressing global environmental change.[106]

One of the clearest legacies of the Marshall Plan both after the ECA's four-year term and for decades to come, was America's continued willingness to provide financial and material support to foreign nations and people in need. This was not strictly a matter of charity, even when assistance was given rather than loaned or sold. Foreign assistance advanced American vital interests and national security. In the critical, tenuous years after World War II, American policymakers and citizens turned away from their historical preferences for staying out of foreign affairs and became deeply invested in the fortunes of people in Europe and around the world. As historian John Gaddis reminds us, in these critical years, the future outcome of the Cold War was unknown. And it seemed at the time that the Soviet Union, possessing in Stalin a leader that continued in power following the end of the war and clear goals for the postwar world, had the advantage.[107] Worries that hunger and want would allow agents with sympathetic to and supported by the Soviet Union to weaken and topple governments in Western Europe—in a kind of *Is This Tomorrow* scenario—did not, to many at the time, seem far-fetched.

In light of what were perceived as major setbacks—the 1949 triumph of the Chinese Communist Party and the Soviet development of a nuclear weapon—American leaders were willing to shoulder the costs of sending surpluses abroad as a display of national power.[108] Not just politicians, but ordinary citizens worried about the Soviet aggression, wanted to bolster

American influence abroad. Perhaps most importantly, policymakers understood that instead of simply contributing to a global food system, America had the heft to create a global food system itself and to place its national interests at its core. Amid a desire for a peace dividend and a return to prosperity only dimly remembered from the years before the Great Depression, and amid hard winters and concerns that failure to help provide freedom from want and fear to areas devastated by World War II might aid the country's emerging Communist foe, Americans were willing to share the bounty of their nation. In doing do, they learned a critical lesson about the value of food power in advancing national interests and ensuring national security.

Fixed Stomachs and Convenience Foods

Abundance and Food in the 1950s

At the 1959 American National Exhibition in Moscow, Marylee Duehring, supervisor of product counselors at General Mills's Betty Crocker Kitchens, led a key battle in the postwar use of food power. Visitors to the exhibition, described by the *New York Times* as "a lavish testimonial to abundance and originality of design," were presented with an array of the kinds of consumer goods that were available to average Americans, including automobiles, home appliances, and model kitchens.[1] General Mills had sent a team of nine people to the exhibition to demonstrate America's modern convenience foods. The team worked ten hours a day, preparing more than forty cakes from boxed mixes (not just cakes but also macaroons, pastries, and "pizza-pies"). They did cooking demonstrations for small groups, as well as, twice daily, events for larger audiences that were broadcast on closed circuit television throughout the exhibition. Visitors, however, could look but not taste: Soviet officials had banned the giving away of free samples. Instead, all the prepared food had to be given to the restaurants at the exhibition, where it would be sold to visitors. The team from General Mills, though, managed to subvert Soviet directives by cutting the food into serving-size pieces, and then turning their backs to allow people to help themselves. As Duehring recalled, "Once in a while a package or a plate of brownies disappear[ed], much to our delight."[2]

Food was prominent in another event at the exhibition: an unscheduled exchange between Vice President Richard Nixon and Soviet Premier Nikita Khrushchev about the merits of capitalist versus socialist systems, in which America's new and abundant foods in the postwar years became emblematic of the advantages of the capitalist system. Dubbed "the Kitchen Debate," the phrase became a shorthand—at the time and thereafter—for the benefits of the American system over the Soviet system.[3] Even Khrushchev accepted Nixon's premise and promised that the Soviet Union would out-produce the United States in consumer goods and foods like milk and meat.[4] The exhibition demonstrated that consuming modern convenience foods was a way for Americans to express patriotism and national identity, including their new "patriotic" Cold War duties. This abundance was marketed at home and abroad in advertisements and films highlighting wealth and comfort as key aspects of postwar American life. That vision of prosperity and consumerism was one of the country's most powerful pieces of propaganda during the Cold War.[5]

But this vision wasn't ephemeral, it had been created by the policymakers, farmers, scientists, manufacturers, and advertisers who were in the process of constructing a new postwar food system. But their vision was not of a planned and centrally managed global food system like the one John Boyd Orr had advocated.[6] Instead, America was taking the lead: during the 1950s, the country took advantage of its agricultural abundance, advances in food science and technology, and food marketing to link local, regional, and national food chains in a world food system that would realize the postwar promise of making sufficient, safe, and convenient food available to all people. Abundance was written into the structure of this system—it depended on agricultural surpluses, the growing desires of American consumers, and the rapidly expanding landscape of American foods. This would become the governing vision for the postwar food system—the strategic deployment of American abundance.

Among the multitude of technological, economic, and social transformations in American life in the 1950s, food was a key marker of American progress. By the mid-1950s, the amount of food produced by American farmers had almost doubled. The average farm worker produced enough food in 1955 to feed 19 other Americans, up from 10 in 1933–35.[7] The yield per acre for corn grew from 22.8 bushels in 1931–35 to 51.7 in 1958; wheat saw less dramatic, though still impressive, increases, rising from 13.1 bushels per acre in 1931–35 to 27.3 bushels per acre in 1958.[8] In 1958, the United States produced 17 percent of the world's wheat, 52 percent of the world's corn, and 58 percent of the world's soybeans.[9] The annual growth in full-factor agricultural productivity rose from the stable 1 percent a year or so it had been for the hundred years before 1935 to at least 2 percent a year between the 1940s and the end of the century.[10] In 1959, *Time* magazine reported, "In the last 20 years, farming has changed more radically than in the previous two centuries."[11] Historian Paul Conkin has found that rapid changes in four areas—machinery, electrification, chemical inputs, and animal breeding—provided the necessary conditions for what he identifies as the most important industrial revolution in American history.[12]

In the 1950s, American food needs and realities were undergoing vast shifts, as technology was making it possible to create more "convenient" foods, such as frozen orange juice concentrate, and even packaged, mass-produced snack cakes. Yet abundance also raised new concerns, such as what constituted a "nutritious" diet, and confusion about the economic effects the postwar food system was having on American culture and values. Policymakers perceived the goals of postwar food prosperity in terms of three criteria: high stable farm prices, low food prices, and a food supply that was balanced between production and demand. The decade saw the exact opposite of all three of these trends. Farm prices were low and variable, American families were spending a higher percentage of their income on food, and surpluses (and the expense of storing them) grew steadily.

The tension between goals and realities would become a central food problem, bewildering to policymakers, business leaders, and economic and marketing experts grappling with the implications of American abundance. One key challenge that emerged was "price spread," the fact that

Americans were paying more for food while farmers were earning less— a quandary that defied traditional logic and exacerbated the problem of ensuring prosperity for farmers. By 1957, urban and suburban American families with average incomes were spending about $500 more per year on food than in 1947, but fewer of those dollars were finding their way to farmers.[13] A 1953 report from the Federal Reserve Bank of Richmond, Virginia, found that whereas most Americans believed that higher food prices meant more money for farmers, the reverse was true. Reporting on the findings, *The Index Journal* of Greenwood, South Carolina, revealed, "Actually, the farmer's share of every dollar the little wife spends at the grocery store is at a postwar low," with farmers receiving 44 cents of each retail food dollar compared to 52 cents in 1946.[14] By the late 1950s, advertising and marketing were being blamed for higher food bills and lower farm returns, with a February 4, 1958 headline from the *Terre Haute Star* declaring, "Big Hunk of Food Expense Grabbed by Publicity Boys." While advertising and marketing executives were easy targets, experts and policymakers investigating the problem learned that the price spread was a signal of deeper changes underway—a realization that complicated the notion of food abundance as an unmitigated good.

Still, this unprecedented abundance provided Americans with a range of options related to the use of food power that few societies had ever possessed. Leaders understood that this was a novel and powerful weapon. For example, when speaking to the Grocery Manufacturers of America in 1962, Henry Cabot Lodge, the former United States ambassador to the United Nations, said that if he could choose one thing to show a communist to demonstrate the superiority and efficiency of the American system, it would be "a supermarket, filled as it is with the products of your industry."[15] His choice of a supermarket was not just a pander to the crowd, but one driven, Lodge went on to say, by his experience escorting Soviet Premier Khrushchev during a visit to America in 1960. "I remember taking chairman Khrushchev and his party into a supermarket in San Francisco, and the expression on their faces was something to behold." An abundance of food provided America with a powerful but peaceful weapon to use in demonstrating the superiority of not just American agriculture and food production, especially when compared to the poor performance of a Soviet system that struggled to provide basic needs, but of the American way of life as a whole.

One strategy to reduce agricultural surpluses was to put them back into products like meat, milk, and packaged food that both used surplus crops, such as corn and sorghum, more intensively, and also demonstrated the ways that science, technology, and big business could improve the diet and standard of living of Americans. This chapter explores the ways that abundance embodied both peril and opportunity in the day-to-day lives of Americans in the 1950s. It begins by exploring the new food land-scape and how it became entwined with an increasingly homogenous and national food culture—one defined by its safety, convenience, and reliance on science and technology. It then examines the food industry as manu-facturers, restaurateurs, and marketers used new technologies to increase profitability not by finding ways to get people to eat more, but by fuel-ing their desires for new foods. Meanwhile, scientific discoveries about nutrition allowed policymakers to open up a wartime "Nutrition Front" to improve the health of military forces and citizens. The popularization of concepts like calories and vitamins meant that universal standards of healthy food and consumption levels were being established, giving Americans a comparative basis on which to judge their own abundance in relation to the rest of the world.

CONSUMPTION, CONVENIENCE, AND FOOD IN THE 1950S

Nothing was as trendy in 1950s America as the sorts of convenience foods that General Mills showcased in Moscow. Such products had spe-cial appeal amid major shifts taking place in the family and in work pat-terns that were attributable, in part, to a considerable increase in the number of Americans who could be classified as middle class (having a family income of between $4,000 and $7,500 in 1953 dollars). This was a group that amounted to 35 percent of all American families in 1953 and held 42 percent of the spendable income in the United States.[16] A critical, though often ignored, driver behind the increase in American families entering the middle class was the growing number of women working outside the home—more than 30 percent of housewives in 1953, up from 24 percent in 1941.[17] The shift affected men, too, a fact that was recognized in food marketing and also in government publications. Writing in 1959, Alfred Stefferud of the USDA Office of Information embraced new roles for men when it came to food. "Food is a big part of a man's world, too. He produces, processes, and markets food. He buys, cooks, and eats food. He earns daily bread, worries about his waistline, and sometimes feeds the baby."[18] In the 1950s, men, like women, struggled to balance expectations of work, childcare, and health and body consciousness. To meet shifting needs and expectations, families turned not to servants and in-home hired cooks, as previous generations of middle-class Americans had, but to foods, as the undersecretary of agriculture Earl Butz described them, with "built-in services."[19]

During the 1950s, policymakers, businesspeople, marketing and advertising experts, food producers, and consumers all understood that the changes taking place were unlikely to reverse themselves. Changes—on both the production and consumption sides of food—focused policymakers and regular people on food and farm issues, all of them with a stake in understanding the emerging shape of the postwar food system.

Closely related to the increasing availability of easy food with "built-in services" was the unexpected increase in the costs of food. By the early 1950s, the average American family was spending 26 percent of its income on food, up from 22 percent in 1941.[20] *Fortune* magazine, in an October 1953 cover story, called this the most baffling of all the upheavals transforming American markets, because it overturned established economic thinking about the relationship between food and income.[21] Since the late nineteenth century, economists had subscribed to Engel's Law (named for nineteenth-century German statistician Christian Lorenz Ernst Engel, not, *Fortune* was careful to point out to its readers, to be confused with the Engels who collaborated with Karl Marx), which held that as incomes rose, people would spend a smaller percentage of their total income on food. Based on Engel's Law, economists expected American spending on food to decline rather than increase.[22]

Congress got involved, launching an investigation into what a House agriculture subcommittee called the central food problem of the 1950s: "the high cost of living for everyone and low returns to the farmer."[23] Experts reported to Congress that the problem was less about opportunism or greed by advertising firms than about these fundamental social shifts. Omer W. Hermann, deputy administrator of the US Department of Agriculture's Agricultural Marketing Service, explained, "Customers are more and more being attracted by convenience and service . . . Under such circumstances retailers, in particular, look for new promotional techniques."[24] Speaking to a canning industry group in 1957, Butz explained that foods, such as canned goods, with "built-in services" and improved merchandising techniques were more costly because they had to sell themselves, and "as a result, vast expenditures for advertising and promotion have become necessary to make consumers more brand conscious."[25] Experts and marketing researchers warned that the trend toward a greater part of the food dollar going to intermediaries, such as processors, transportation people, packers, canners, and middlemen, was unlikely to change in years to come.[26]

At the same time that Americans were spending more on food, they were eating less and, by many accounts, eating better. In 1959, the average American was eating almost 100 pounds less than the 1,600 pounds of food consumed by an average American in 1915.[27] Changes in work and mechanization reduced the amount of heavy labor Americans needed to perform and improved incomes such that diets composed of bulky, starchy, low-cost foods could be abandoned.[28] Yet, while Americans were eating less food by weight, they were consuming more of what had once been considered luxury foods. Compared to the period just before World War II, Americans in the mid-1950s were eating 30 more pounds of meat per person, as well as 5 percent more fresh vegetables, 38 percent more cheese, 39 percent more eggs, 79 percent more chicken, and 36 percent more canned fruits.[29] But they were also spending their food dollars

differently, particularly favoring the new processed and packaged convenience foods.[30]

Americans had developed a taste for these new kinds of foods. Packaged
cake mixes were first introduced in 1947, and by 1957 accounted for more
than half of the homemade cakes in America.[31] Changes even impacted
consumption of foods like meat. Instead of buying a whole chicken that they
then took apart at home, Americans began to show a preference for frozen
chicken livers, canned breast of chicken, and dehydrated chicken soup. As
Fortune described the trend, "With babies to take care of, jobs to hold down,
and maids scarce, housewives looked to the food processors to perform
many of the services formerly carried on in the family kitchen."[32] Reflecting
these shifts, home production of foods continued to decline, from at least
one-third of America's food production before World War I to 18 percent in
1942 to just 8 percent in 1955.[33] Even increases in the consumption of meat
and dairy were related to growing preferences for processed and prepared
foods. For example, while Americans in the 1950s ate 20 percent more eggs
than in the 1910s, much of the increase was due to the egg content of prepared foods. Likewise, Americans consumed almost 100 pounds less per
person of raw flour, but much more flour in the form of purchased bread
and other bakery products.[34] Consumption of coffee, another luxury food,
increased because manufacturers made it more convenient. In 1953, *Fortune*
reported that "one out of every five home-made cups of coffee drunk in
the U.S. today is made from a soluble preparation, and the proportion of
"instant" is rising about 5 percentage points a year."[35] Changing food preferences helped grow the food market to $60 billion industry in 1953, $10
billion dollars more than industry specialists had predicted.[36]

Advances in food science and technology in the 1950s enabled many
of the new kinds of convenience foods that Americans desired. Theses
ranged from cheaper, more secure packaging to food sterilization processes that better preserved the food's texture and flavor. For instance,
by using cold rolled steel and protective enamel liners, manufacturers
improved the safety, stability, and palatability of foods stored in cans,
reduced the danger of corrosion, and diminished packaging costs.[37] More

precise understandings of the heating time required to kill off food safety threats like bacteria produced canned fruits and vegetables that retained more of their natural color and texture. Batch pasteurization replaced older methods that involved heating liquids at about 165 degrees F for 15 to 30 minutes in favor of techniques that rapidly heated fluids for as little as a fraction of a second and then cooled them through a series of coiled tubes, resulting in liquids with better flavor and color. Advances in freeze drying technologies improved texture, taste, and mouth feel and allowed scientists to create modern staples like instant mashed potatoes and soup mixes. Additives like calcium propionate helped preserve baked goods and extend the shelf life of breads and cakes considerably. New forms of hydrolyzed starch that could withstand temperature changes helped smooth puddings, gravies, stews, and baby foods. New artificial flavoring agents helped liberate companies from production bottlenecks because of dependence on natural fruits and flavors. All told, during the 1950s, food scientists developed more than 400 new additives for use in preserving and processing foods. While not all of the ideas panned out—such as selling upgraded versions of individually packaged military meals to consumers or producing meals-in-a-capsule by dehydrating foods and reducing them to powders—science and technology augmented the bounty of American agriculture.[38]

A key area of technological change came in the area of frozen foods. Before the war, frozen food was a relatively low-volume, specialized market that supplied high-priced foods. By the early 1950s, frozen foods represented the fastest growing segment of the food sector, and industry officials had transformed frozen food into a product seen as a low-cost, high quality food that formed a core component of Americans' daily diets. Improvements in rapid freezing technologies made possible such innovations as frozen concentrated orange juice, which tasted better and retained more vitamin C than canned juice, and quickly become popular with consumers. By 1953, frozen orange juice accounted for 20 percent of the total poundage of frozen food sold.[39] Hand in hand with, and making possible, these improvements was the more widespread availability of home refrigerators with freezer compartments. Consumers were presented with a variety of food storage appliances, such as the Cycla-matic Frigidaire, which featured "the meter-miser, the greatest cold-making mechanism ever built," or the Hotpoint two-door refrigerator that never needed defrosting.[40] The greater availability of frozen foods and home freezers also gave rise to a trend for frozen food clubs that offered members bulk purchasing of frozen foods that were delivered directly to their homes. By 1953 such clubs had nearly 300,000 subscribers and were being watched by restaurants and supermarkets worried about the loss of so many diners and shoppers.[41]

These technological changes, however, also produced products that were roughly equivalent to each other. As a result, marketing and advertising strategies made clever use of new technologies such as television and played on consumers' concerns about social status and mobility to convince them to favor one brand over another. Tying consumer's identity and sense of themselves to certain kinds of product choices allowed stores, chains, and brands to not only pitch a particular product, but also to build and maintain brand loyalty. Marketing used messages about health, safety, and even patriotic duty to build shopper's loyalty. For example, one grocery store advertisement from 1955 urged shoppers to stockpile only quality IGA brand foods to prepare for a nuclear attack.[42] Efforts to boost store brand sales, however, paled in comparison to the success of mass-advertised foods. A 1960 survey found that "seven out of ten purchases of packaged foods continue to be of major brands."[43] In addition to changes in technology and advertising, new business models, such as the emergence of integrated long-haul trucking companies allowing more rapid transportation of foods, also brought major changes to American tables.[44]

FIXED STOMACHS AND NEW FOODS: THE FOOD INDUSTRY IN THE 1950S

As Americans struggled to navigate the changing food landscape of the 1950s, the modern American food industry continued to develop, expanding what people ate, how they ate it, and how much they paid for it. In particular, the 1950s represent the rise of "Big Food," an assemblage of food manufacturers that came to be key actors between consumers, on the one hand, and the farmers, ranchers, and fishers who produced food, on the other. The collective impact of changes in technology, processing, and packaging changed almost every aspect of the American food system, including how food was grown, processed, purchased, prepared, and consumed. Companies navigating the consumer landscape faced a number of challenges. Chief among them was was the problem of "fixed stomachs," the fact that Americans were unlikely to eat more food. Increased consumption of one type of food meant decreased consumption of another type of food. It was an issue that had troubled food companies since the late nineteenth century, when they realized that once consumption increased to the point that consumers received sufficient calories and nutrients from their diet, increases in food consumption would result not from consumers eating more food but from the substitution of one food for another.[45]

This problem, however, did not lead business observers to believe that there wouldn't be growth in the food industry. In 1956, Paul Willis, president of the Grocery Manufacturers of America, predicted that food consumption would rise by about $100 million per year by the mid-1960s.[46] To achieve this growth, processors focused not on selling more foods but on increasing profits through economies of production and scale and by adding value to foods through processing and packaging to provide the convenience consumers wanted. Food companies invested heavily in new equipment that would allow them to shift from small-batch production to continuous mechanized operations that reduced or removed human involvement from various aspects of food production. Companies turned efficiency into the signature feature of their businesses. For example, Krispy Kreme Doughnuts, founded in 1939 in Winston-Salem, North Carolina, remodeled their stores so that customers could watch the clean, modern process that made donuts with machines such as the Ring-King Junior Doughnut Machine, which was capable of producing 60 dozen donuts an hour.[47] The drive for increased efficiency had a similar effect in agricultural production, as the companies that were willing and able to invest in technology and mechanization did so, often edging out smaller companies. Even a sector like canning, which had been a good market for small, rural-based companies, was affected—the number of canning companies declined by almost 25 percent from 1947 to 1954, even though the total production of canned goods increased dramatically, as larger, more mechanized producers took over the sector.[48]

As companies sought to improve efficiency, the watchword in the industry—as for consumers—was convenience. Companies could appeal to consumers' desire for convenience and time-saving by selling products with longer-shelf lives and more preprocessing that meant less preparation at home. In producing time-saving products, however, companies found the need to maintain a delicate balance between ultimate convenience and products that reinforced the home cook's sense of skill and satisfaction. General Mills, for example, found that a cake mix that only required adding water was less well received than one that required adding water *and* an egg, as home bakers liked to have a sense that their contributions were meaningful. By 1954, the USDA reported that the value added by manufacturing and food processing had risen considerably and Americans were paying $4 billion a year more (adjusted for price changes) than they did in 1939 for the convenience of products that transferred some of the work of food preparation from the home to the factory. Yet, these changes in foods and food technology, perhaps surprisingly, did not actually change American eating habits. Americans continued to like foods such as steak, mashed or French fried potatoes, bread, apple pie, cake, and coffee. It was only the methods, products, and processes used to produce and prepare the desired foods that changed in the 1950s.[49]

Changes in food preferences and technology also affected dining out in this period. While Americans continued to favor restaurants that allowed them to eat in their cars, restaurants shifted toward business models for providing faster service. Drive-ins had been around since the 1920s, but the 1950s innovation of the "drive through," pioneered in 1948 by In-N-Out Burger in Baldwin Park, California, allowed customers to line up in their cars and order through a speaker system.[50] The most popular restaurants during the 1950s continued to serve American-style meals with the emphasis on steak, lobster, and roast beef. Guides to fine dining continued to rate restaurants that featured classic American cuisine highly, though cultural cuisines were making some small inroads. For example, in 1954 the committee that compiled Ruth Nobel's *A Guide to Distinctive Dining* included only two French restaurants, two Italian restaurants, and three Mexican restaurants.[51] American attitudes toward food even impacted their views of foreign cuisine. While traveling in Europe, American restaurant critic Duncan Hines rated Britain as the best cuisine in Europe because it was possible to get good roast beef and steak-and-kidney pie there, though he came away from the trip still convinced that American cooking was the best in the world. In his guides, Hines stressed the superiority of American-style cooking and also the importance of cleanliness and sanitation, rating family-friendly restaurants, such as Howard Johnson's, highly.[52]

One of the biggest challenges facing restaurateurs in the 1950s was the need to implement the same efficiencies of production that food producers sought in the effort to overcome the problem of fixed stomachs. Even when they ate out, Americans tended to eat the same amount as, or sometimes less than, previous generations. Profitability for a restaurant, then, came from finding ways to cook foods faster and more cheaply than in the past. A notable example of this tendency was the method pioneered by the McDonald Brothers of San Bernardino, California. Ray Croc, an inventor who had approached the brothers to see if they would purchase more of his multi-mixers (capable of making five milkshakes at once), came away impressed with their business model.[53] The brothers' restaurant, along with competitors such as Burger Chef, a chain that began in 1954 in Indianapolis, Indiana, were successful because production systems removed skill from food preparation. Production-line techniques allowed cheaper, faster food production and also helped overcome a postwar labor shortage that meant that skilled cooks were so in demand they could not be retained at quick-service restaurants.[54]

Changes in foods, technology, and restaurants in America during the 1950s also supported the notion of America as a classless society. As marketers created a vision of a new American cuisine, one targeted to the growing middle class, what they served up rapidly became standardized.

Historian Harvey Levenstein describes the American table in the 1950s as one that transcended regional and class divides. "The weekday dinner table at a corporate lawyer's household in upper-middle-class Flossmoor, Illinois, looked little different from an insurance company clerk's in Levittown, New York: Campbell's canned or Lipton's dried soup, broiled meat, frozen French fries, and a frozen green vegetable with supermarket ice cream or a Jell-O concoction for dessert."[55] This preference for simple food exemplified America's sense of itself and its place in the world. Consumer satisfaction with the food landscape was demonstrated by a study in 1960, which reported to the Grocery Manufacturers of America that of 1,173 shoppers surveyed outside a supermarket only 4 percent had any suggestions about how food companies could make their products better.[56] It was evidence, along with the industry's record profits, that the changes in American food accorded well with Americans' sense of the good life in the postwar world.[57]

Companies also embraced new mediums and methods in an effort educate the public about new foods. Publishers put out new versions of such staples as the *Joy of Cooking* and *Better Homes and Gardens New Cook Book*, and women's magazines provided a continual stream of new recipes and tips about how housewives could improve their cooking, for example, by using new ingredients like soy sauce and garlic powder. The rise of large supermarkets meant a decline in the ability of grocers and stock clerks, who had once made careful decisions about the stock they would carry and had personal relationships with their customers, to influence purchasing decisions. This placed even greater emphasis on mass-media advertising and led to the deployment of new marketing strategies, such as coupons, specials, in-store displays, and redesigned packaging intended to attract attention and provide easy-to-read information that helped sell the product. Television and film became powerful mediums for conveying messages about health and prosperity and for teaching Americans, particularly young Americans, about the changing food landscape.[58]

Much of this education took place in home-economics classes and though outreach. Having enjoyed a long-standing and mutually beneficial relationship, the food industry and home economists sought to educate the public about the need to adopt a modern attitude toward food that dispensed with anecdotal evidence and teachings from the past.[59] In *Why Study Home Economics?* (1955), a film produced by the Centron Corporation with technical asstance from the Department of Home Economics at the University of Kansas, a young woman, Janice, explains why she is studying home economics. When her sister says that their mother can teach them enough to just get by, Janice replies: "But I don't want to just get by. If I'm going to be a homemaker for the rest of my life, I want to know what I am doing."[60] Other films conveyed messages about the importance of being a savvy consumer. For instance, *Buying Food* (1950) took viewers on a series of shopping trips so they could learn how to make good food choices. The film opens with the reminder that the American housewife has an important and responsible occupation that includes many roles: wife, mother, laundress, counselor, mate, chef, and purchasing agent. The film's narrator intones a number of standards to guide the young housewife in shopping wisely and fulfilling her "duty to be sure that what she has to spend buys the most in healthful, nutritious food for her family."[61] The film offers a number of tips, including using a shopping list to eliminate impulse buying. According to a 1949 study for DuPont, impulse buying accounted for well over two-thirds of the purchases of candy, pie, and dessert mixes.[62] Although the food industry may have desired impulse buying, films like *Buying Food* demonstrate the role home economistst felt that proper eduction could play in creating savvy consumers. Other strategies for purchasing wisely included matching the quantities purchased to the food requirements of the family, based on factors such as family size, storage capacity, and family members' food preferences.[63]

As *Buying Food* suggests, by the early 1950s food shopping had become a complex activity that required shoppers to be vigilant to ensure that they were not giving in to impulses or being swayed by advertising claims but were instead making wise food choices guided by values such as thrift, health, and the needs and preferences of their modern families. These films reinforce the idea that the state, working through mechanisms like Home Economics departments at land grant educational institutions, had an important advisory role in the cultivation of citizens, especially young citizens. Through educational strategies, such as films shown in home economics classes, home economists were able to emphasize the importance of strong American families guided by core values such as thriftiness, practicality, and wisdom.[64] Patriotism and performing one's civic duty through responsible consumption were strong themes in these materials. *Buying Food*, for example, to the extent that it stresses the importance of economizing, smart shopping, and home food-preservation techniques, echoes the home-economics teachings that had guided Americans through the war years. The film also promotes the idea of substitutability, explaining that since all forms of protein are similar to the proteins found in the body, ground beef, or an even cheaper form of protein such as chicken or beans, could be substituted for a T-bone steak. Films like *Why Study Home Economics?* and *Buying Food* helped arm future American housewives with the knowledge that would enable them to build strong families that could serve as bulwarks against a dangerous and rapidly changing world.[65] Efforts to shape American food consumption and help Americans navigate the changing food landscape of the 1950s relied heavily on new scientific ideas of nutrition and health.

THE "NUTRITION FRONT": NUTRITION IN A TIME OF ABUNDANCE

The scientific ideas critical to American food power, however, did not emerge in the 1950s; instead they had developed over the preceding decades as part of a series of efforts to better understand the composition of food. American understandings of nutrition and what constituted a healthy diet, coupled with developments in nutritional science in the nineteenth and early twentieth centuries, contributed to notions of food as a complex substance. Experts explained that food contained distinct components such as proteins, fats, carbohydrates, and vitamins that performed different functions and could be scientifically assessed and compared using measures such as the calorie.[66] This scientific, measurable

conception of food, Nick Cullather has argued, "popularized and factual-
ized a set of assumptions that allowed Americans to see food as an instrument of power."[67] The understanding of food as an artifact composed of
parts that could be measured and compared, especially with regard to
caloric value, was an essential element of seeing food as a marker of prosperity. Understanding food as a resource that provided energy, vitamins,
and nutrients also allowed policymakers to develop strategies to utilize
food for wartime needs and as an element of national power in the postwar world. A firm command of calories and nutrients underlay American
strategies to promote healthy eating at home and address the problem of
global hunger abroad using food and development aid as a way to expand
America's global influence. In this way, domestic notions of nutrition
became the basis for American expectations and hopes for the deployment of food power both at home and abroad.[68]

Initial developments in nutritional science came in the late nineteenth
century amid efforts by American scientists, philanthropists, and home
economists, such as Wilbur Atwater, Edward Atkinson, Mary Hinman
Abel, and Ellen Richards, to improve the lives of the poor by changing
their eating habits. A critical precursor to the work of these American
experts was the discovery by scientists, such as the German chemist Justus
von Liebig in the 1840s and 1850s, that food was composed of different
components. Each constituent part of food, such as water, protein, carbohydrate, fat, and minerals, performed specific functions and had different
physiological effects on the body. For instance, both carbohydrates and
fats provided energy, albeit in different forms, while proteins helped repair
damaged tissues. These understandings of nutrition formed the basis for
what historian Harvey Levenstein calls the "New Nutrition," a set of ideas
that encouraged people to consume food based not on what they liked or
its taste or appearance but on the nutrients it contained.[69]

Using these principles, Wilbur Atwater, who was a chemist, began
applying new research techniques to better understand the American diet.
He was convinced that Americans had developed unhealthy and uneconomic eating habits chiefly because they used cost as a way to distinguish
the quality of food. The body metabolized component parts of food in

the same way, whether the food was cheap or expensive. This meant, for example, that the protein contained in the most expensive cut of beef was nutritionally equivalent to the protein in fish or beans. What mattered to a healthy diet, Atwater believed, was not price of food but its function. An ideal diet could thus be identified and managed much more precisely, and economically, using such guides as "nutritive efficiency" than by reference to the cost of food. Efficiency, in this instance, meant eating only as much protein, carbohydrates, and fats as were needed to meet dietary requirements and choosing the lowest-cost sources of those nutrients.[70]

Atwater felt that many people, especially the poor, ate too little protein and far too many carbohydrates, especially carbohydrates from sweets. Consuming many unneeded nutrients and too few necessary nutrients thus constituted a form of waste. Ignorance about food, he believed, was a barrier to improving the lives of Americans, especially American workers. In the eyes of nutritional reformers, Americans of all classes spent too much on the wrong things, favoring diets rich in butter and beef tenderloin. Cooking methods also inhibited American nutritional efficiency, with a preference for roasting beef and an aversion to cooking soups and stews, which were economical and retained far more of the ingredients' nutrients, effectively combining nutritional and economic efficiency. Reformers felt that if dietary intake could be aligned with dietary needs, American nutrition could be considerably improved while spending on food would be reduced.[71]

The idea to improve American diets through better eating choices rather than greater expenditures on food, which would have required higher wages, was especially attractive to late nineteenth-century industrialists, philanthropists, and social reformers. Dominant economic ideas of the time, such as David Ricardo's "iron law of wages," held that wages would fluctuate and settle around a level that provided workers sufficient income to subsist rather than thrive. With policymakers and philanthropists under the sway of such ideas, it was seen as unwise to try to improve the lives of the poor by increasing their income. The "New Nutrition" thus offered alternative way to improve the lives of the poor—and, by extension, all Americans—by teaching them to make better informed eating

choices. A number of dietary reform efforts at the time sought to trans-
mit the new ideas of nutritional efficiency. Philanthropist and inventor
Edward Atkinson, for example, tried to improve the eating habits of poor
Americans with his design for the "Aladdin oven." The oven, consisting
of a tin-lined box with a hole in the bottom into which a kerosene lamp
could be inserted, used fuel more efficiently than kitchen ovens at that
time, but it was slow to heat and had trouble reaching higher tempera-
tures. Although it was cheaper to use, the oven could not reach the high,
sustained heat necessary to for cooking a roast. But it was ideal for making
the soups and stews nutritionists believed were healthier.[72]

In 1889, Atkinson joined with Mary Hinman Abel and Ellen H. Richards
to promote the Aladdin oven as part of an effort to develop public kitchens
in the United States. Abel, who had studied German scientific methods
while her pharmacologist husband was being schooled in Germany, and
Richards, a chemist who was the first female graduate and first female
faculty member of the Massachusetts Institute of Technology, sought
to address the difficult problem of changing home cooking methods by
developing public kitchens that would cheaply provide workers with
nutritious meals. Modeled on the people's kitchens that Abel had visited
in Berlin, the idea received a great deal of attention but failed to gain widespread acceptance in the United States. The departure from traditional
diets, denigration of immigrant cooking styles, along with public state-
ments by backers such as Atkinson that new food habits would alleviate
the need for higher wages—an idea not popular with labor reformers and
union leaders such as Eugene V. Debs—presented a series of insurmount-
able challenges to proponents of the idea. The limited understandings of
nutrition at the time also contributed to the problems. Nutrition advocates
and researchers did not yet understand the important role of vitamins and
minerals in the diet, and thus reformers tended to denigrate foods like
fruit and vegetables in favor of protein and starchy foods.[73]

In addition to the difficulty of changing eating habits, reformers also
encountered questions about how to compare foods and establish a
clear, easy-to-understand measure of what constituted sufficient food
and a healthy diet. An answer to the problems of measurability and

comparability of food came in the form of the calorie. The use of the word *calorie* to represent a unit of heat emerged sometime between 1787 and 1824 in France. By the 1880s, when Atwater traveled to Germany to study under German chemist Carl Voit, *calorie* was commonly used to refer to energy supplied by food. In 1887, after the government established federal agricultural experiment stations, Atwater accepted a position as director of the Storrs Agricultural Experiment Station in Connecticut, where he worked to develop a system that would allow people to select foods based on a rational assessment of their nutritive value. At the time, however, the federal government did not support pure scientific research, and the station's initial work focused on improving understanding of animal, rather than human, nutrition. By 1893, however, Atwater, with help from Atkinson, was able to to persuade Julius Sterling Morton, a Nebraska newspaper editor who served as Secretary of Agriculture under President Grover Cleveland, to request congressional funding of studies of human nutrition. Atwater was able to secure the funds needed to build a respiration calorimeter. Unlike previous studies, in which reasearchers had to estimate nutritional requirements and energy values of food, the respiration calorimeter, a sealed chamber in which animals or people could live for days, allowed precise measurements. Atwater's link between pure and practical science helped convince Congress to fund his experiments and also persuaded Governor Luzon Morris and the General Assembly of Connecticut to help fund the building of a calorimeter in Atwater's laboratory at Wesleyan University.[74]

Using the new calorimeter, Atwater and his colleagues developed concrete understanding of how the human body consumed and used food. The work attracted attention from media outlets that prognosticated about its importance for human societies. In April 1896, for example, the *New York Times* reported that Mr. A. W. Smith had lived in the calorimeter apparatus for twelve days and six hours, the longest continuous experiment to date. The *Times* noted that while experiments were still ongoing, "when fully completed, they will doubtless throw very valuable light on the quantities of food materials used by the body when at rest and when the person is engaged in intellectual and muscular work and also upon the relations of energy to the bodily functions."[75] In 1899, the *Times* reported that Atwater's research had allowed for the discovery of what they characterized as a scientific law governing the consumption and utilization of food by the human body.[76] Atwater's data had made it possible to create numerical tables that assigned calorie counts to specific foods and indicated the number of calories burned in various activities, from working to sleeping to reading. His success led to the creation of additional calorimeters in Washington, DC, by the USDA; at Harvard University, with the support of the Carnegie Institute; and at Pennsylvania State College (now Penn State University), where a calorimeter was central to the experiments by the Institute of Animal Nutrition in studies the energy metabolism of cattle.[77]

Armed with Atwater's findings, various constituencies considered how to use the data to improve American life. Members of the clergy were bolstered by findings that the human body produced energy more efficiently than a steam locomotive. The Women's Christian Temperance Union did protest against Atwater's work, when in one experiment he had a subject subsist for six days on a diet that largely consisted of alcohol, with the finding that alcohol was a good source of energy. But others, such as Carroll D. Wright, the US commissioner of labor, saw the potential to use Atwater's findings to change the diets of city slum dwellers. Other experts saw the potential to revolutionize management of factories, prisons, and armies and argued that the findings could be used to measure and compare the diets of different cultures, social classes, and nations. Atwater did little to tamp down the discussion of his work's revolutionary effects. In an 1891 article in *The Century Magazine*, for example, he addressed the concerns of the English cleric and scholar Thomas Robert Malthus, who worried about the inevitability of food crises arising from the different rates of increase in agricultural production and in the human population. Atwater assured *Century*'s readers that modern science had solved the problem of food shortages and famine and that "the prospect for the future of the race is not one of Malthusian dreadfulness, but full of inspiring hope."[78] By the early twentieth century, the calorie had become an international measure of food value, providing scientists and policymakers with a way to assess and manage food supplies in an ordered, empirical manner, which would be central to later efforts to use food as symbol of American security and prosperity.[79]

Further developments necessary for the conceptualization and deployment of food as a form of power occurred during the first decades of the twentieth century. The discovery of vitamins, for example, revolutionized nutritional and food science and shifted understandings of health. In 1912, Polish chemist Casimir Funk identified what he called "viatmines," previously unknown elements of food that were essential to good health. In 1911, Funk discovered a water-soluble nutrient, later named vitamin B. Other scientists also began to identify vitamins. Elmer McCollum at Yale identified a fat-soluble vitamin related to the maintenance of good vision and health, which he called vitamin A. In 1916, McCollum identified a critical link between a deficiency of vitamin B1 (thiamine) and beriberi, a set of health conditions related to thiamine deficiency. In the early decades of the twentieth century, efforts to develop artificial foods—often for infants—using the approach developed by Atwater and his contemporaries for producing foods from proteins, carbohydrates, fats, and salts, yielded foods that did not provide sufficient nutrition. But studies on rats, begun by McCollum and other scientists at Yale, increased our understanding of problems related to vitamin deficiencies, even if other food components were present in sufficient quantities. At the time, scientists and physicians were developing the germ theory of disease—which would revolutionize medicine and public health—popularizing the understanding that health could be negatively impacted by the presence microscopic foreign agents in the body.[80] If scientists now understood that the presence of harmful germs could cause ill health, the identification of vitamins showed that health could also be negatively affected by the absence of beneficial substances.[81] Vitamins C and D were identified, which led to an awareness that eating certain foods, such as citrus fruits, could have a protective effect on health. For instance, in 1934 the California Fruit Growers Exchange claimed, based on the testimony of a Chicago doctor, that consumption of Sunkist orange juice and lemon juice reduced children's gum troubles and tooth decay.

Because methods for manufacturing vitamin pills and measuring the amount of vitamins in food would not be discovered until the 1930s, the discovery of vitamins was initially a boon to hucksters, faddists, and unscrupulous companies making all sorts of extravagant claims about the health benefits of, for example, eating yeast cakes, drinking fruit juice, or eating vitamin-packed chocolates. Despite the actions of hucksters, during the 1920s, most Americans became familiar with the message that a healthy diet consisted of eating a mix of foods, rather than just the foods that one liked. Food companies in particular, learned to trumpet the latest research that gave a boost to their products or, at the very least, to make the most of inconclusive studies that allowed making claims. By the early 1930s, however, reliable methods to measure the amounts of vitamins in food had been discovered, and this newer understanding of nutrition contributed to diet and health knowledge during the Great Depression and World War II.[82]

At the beginning of World War II, policymakers and scientists understood that the discovery of vitamins made the dietary advice from World War I obsolete. Scientists now spoke of revolutionary changes in nutrition that would help the United States win the war. In January 1941, the *New York Times* wrote, "In 1917 the slogan was: 'Food will win the war.' With present-day knowledge that would be revised; read 'vitamins' for 'food.'" Dr. M. L. Wilson of the USDA elaborated on connection between nutrition and the war effort: "Proper nutrition is exactly as important to the country now as are 50,000 airplanes that will fly 400 miles and hour. There is, now, a Nutrition Front."[83]

Understanding the importance of nutrition also helped fuel concerns about malnutrition and encouraged the federal government to for the first time take a stance on what constituted a healthy diet. In 1941 it released its Recommended Dietary Allowances, developed by a subcommittee of the National Research Council's Committee on Food and Nutrition, led by Lydia Roberts, a home economist at the University of Chicago, the first government-promulgated standard that could be used to assess the dietary sufficiency of the entire American population.[84]

By the 1950s, nutritional science had developed a much more robust understanding of the composition of food and the role of food in maintaining heath. The USDA emerged as the key government agency for managing food and nutrition in the United States. Secretary Benson, writing in USDA's 1959 *Yearbook of Agriculture*, commented, "The Department of Agriculture is, in a sense, a department of food—food for health and fitness."[85] As described by Dr. Hazel Sterling, director of the USDA's Institute of Home Economics, the agency took a broad view of the importance of food, holding that "food contributes to physical, mental and emotional health. Food nourishes our bodies. When we eat in a favorable setting, we get another kind of well-being: A sense of belonging and other psychological and social values accrue from the pleasures of mealtime and from having our food with friendly companions."[86] As Sterling recognized, food played many roles in the lives of Americans during the 1950s and was a critical component of not only nutrition, but also the cultural, social, and economic areas of daily life.

Dietary advice began coming at Americans from a dizzying array of sources, including media outlets, food companies, and health experts. Government agencies and bodies supported this effort by updating standards and guidelines, publishing a revised version of the Recommended Dietary Allowances in 1958.[87] The initial guidelines had been developed during wartime "so that nutritional knowledge could be utilized to best advantage in planning the health and productivity" of the United States. The 1958 revisions focused on a broader goal and were "designed to maintain good nutrition in healthy persons.[88] The revisions made a number of important changes that reflected the prosperity and health of the country during the 1950s and represented, scientists and physicians were careful to point out, only the minimal requirements.[89] While the federal and state governments did have authority over some areas of the food system, such as product labeling and safety, government policymakers and scientists were more comfortable in an advisory, rather than a controlling, role when it came to questions of food and health.

But despite having a better understanding of nutrition and no shortage of advice about how to eat, American consumers, producers, and policymakers confronted food problems in the 1950s. Amid agricultural, scientific and technical plenty, abundance itself would emerge as a central food

problem—of more food available, higher food costs to urban and suburban consumers, and lower returns to farmers. Policymakers, businesses,
farmers, and consumers struggled in the 1950s to understand and navigate a changing food landscape. By the middle of the twentieth century,
a convergence of global trends, including postwar economic recovery, a
revolution in agricultural productivity, and dramatic changes in the food
industry converged to dim early hopes that abundance would easily lead
to shared prosperity for all. Even the changing market for food could not
absorb all of the food being produced by farmers, fishers and ranchers in
a way that brought prosperity for all Americans.

Ultimately, policymakers settled on agricultural surpluses as the root of
the food problem. If only, they argued, the surpluses could be eliminated,
farmers would make higher incomes and food prices would fall as supply
was brought in balance with demand. Addressing the significance of food
to America, Secretary Benson wrote, in 1959, "Food is important in keeping our people and our country strong.... An abundance of food is one
of our blessings. The problems caused by our excessive supplies of a few
commodities are quite in contrast to the hunger experienced daily by large
number of people in many countries of the world." He concluded by noting that he was "grateful that we struggle with problems of too much rather
than too little."[90] Abundance thus presented both peril and opportunity.

Perhaps, American leaders reasoned, if food could not be absorbed
in domestic markets, it could be harnessed as a powerful and deployable
weapon to use in addressing foreign policy goals. Coupled with understandings of nutrition that allowed food to be seen as a uniform, com-
parable, and transferable resource, American policymakers came to see
food as a valuable tool in international affairs.[91] But leaders struggled to
understand how America could strategically use food power to be more
than just an advertisement for America. Was an abundance of food a
weapon to be deployed on terms that brought maximum advantage to
the United States? Was an abundance of food a basic human necessity
that the United States had an obligation to give out to ease human suffering and respond to unexpected shocks in global food production?
Was an abundance of food a great resource that could be packaged and

stockpiled in bomb shelters to help provide deterrence by increasing the difficulty of successful Soviet atomic attacks and that would help with recovery in the event of a nuclear war? In this way, Cold War debates about food reflected debates in Cold War security thinking as policymakers, scholars, military officials, and scientists sought to understand the sudden shifts of tactics and strategy brought about by the advent of nuclear weapons and other weapons of mass destruction.[92] As with nuclear weapons, American policymakers and experts struggled to understand and develop a doctrine for the deployment of food as an element of national power.

Freedom to Farm

Prosperity, Security, and "the Farm Problem" in the 1950s

In a photo from October 1958, an unnamed farmer sits on his tractor in the middle of a large cornfield near Kasson, Minnesota; he is looking, somewhat forlornly, at the camera. The photo accompanied a *New York Times* story entitled, "Minnesota Farm Disquiet Found Aiding Democrats."[1] Indeed, it was an unsettled moment for American farming, as small-scale farmers found themselves at the center of the political debate over the farm problem: despite the agricultural abundance of the postwar years, farmers were making less but consumers were paying more for food. The lonely Minnesotan sitting forlornly in his field seemed to foretell, not simply an end of sorts, as the family farm faded from reality to myth, but also a shift in the place that agriculture occupied in the American policymaking landscape. The abundance of the 1950s altered American perceptions of food at home, but those shifts were undergirded by the growing notion that food could be a strategic resource—one that could, if managed properly, make both the home front and the international arena a safer and more stable for the United States.

This shift was apparent in domestic politics, and concern about agriculture was a topic of considerable discussion in Minnesota and across the country as discontent over farm policy emerged as a key issue in the 1958 mid-term elections. Since his appointment in 1953, President Eisenhower's secretary of agriculture, Ezra Taft Benson, had been promoting an approach to agriculture he felt would allow farmers to farm unfettered by complex systems of government agricultural controls. Benson wrote, "The farm problem is not a passing problem; nor one simple of solution. Yet it is vital that a solution be reached. Many civilizations have come into being and have flourished and then have fallen into decline and finally into virtual extinction because they failed to meet their agricultural problem."[2] The farm problem was thus not something Benson viewed merely as a matter of convenience or ensuring a wide range of food choices, but as a question that was fundamental to the security and stability of the United States.[3]

Benson, who had grown up on a farm in Idaho, had carefully built a career as a solid member of the agricultural community. Despite some efforts by Congress and the Truman Adminstration to reform the system of rigid farm price supports that had been in place since World War II, postwar reconstruction and the Korean War had hindered previous efforts reduce the government's role in agriculture. Benson's efforts to reduce the role of government found support from farm organizations, such as the Farm Bureau, and many representatives in Congress, both Democratic and Republican, from both cities and the newly emerging suburbs. But he encountered opposition from such groups as the National Farmer's Union as well as from both Democrats and Republicans representing the farm states. Some of Benson's most vocal congressional critics were Republicans, who blamed his style and policies for the party's failure to regain control of Congress in 1954 and fretted over the possibility of further losses in the mid-term elections of 1958.[4]

Across America, many farmers saw Benson as the embodiment of changes and trends in agriculture that were making farming more challenging, especially for the smaller producers often discussed as "family farmers." In that October 1958 article, the *New York Times*, had also reported that in many farm communities, Benson's name "was pronounced in sour tones, often in anger," quoting Mrs. C. A. McEvers, of Sabin, Minnesota, who said bluntly, "Benson doesn't dare come up here."[5] Benson's support for the industrialization of agriculture and easing of government price supports drew the ire of small farmers, such as one Minnesota farmer who commented, "In other words you've got to get big or get out ... Benson has said as much, and we family farmers don't like it."[6]

These reactions illustrate the difficulty policymakers faced in trying to balance the desire of producers for higher farm prices with those of consumers for low food prices. But, as Benson was well aware, broader international concerns were at play as well. The push for a more global-ized perspective on food was a key driver of American policymaking, and Benson, among others, argued that to compete in the changing global economy, American farmers had to embrace the technological and meth-odological changes offered by intensified agricultural production, even if that led to overproduction. This, however, also meant embracing the downsides of abundance—one of which seemed to be the intractable "farm problem." While US farmers boosted production, increasing the food sup-ply, policymakers were faced with the new task of avoiding surpluses and supporting farmers' incomes while also ensuring low food prices for con-sumers and reducing the cost to government of farm-policy programs.[7]

The need to balance these competing interests bedeviled the Executive Branch and congressional policymakers throughout the 1950s. Benson and other policymakers implemented a number of strategies to address the problem of abundance, for example, trying to limit oversupply by making agricultural production more sensitive to market forces in order to reduce the costs of government agricultural programs and provide farmers with freedom from government control. Yet these policies had a limited effect. Unable to contain abundance with supply management, Benson then advocated opening up new markets and advancing foreign policy goals by exporting American commodities through sales, loans, and gifts of food aid. If abundance couldn't be reduced or avoided, the argument seemed to go, perhaps it could be utilized to advance the vision of world that the United States wanted to see. During the early stages of the Cold War, as politicians worried about courting voters in farm states and stabilizing the domestic economic situation, food politics was becom-ing increasingly intertwined in geopolitics abroad. Indeed, Benson's most important legacy ended up not being his adept management of agricul-tural surpluses, but his support for the development of multiple pathways to deploy those surpluses through strategies such as opening up new markets for American agriculture and formalizing food aid programs. Although Benson's policies would not achieve the goal of eliminating surpluses in the 1950s, the policy directions set during his tenure would pioneer a new approach to using food as a lever of international power and eventually help to end agricultural surpluses by the early 1970s.[8]

Policymakers sought to harness and deploy America's food power, both offensively abroad and defensively at home, to advance American security and prosperity. Yet, as this chapter explores, their efforts were complicated by the traditional problem of balancing supply and demand that had plagued American agricultural policy at least since the New Deal but also seemed newly salient in a period of agricultural abundance, to which there appeared, in the intense international competition of the Cold War, a new solution. This solution, if harnessed correctly, would benefit farmers, politicians, and America's geopolitical position. The chapter first reviews the history of agricultural policy in the United States and the ways the history of farm policy informed the debates and concerns of the 1950s. It then examines efforts by policymakers to come to terms with the farm problem through changes in domestic policy, followed by concerns about rural prosperity during the 1950s. Finally, it explores policymaker's efforts to offensively deploy food to solve the food problem at home and buttress American national security abroad.

FARM POLITICS AND FARM POLICY IN THE 1950S

In 1952, presidential candidate Dwight D. Eisenhower knew that he needed to satisfactorily address the farm problem if he were to secure enough votes from American farmers to avoid the fate of Thomas Dewey. Dewey had narrowly lost the 1948 presidential election to Harry Truman in part, the conventional wisdom held, because of his failure to convince farmers that the Republican party offered a better plan for farm policy through efforts that would boost farm income while also enchancing the autonomy of farmers. But it was not just the memory of 1948 that weighed on Eisenhower and the Republicans in 1952. Going into the election, Republicans had lost five presidential elections in a row. Many believed that Eisenhower was the candidate who could end that losing streak: the retired five-star general had served as the Supreme Commander of the Allied Forces in Europe, the first supreme allied commander of NATO, Army Chief of Staff under President Truman, and president of Columbia University. Yet Republicans, especially in the Midwestern farm states, worried that Eisenhower's self-professed lack of detailed knowledge about farm policy would hinder his efforts to reach out to the farm bloc and doom the Republicans to another loss.

The challenge Eisenhower faced was rooted, in part, in the complicated history of US agricultural policy. By 1952, American farm policy had gone through two main phases. The first, running from the beginning of the nation until the late nineteenth century, grew out of the problem of scarcity, and was primarily focused on boosting productivity. This effort included the trade and economic policies of the early republic, efforts to balance agrarian interests with the emerging industrial economy in the mid-1800s, and the challenge of finding ways to smooth out the economic boom and bust cycle of agricultural production during the late 1800s and early 1900s. The second major period of American agricultural policy began after World War I. Now, the overarching problem in American agriculture was not scarcity but abundance. Global needs for food during the war had boosted prices and sparked growth in domestic agricultural production. Following the war, American production at those levels continued; but as countries devastated by the war gradually resumed agricultural production, the demand for American food and fiber crops like cotton decreased. American farmers thus felt the onset of economic difficulties early in the 1920s, before other sectors of the American economy.[9]

By the late 1920s, challenges in the larger economy began to exacerbate the problems faced by farmers. For example, in the 1920s and early 1930s, many farms carried mortgages for periods of three years or less. As banks sought to improve their financial balance sheets during the banking crises that began the Great Depression, one easy way for banks to boost their bottom line was to stop rolling over, or refinancing, farm mortgages.

The Agricultural Marketing Act of 1929, under the administration of Republican president Herbert Hoover, created the Federal Farm Board to help stabilize prices and promote the sale of American farm products through the organization of marketing cooperatives , but with only a half billion dollars in funding and a relatively limited mandate compared to subsequent farm programs, the board was unable to deal with the magnitude of the problem. The board's failure, combined with the general perception that Hoover was less than sympathetic to the plight of Americans in the early years of the Great Depression, led to a realignment of American politics, as farmers joined with industrial workers, urban voters, and liberal intellectuals to support Franklin D. Roosevelt, and his New Deal that promised to protect Americans from economic disruptions.[10]

The result were New Deal–era policies that sought to manage some of the country's most persistent economic problems, creating tensions that would continue into the 1950s and establish the policy reality that Eisenhower would face during the elections. With the Agricultural Adjustment Act of 1933 (AAA), Midwestern Republicans joined with New Deal Democrats to establish a system of government support of farm prices. Initial efforts, in 1933, focused on lowering production by allowing farmers to enter into voluntary agreements with the federal government to reduce production in exchange for benefit payments or supplemental income. The act also sought to boost farm income by increasing the ability of farmers to achieve equality with workers in other economic sectors. The standard used by agricultural policy to compare the economic performance of farmers to other American workers is called agricultural parity. It is a measure developed by economists and policymakers to provide farmers with economic justice. Parity prices were calculated to maintain farm prices at a prescribed ratio of predetermined prices, initially between 52 percent and 75 percent of an average of farm prices between Janaury 1910 and December 1914, years of high prices and general rural prosperity. Parity was introduced as a measure that could be used to guarantee farmers a certain percentage of past farm prices, regardless of what prices the market set for their products at the time they sought to sell them.[11] Early New Deal efforts also included the

Emergency Farm Mortgage Act and the Farm Credit Act, both of 1933, which addressed the problem of ensuring adequate credit to the farm sector. Amendments to the AAA in 1938 consolidated federal policy efforts to reduce surpluses through establishing new loan programs on corn, wheat, rice, cotton, and tobacco that were only avalible to farmers who accepted production controls. The act also allowed farmers to use crops at harvest as collateral for loans.[12]

Links between full farm production and national security were established by changes in agricultural policy necessitated by the wartime needs of America and its allies. As in WWI, increased demand for agricultural production during World War II strengthened prices and resulted in an increase of parity prices to a fixed 90 percent of parity to ensure maximum production. Once established, this system of fixed prices would prove hard to remove. After the war, when policymakers were worried about a return to surpluses and economic downturn, pressure from farmers wanting to share in the postwar prosperity made Congress hesitant to lower the fixed parity levels. In the Agricultural Act of 1948, Congress extended the temporary system of rigid price supports to 1950, but also established, in Titles II and III of the Act, a new system of more flexible price supports that would take effect that year.[13]

Called "flexible parity," the new system broadened the range of price supports to between 60 percent and 90 percent and updated the base period used to calculate the percentage to incorporate an average of prices from the previous 10 years as well as the base period of 1910–1914. The system was designed to return a measure of free market activity to agricultural sector. Although the 1948 act was based on suggestions from his sececretary of agriculture, Clinton Anderson, President Harry Truman was largely opposed to the new system. Truman did sign the act, however, chiefly, he said, to ensure the continuation of the price-support programs that were "vital elements in our agricultural and national prosperity," stipulating, however, that the act did not "provide the basic declaration of long-range agricultural policy" that he felt was needed.[14] Truman made the act an issue in his 1948 re-election campaign, suggesting that it was evidence the Republican-majority 80th Congress was intent on overturning New Deal policies and reducing farm income. He pointed to other farm-policy problems as well, such as reduced funding for the Commodity Credit Corporation, which stored the food and fiber crops in surplus held by the federal government, as well as Congress's failure to fully fund market research or establish a program to improve the diets of low-income Americans.[15] Following his re-election, Truman turned to his new secretary of agriculture, Charles Brannan, to develop a long-term vision for postwar farm policy.[16]

In an effort to simplify and modernize agricultural policy, Charles Brannan announced a grand plan in 1949 that had it been enacted would have amounted to a major overhaul of agricultural policy, needed, Brannan argued, because "the prosperity of our agricultural producers is closely tied up with the prosperity of our entire country."[17] Using logic similar to that underlying the New Deal reforms, Brannan reasoned that if farmers had more disposable income, then they would spend more, which would benefit other sectors of the economy. Brannan's proposed methods for achieving this goal, however, was sharply divergent. Rather than a complicated parity formula, he wanted to provide farmers with direct payments from the federal government. Brannan wanted to put in place an income standard based on a ten-year average, starting with the period 1938–1947. Brannan's plan was intended to ensure high income for farmers and low food prices for consumers, but would have entailed a dramatic expansion of federal involvement in agriculture. Old policies, such as loans and crop storage, would have been replaced with new payments that would rigidly control farm output using acreage alotments and marketing quotas, at a high cost to American taxpayers. The plan had Truman's support, but the reception in Congress and from farm organizations was mixed. Groups such as the National Farmers Union supported it, but many other organizations, such as the American Farm Bureau Federation and the National Council of Farmer Cooperatives, were against it. Many people felt it was an effort to permanently tie farmers to the Democratic Party, and it became a topic of great debate across the country. Ultimately, Congress voted opted instead to pass the Agricultural Act of 1949, which continued 90 percent price supports through 1950. Although it failed, the debate over the Brannan Plan represented the first major conversation about the shape of the postwar American food system.[18]

The 1949 act, passed with considerable Republican support, repealed the price support sections of the 1948 act, developed a new modernized parity measure for price supports, and postponed the transition to flexible price supports until 1952. Further, the Act provided that until 1954, the secretary of agriculture was required to use the higher of either the old 1910–14 parity measure or the new "modernized" measure in the 1949 bill, so as to guarantee farmers the highest income. Refusing to admit defeat, Brannan promised to take his appeal directly to the American people, but his efforts were unsuccessful. The outbreak of the Korean War prompted Congress to extend rigid price supports for two more years, postponing flexible price supports until 1954. Although the war increased demand, the postwar recovery of Europe and Asia meant less demand for food from America. Brannan's assault on price controls and the failure of Truman to enact the long-term agricultural reform he had called for combined to create favorable conditions for the Republicans in the lead up to the 1952 presidential election.[19]

Though it was far from the high point of public interest in farm policy occasioned by the debates around the Brannan Plan, in 1952, farm policy was once again a critical issue for the presidential campaigns. Farmers had emerged as a vital and almost independent bloc of voters in the late 1940s and early 1950s; states in which farmers' votes were decisive became known as "farm states." The farm belt stretched from Ohio west across the Mississippi to the states of Iowa, Wisconsin, Minnesota, the Dakotas, Nebraska, and Kansas. By the early 1950s, the farm bloc was seen as chiefly interested in their pocketbooks, but also concerned about a set of larger issues that impacted farm productivity and farm prices—including, most of all, national security, which they saw taking their children and needed workers from farms in the form of the draft. Farmers also worried about the effects of national security on the farm sector's economic health and the effects of wartime conditions on markets, income, and available goods. Farmers were regarded as traditionally Republican but willing to display a measure of independence and to switch parties between presidential and off-year elections. The election of Truman in 1948 illustrated this trend. Republicans realized that with only a few of the farm votes that went to Truman they could have won the election. In the 1950 mid-terms elections, Republicans picked up twenty-eight seats in the House and six in the Senate, which positioned them to potentially win majorities in both houses in 1952. Approaching the 1952 election, both parties felt they needed the farm vote to be victorious. Republicans were hopeful that with the right candidate, and the right message on farm policy, they could secure the farm vote and break their presidential losing streak.[20]

Republican hopes were buoyed by the Democratic Party's choice of Governor Adlai Stevenson of Illinois as their candidate and by recent crop storage scandals which focused attention on farm policy problems. Stevenson's farm policy views were relatively unknown, despite his having served as governor of a farm state for four years, and he took a relatively safe line by endorsing the continuation of price supports at 90 percent of parity. He also supported policy modifications, such as removing perishable products such as potatoes from the price-support system—a policy change necessitated by public outrage over the "great potato fiasco," when significant amounts of the government's holdings of potatoes rotted while in storage.[21] Given the uncertainty about Stevenson's farm policy views, Eisenhower's farm advisers, including Senator Frank Carlson of Kansas and Senator Fred Seaton of Nebraska, encouraged him to embrace the 90 percent standard as well. Other advisers, such as Representative Clifford Hope of Kansas, considered during the campaign a likely contender for secretary of agriculture, likewise felt Eisenhower needed to declare that he was clearly in favor of high, rigid price supports. Eisenhower, however, was hesitant to take such a strong stance, personally believing that government control over agriculture needed to be reduced. He was, however, aware that clearly stating those beliefs to farm-state audiences would undercut Republican efforts to compete for the farm vote.[22]

In a wide-ranging speech on September 6, 1952, at the National Plowing Contest in Kasson, Minnesota, Eisenhower laid out his views on agriculture. He expressed his support for land conservation efforts and reminded attendees of his own Midwestern origins, saying "man draws his strength from the land," though he was careful to acknowledge the limits of his farm expertise. "In discussing one phase of the farm program with you, I am not going to pretend to be a farmer. My farm activities belonged to the day of the percheron and the mule; the walking plow and the wheat binder; the traveling thresher and husking corn by hand. Things have changed."[23] Before turning to issues of farm policy and farm income, Eisenhower first addressed the national security concerns of the farm bloc by asserting, "We owe it to ourselves and to our children to give them the chance to remain here on these fertile, peaceful lands, to establish families of their own—and not to be sacrificed to stupid blunders in world politics." He promised he would first and foremost work with other nations to "establish peace and maintain freedom," stressing that "a productive, prosperous agriculture is a foundation stone" of the strong, secure, solvent United States he hoped to lead. Turning to farm policy, Eisenhower invoked what he saw as a bipartisan heritage of farm policy "based on the sound principle that the Government should aid farmers to aid themselves." Yet, he warned, farm policy had strayed from this bipartisan foundation and been taken over by "Washington agricultural autocrats" or "agricrats." He cited the great potato fiasco and another scandal, known as "the grain storage hoax of 1948" as warnings against believing Democratic claims about Republican farm policy positions.[24] According to Eisenhower, it was the Democrats who were trying to do away with New Deal era polices, whereas the Republicans promised continuity for existing programs and support levels..[25]

Eisenhower vowed that "the Republican Party is going forward with positive, aggressive farmer-run farm programs." In terms of specifics, he pledged, "Here, and now, without any 'ifs' or 'buts,' I say to you that I stand behind—and the Republican party stands behind—the price support laws on the books . . . to continue through 1954 the price supports on basic commodities at 90 percent of parity." In the speech, Eisenhower not only endorsed existing law and promises, which he called "a moral and legal commitment which must be upheld," but also carefully laid the groundwork for his longer-term goal of helping famers get "a full, fair share of the national income," a goal that must be achieved "in ways that

minimize Government control and protect farmer's independence."[26] In
the Kasson speech, and again in a similar speech delivered on October 6,
1952, in Memphis, Tennessee, Eisenhower endorsed the high, rigid price
controls and pledged to develop a new plan that would give farmers full
income parity with other Americans while lessening the government's
involvement in agriculture.[27] The pledge seemed unequivocal, but as historians Edward Schapsmeier and Frederick Schapsmeier observe, in reality, Eisenhower only committed to maintaining existing policy until its
expiration in 1954.[28] Nevertheless, Eisenhower accomplished the goal that
he and his advisers had hoped for, a success demonstrated when Truman
accused him of attempting to steal the Democratic record on farm policy.[29] Eisenhower's farm platform, combined with his personal charisma,
contributed to the Republican landslide victory in over Stevenson—his
farm bloc support had allowed him to win five states—Illinois, Iowa,
Oklahoma, Texas, and Colorado—by greater margins than the Democrats
had in 1948.[30]

FARM POLICY IN THE EISENHOWER ADMINISTRATION

President-elect Eisenhower entered office determined to keep his campaign pledges but also to address overproduction and farm income issues
by bringing modern science, technology, and expertise to bear on the
farm problem. The immediate task facing him was selecting his secretary
of agriculture. Ezra Taft Benson would profoundly shape the Eisenhower
administration's efforts to limit the farm subsidies that continued to fuel
the production of huge agricultural surpluses. When those efforts were
largely stymied or proved unsuccessful in addressing the problem, Benson
would then support a new policy of directing those surpluses to offensive uses. Benson had a deep knowledge of agriculture and had cultivated
broad networks within its most powerful political organizations. While a
student at Utah State Agricultural College (now Utah State University), he
had spent alternating semesters working on his family's farm. He earned
a master's degree in agricultural economics from Iowa State College

(now Iowa State University) and helped start cooperative associations when he worked for the Idaho Extension Service. From 1939 to 1944, Benson served as executive secretary of the National Council of Farmer Cooperatives, an organization of more than 4,600 cooperatives; thereafter, he directed the Farm Foundation, from 1946 to 1950. Benson gained political experience as a member of the National Agricultural Advisory Council during World War II and testified before Congress representing the interests of farm cooperatives. He was also deeply religious. Despite his expertise in agriculture, Benson thought of himself as a clergyman first; he was a high official in the Mormon Church and a member of the Council of the Twelve Apostles.[31]

Benson's nomination was supported by a range of farm organizations. Allan Kline of the American Farm Bureau Federation called it was a "top-notch appointment." Herschel Newsom, the master of the National Grange, commented, "President Eisenhower is to be commended on his choice"; while James Patton, president of the National Farmers Union, said, "He will hold the balance level between farm organizations, which is all we ask. . . . All in all, I think this is one of the best of Mr. Eisenhower's cabinet appointments, one which promises well."[32] The confirmation hearings were not without a few rocky moments. Some farm-bloc senators, such as Republican Milton Young of North Dakota and Edward J. Thye of Minnesota, tried to get him to commit to supporting a permanent 90 percent of parity subsidy, or at least to extend it beyond 1954; the nominee would only affirm his support for the Eisenhower's election pledge. Ultimately, however, Benson was easily confirmed.[33]

Benson's ideas about agriculture became much more widely known after a February 5, 1953, press conference, when, in front of about a hundred reporters gathered in the USDA administration building, he announced there would be no sweeping changes in the Department of Agriculture or an immediate farm policy proposal from the administration, pledging, "There would be no Brannan Plan type of approach, to change the whole face of American agriculture and make farmers wards of the federal government."[34] He distributed the "General Statement on Agricultural Policy," a two-thousand-word document drafted by Benson, vetted by the

National Agriculture Advisory Commission, and reviewed by key members of Congress and the farm organizations.[35] The document recognized "that the development of modern, mechanized, high investment agriculture had placed the family farm in a somewhat vulnerable economic position, it cautioned against an undue concentration of power in Washington and warned against subsidizing inefficiency in agriculture by endlessly continued 'emergency' programs."[36] The statement also affirmed that the existing price-supports would continue for 1953 and 1954.[37]

But Benson also indicated he would take up the goal attempted by Brannan, pledging that before the expiration of current law in 1954, he would work to formulate a longer-term program for American agriculture.[38] Describing his intentions for such a program, Benson explained that "price supports should provide insurance against disaster to the farm-producing plant and help stabilize national food supplies. But price supports which tend to prevent production shifts toward a balanced supply in terms of demand and which encourage uneconomic production and result in continuing heavy surpluses and subsidies should be avoided."[39] Benson described a vision of American agricultural policy that would, he believed, provide farmers with stability and prosperity, but also give them increased freedom in decision-making. Then he took questions, answering more than sixty questions over the course of an hour, which, he recalled, was "the most thorough quizzing I had ever had."[40] Benson's statement, and his exhaustive press conference, introduced the country to his thorough, dogged approach to policymaking. Along the way, he articulated his philosophy that reducing the role of government would, he hoped, promote the moral enrichment of farmers by encouraging self-sufficiency.[41]

Beyond the cost of government agricultural policies, Benson worried about the distorting effects of government intervention. His concerns were twofold. First, he was concerned that current government price support programs encouraged farmers to make different farming decisions than they would otherwise. In his memoirs he recalled, "A good many farmers were taking government help against their own better judgment, even contrary to their consciences. Some of them told me, 'Well, we've been taking these government handouts for lime and fertilizer, but we've

never felt quite right about it.' Others were growing corn, wheat and cotton, not for sale in the market, but to turn it over to the government for the
guaranteed 90 percent of parity."[42] In the best-case scenario, he believed,
price supports should be done away with entirely; but, at the least, long-
term agricultural policy had to incorporate a greater degree of flexibility.[43]

The other concern that troubled Benson was the corrosive moral effect
on farmers and rural people of taking of handouts but "not feeling right
about it." Rural people were, to Benson, "the bulwark against all that is
aimed at weakening and destroying our American way of life."[44] Benson
argued that government intervention was weakening farmers' self-sufficiency at precisely the time when the Cold War required the effort of all
American citizens to support freedom and independence. Benson believed
that the government supports were little more than a security blanket for
farmers that inhibited innovation and prevented them from doing things
for themselves. He wrote, "It seemed to me that if there was a grain of
truth in the Fascist jibe of the 1940s and the Communists [sic] contention
of the 1950s that the U.S. was a 'decadent democracy' the answer might be
found in the tendency to look more and more to Washington for the solution to all problems."[45] At a time when there were increasing debates about
the fate of small farmers in America amid pressures for farmers to indus-
trialize and mechanize, Benson worried that government farm policies
ended up hurting all farmers and prevented adaptation and innovation
by the most successful farmers. Rather than lock farmers into producing crops to sell to the government, "price supports should provide insurance against disaster," not be a means for the government to pick winners
and losers in agriculture by supporting some types of farmers over others,
especially since, as he believed "inefficiency should not be subsidized in
agriculture."[46] Benson worried that government policies were preventing
creative adaptation at a time of dramatically changing market conditions,
such as shifting food preferences, the development of synthetic fibers, and
the recovery of agricultural production in Europe and Japan.[47]

Moreover, Benson was convinced that the focus on price supports
meant that Washington was not generating policies to address what
he saw as a key problem: that some farmers were significantly more

prosperous than others. Government policies exacerbated this gap by distributing aid unevenly. Benson described a vast chasm that "separated the efficient, mechanized commercial farm run by a highly skilled operator from the small, ill-equipped, poor soil farm run by an operator with sub-par education and skill and very little capital."[48] Government programs tended to benefit the former, while not offering much to the "families who needed help and weren't getting much," a category that in the early 1950s included 1.5 million families living on farms that had an estimated cash income of less than $1,000 per year.[49] For the next six years, from 1954 to 1960, Benson would effect important changes in agricultural policy, but he would fight a losing battle to bring American farm policy into line with his, and the president's, beliefs. Among his accomplishments, after years of effort, was the enacting a system of more flexible price supports. He would also help develop a permanent American program to send American grain and other food supplies needy nations overseas to help reduce agricultural surplus at home and support US diplomatic efforts abroad. As noted earlier, Benson was not able to eliminate agricultural surpluses in the 1950s, but their continuation would provide the United States with the abundant food supplies necessary to establish America's international food power policies

The government conducted a six-month investigation into all aspects of farm policy, which included Benson taking a number of trips across the nation in 1953 to learn first-hand about farmer's concerns, after which the administration submitted new farm program to Congress on January 11, 1954.[50] The proposal reflected a compromise between Benson's desire to reduce price supports and "gradualism," Eisenhower's condition that the reductions be incremental. It outlined a new system of flexible price supports to take effect after 1954, along with a new, modernized parity standard that would take effect on January 1, 1956. The program was designed, Eisenhower wrote to Congress, to address the fundamental causes that led to the overproduction of farm commodities by lowering price supports to reduce production and stimulate competition.[51]

To generate support for the administration's plan, Benson again toured the country, speaking to a broad range of farm groups. He spoke at meetings of the National Council of Farmer Cooperatives and the National Farmers Union, at a Farm and Home Week Conference in Ithaca, New York, and to the Cache Valley Breeding Association in Utah. On one stop in Kossauth County, Iowa, he gave four talks in five hours, including one at the John Ludwig Farm and another at the Kiwanis club.[52] Speaking to representatives of the frozen food industry on the occasion of their group's 25th anniversary, Benson advocated for the important role of government in supporting the foundation for agricultural prosperity through public investments in research and marketing. Benson reminded the organization's members that it had been government research that helped start their industry and told them that he was "thoroughly convinced that most of agriculture's present problems can be met through increased research and education and improved marketing methods."[53] The farm problem would ultimately be solved, he argued, by finding new ways to utilize American agricultural abundance through support for research, education, and improved marketing of agicultrual products.[54]

Despite these efforts, Congress was resistant to the proposed changes, seeming to prefer further extending the 90 percent of parity price support. Benson then took the administration's message directly to the American people. He joined Vice President Nixon at the Capitol to record a joint appearance on the ABC radio network. On the program, Benson tried to convey the urgent need for agricultural policy reform, and cited the costs of current policies, both the payments to farmers and of storing surplus commodities. At the end of World War II, he explained, "We stopped all-out production of munitions and ships. But we didn't put a stop to all-out production of surplus food."[55] He argued that high levels of government intervention in agriculture may have been necessary during the Great Depression and to meet wartime demand, but said that continuing such policies no longer made no sense. Even the president got involved, giving a speech about the program to the opening session of the National Citizens for Eisenhower Congressional Committee.[56] Despite these efforts, Eisenhower, Benson, Nixon, and other administration officials were not able to overcome congressional resistance.[57]

Besides the entrenched opposition in Congress to altering agricultural policy, the approaching the mid-term elections in 1954 meant that
Republicans were wary of upsetting the farm bloc; at the same time,
Democrats had little incentive to fix policy problems, hoping that the agriculture problems of the Republican administration could help them regain
control of the House and Senate. Against these headwinds, it became clear
that Benson's push for flexible price supports with a range from 75 percent
to 90 percent of parity was not an achievable goal. Eisenhower agreed to
a compromise, suggested by Representative Charles Halleck of Indiana,
to reduce the range to 82.5 percent to 90 percent. The Agricultural Act of
1954 was then passed by Congress and signed into law by the president
on August 28, 1954.[58] In addition to implementing a flexible price support
system, the act also allowed the setting aside of up to $2.5 billion in surplus
commodities to be used for school lunch programs, disaster relief, aid to
foreign countries, and stockpiles in the United States that could be used in
the event of war or other national emergency.[59] Eisenhower also noted that
the 1954 act was only a part of the administration's broader agricultural
program, which included the authorization of the St. Lawrence Seaway,
the Watershed Protection and Flood Prevention Act, and the creation of
new mechanisms to develop foreign markets for US agricultural products.

Reaction to the bill was strongly supportive. *The Sedalia Democrat* in
Sedalia, Missouri, ran the headline: "Farm Leaders Credit Benson with
Victory in Bill Passage," while the *San Bernardino County Sun* edito-
rialized, "While the American people are the real winners of the decision, it is a particularly gratifying victory for the agriculture chief."[60] The
Kiplinger Letter wrote, "The principle of flexibility is established to replace
rigidity. To ram this through Congress took guts . . . in both Benson and
Eisenhower. . . . It was principle vs. politics, and much of the betting was
on politics. Yet principle won."[61] While the act was not all that Eisenhower
and Benson had hoped for, they both stated belief that important steps had
been taken in a new direction that injected some level of flexibility into
American agricultural policy.[62] Ultimately, they hoped, such efforts would
begin to pare down the agricultural surpluses that were widely believed to
be causing the "farm problem." Those reductions, however, would not be

immediate. The nation would have to find another way to deploy its agricultural surpluses. Benson and other policymakers were already laying the groundwork for that pathway forward, too.

FARM POLICY AND RURAL UNREST IN THE MID-1950S

By the fall of 1955, declining agricultural prices and concerns about Eisenhower's viability as a presidential candidate following a heart attack led administration officials to look for short-term ways to boost agricultural prices, buying time until the 1954 Act would take effect and raise prices by lowering surpluses. They settled on a strategy to aid American farmers that policymakers, including Benson and Nixon, felt would gain rural support but that also had economic and policy merit. In addition to flexible price supports and surplus commodity disposals already in place, Benson proposed adding a land-retirement system to take land out of cultivation, under the auspices of a Soil Bank program to be administered by USDA. The Soil Bank, which was enacted as Title I of the Agricultural Act of 1956, established two kinds of land retirement programs. The first, an Acreage Reserve Program, would apply to highly productive crop and pasture lands, while the second, the Conservation Reserve Program, would allow farmers to enroll land that had been used for any crop for a period of three to ten years, or fifteen years if farmers agreed to plant trees on the land. As the administration laid out plans for the Soil Bank, rural discontent was rising. Despite decades of federal farm assistance, rural poverty remained widespread. A USDA report found that more than half of America's 5.3 million farmers had annual incomes under $1,000. Changes in the nature of farming in the 1950s meant that increased amounts of land, capital, technology, and knowledge were required for farmers to be successful and prosperous. The administration, however, found support for a major rural development program lacking in Congress, farm organizations, and among the American people.[63]

Among farmers though, concern galvanized action, especially among small farm operators. A new farm group, the National Farm Organization

(NFO), emerged in Iowa, supported by former Iowa Governor Dan Turner, that demanded 100 percent parity for farm products as well as other steps to establish floor prices for hogs and cattle. The NFO accepted only actual farmers as members and grew rapidly in areas where small farmers were commonplace, pushing for collective bargaining to allow farmers to nego-tiate prices for commodities. The NFO, like other farm organizations, was not excited about the administration's plans to address rural prosperity through a land retirement program. Three observers of a Grange meeting in Pecatonica, Illinois, in the fall of 1955 reported that unrest was real and tangible, one of them telling the White House that "Republicans are in real trouble among farmers by 1956. . . . If something isn't done, the dissatis-faction could reach to Eisenhower personally."[64] administration officials took such concerns seriously and farm problems topped the list when they initiated "Operation Arrowhead" to focus attention on potential trouble spots for the 1956 election.[65]

Republicans were not the only ones to notice this dissatisfaction with the administration's farm policies. Congressional Democrats, supported by Midwestern Republicans, sought to appeal to farmers by developing a new farm bill that revived high fixed price supports. As Senate majority leader Lyndon Johnson summarized the Democrat's position, "Republicans worry about the economic problem and the percentage points and dollar symbols, but the Democrats worry about people."[66] Congress delivered the administration's Soil Bank bill, but included it in a package that returned price supports to 90 percent of parity, introduced a standard of dual parity that would apply only to 4 of the 160 parity crops, and created mandatory price plans for feed crops. Despite pleas from farm bloc Republicans who supported the bill and asked Eisenhower to sign it, the president vetoed it. In doing so, he heeded the council of Benson and other prominent voices, such as Kansas newspaper editor William Allen White who, in a letter to the president, called the administration's approach, "the only sane one—the only healthy one—from the standpoint of the actual farmer, not the politicians who by distortions and lies are trying to squeeze votes out of the farmer."[67] In announcing his veto, Eisenhower announced that the adminstration would set price supports for 1956 at at least 82.5 percent of parity.[68] This was not as high as the 90 percent advocates of the farm bill had hoped for, but neither was it as low as the 75 percent allowed under the 1952 act. Worried that Eisenhower's popularity would make it difficult to override the veto and wary of impeding any farm legislation lest rural discontent become focused on them, congressional leaders agreed to a compromise that left prices at 82.5 percent of parity and enabled the creation of the Soil Bank. Eisenhower was not pleased with all aspects of the new arrangement, but he did sign it into law as the Agriculture Act of 1956.[69]

Responding to calls for action to address the concerns of farmers, Congress and the Eisenhower administration sought to reduce agricultural surpluses and boost output by paying farmers of the six basic crops— wheat, corn, cotton, tobacco, rice, and peanuts—to take acres out of production. The Acreage Reserve Program, more popularly known as the Soil Bank, was in effect from 1956 to 1958 and allowed farmers to remove land from production and receive a payment from the government based on the net income they would have received from growing crops on the removed land. By 1957 almost 21 million acres were covered by the program, though the effect of the Soil Bank on reducing surpluses was limited given improvements in productivity that continued to increase output on the remaining crop- and pasturelands. Changes in policy in 1958 that limited participating farmers from increasing acres planted in other crops caused many farmers to withdraw from the program, which led to its discontinuation.[70]

The Conservation Reserve Program of the Soil Bank allowed farmers to retire low-yield lands that had been used for producing any kind of crop, not just the six major crops under acerage controls. In return, farmers received a low rent for the land as well as additional payments if they implemented on other conservation measures, such as planting trees, protecting wildlife, or improving water quality. The amount of land retired under the Conservation Reserve eventually exceeded that retired under Acreage Reserve, reaching 28 million acres. Most of the land entered into the program however was marginal, low-yielding farmland, so the program, too, had little effect in reducing surpluses

and was discontinued, with final agreements issued in 1960. The immediate effects of the programs were minimal. Since land had been planted
before the law was passed, only a small number of farmers took part
in the program the first year, though participation increased in future
years.[71]

There were a number of reasons for the failure of the Soil Bank programs. Although the administration did create new land diversion policies,
farmers tended to creatively take advantage of things like land retirement
to set aside unproductive land while simultaneously investing resources
in machinery and other inputs that allowed them to increase yields on
their remaining land.[72] The programs to promote the reduction of acreage
farmed, combined with other policy steps, would eventually help eliminate surpluses, in the early 1970s, but they did little to solve the complex
problems of modern agriculture that were behind the political unrest of
the mid-1950s. Unable to reduce surpluses and boost farm prices through
domestic programs, policymakers in the 1950s also sought to accomplish
their goals through other means abroad.

FOOD AS FOREIGN ASSISTANCE

In the mid-1950s, the administration still hoped that the limited success it
had in establishing flexible price supports might reduce surpluses. Benson
worked with scientists at the USDA as well as with private-sector food
companies to try to come up with packaging and marketing innovations
and new directions in research that might provide longer-term pathways
to reduce surpluses.[73] But such solutions offered little in the way of immediate fixes. By 1956, the Commodity Credit Corporation (CCC), a gov-
ernment-owned corporation created in 1933 to support farm prices and
farm income by purchasing and storing surplus commodities, had more
than $9 billion invested in storage of surplus crops (an amount equal to
the entire federal budget of 1940), the majority of it invested in wheat,
corn, and cotton.[74] If ways could not be found for American farmers to
produce less, or if new ways to use more of the key commodities could not

immediately be found at home, perhaps, policymakers reasoned, more outlets could be found for America's agricultural bounty abroad.

A world filled with plenty had been key element of the visions of hope, prosperity, and peace depicted by the United States during World War II. The United States turned to foreign countries to utilize its agricultural abundance to promote American goals at home and overseas For example, even when the the Marshall Plan ended in 1951, the United States continued to provide food assistance to friendly nations in need on a case-by-case basis. In 1953, Congress passed Senate bill 2112, which allowed the donation of surplus wheat to Pakistan; Senate bill 2294, to allow the president to donate up to $100 million in surplus commodities for famine relief worldwide; and section 550 was added to the Mutual Security Act of 1951 that authorized the sale of surplus commodities to needy nations.[75] Such efforts, though, were dependent on need or offered limited conditions for action by the president and Executive Branch agencies. Following the failure of farm policy reform efforts, and in recognition of continued need abroad led policymakers, including Secretary Benson, the assistant secretary of agriculture Earl Butz, and economic adviser Don Paarlberg, to take a greater interest in the possibility providing the President more permanent authority for dispensing food aid. A similar goal was persued by Democratic senator Hubert H. Humphrey of Minnesota who had introduced a number of bills, starting in 1951, that sought to develop a comprehensive program of food aid. In 1953 Republican senators Andrew F. Schoeppel of Kansas and Robert Harrison of Nebraska introduced a bill that would have allowed use of up to $500 million of CCC stocks of surplus food for sales abroad. When the House Agriculture Committee threatened to develop its own plan, administration officials decided to support the proposed Agricultural Trade Development and Assistance Act that was making its way through the congressional approval process, which would establish America's first permanent program of international food assistance.[76]

The act was passed by both the House and Senate in mid-June and signed into law by Eisenhower on July 10, 1954. Public Law-480 (PL-480) as it was known, allowed the CCC to use more than $1 billion of its stored surplus commodities over a three-year period in order to expand international trade between the United States and friendly nations, to promote the national welfare and economic stability of agriculture in America, and increase consumption of US commodities in foreign countries to further the foreign policy of the United States. The act operated through three titles. Title I allowed the sale of surplus agricultural commodities in exchange for foreign currencies (rather than requiring payment in US dollars) up to an amount of $700 million per year. It also enabled the president to use any foreign currency that accrued from such sales to establish stockpiles of strategic and critical materials such as aluminum, copper, and mercury. The Title II authorized the president to send up to $300 million of excess agricultural commodities to friendly nations in the form of emergency assistance, such as famine or other urgent relief over the three-year period. Finally, Title III empowered the president to use any farm commodity or product owned by the CCC for domestic relief in the case of disaster or acute distress, such as unemployment. PL-480 also carried restrictions, such as prohibiting sales to "(1) the U.S.S.R. or (2) any nation or area dominated or controlled by the foreign government or foreign organization controlling the world Communist movement," and a stipulation that "on each package or container" of American commodities sent overseas be labelled "furnished by the people of the United States of America" and that commodities sold under the Act had to be shipped in American vessels.[77] PL-480 would become the foundation of American humanitarian assistance programs. During the two decades from 1955 to 1975, more than $24 billion in farm products were deployed abroad to a diverse range of nations including India, Pakistan, Poland, Yugoslavia, Indonesia, Brazil, and Israel.[78]

Implementing of PL-480 faced a number of challenges as well. By the fall of 1954, Eisenhower had taken action on the programs allowed under PL-480, including giving Benson authority over Title I operations. Decades of subsidies to domestic agricultural producers had made American goods like wheat, cotton, and butter more expensive on the world market than were the alternatives from Canada, Egypt, or Australia. If America sold goods at preferential, below-market prices, it ran the risk of disrupting channels of international trade and running afoul of provisions of the General Agreements on Tariffs and Trade (GATT). The congressional requirement that goods had to be shipped in American vessels caused resentment from other nations, and delays when American vessels weren't available. There were also complaints from some of the recipient countries about the quality of the surplus commodities, some of which had been stored for a considerable amount of time prior to being delivered. For instance, there were complaints that mechanical harvesting had damaged corn and that wheat was damaged or contaminated with leaves and other debris. Some of the surplus foods sent abroad were unfamiliar and thus initially unpalatable to people in recipient nations. Wheat for example, was initially regarded with skepticism by consumers in Japan, though promotional efforts, such as presenting the American Wheat Cup to the winner of the annual Japanese Grain Importer's Association golf tournament and the creating a training school for bakers in Japan, sponsored by the Oregon Wheat Grower's League, helped to increase the acceptance of wheat.[79]

Nonetheless, since many of these problems could be avoided by increasing direct sales of American commodities to foreign countries, Benson expended a great deal of time and energy on boosting trade ties. On a whirlwind tour of the Caribbean, from February 19 to March 8, 1955, he stopped in Puerto Rico, Cuba, Trinidad, Costa Rica, Nicaragua, Guatemala, the Virgins Islands, Panama, Mexico, Colombia, and Venezuela.[80] While Benson was primarily seeking new markets for American grain and whole milk (including milk products like butter); he instead encountered complaints about high American trade barriers to such goods as Cuban sugar or South American coffee. Officials in these countries wanted the United States to promise that it would not simply dump surplus commodities in Caribbean nations at below-market prices. The Caribbean and South American nations were not alone in expressing concern this concern.[81]

Benson sought to reassure foreign nations that the United States that its food assistance goal was to help those in need, not to undercut the production of foreign nations. At an address to the International Federation of Agricultural Producers in Rome, Benson repeated his commitment that the United States would not dump products on foreign markets and appealed to policymakers in the nations he visited for an easing of the trade barriers that protected markets and inhibited private commerce.[82] By 1956, he had logged 284,000 miles of official domestic and foreign travel (only 25,000 less than the US secretary of state, John Foster Dulles) to promote administration polices.[83] Benson was not alone in these efforts. Clarence Francis, the chairman of the Interagency Committee for Agricultural Surplus Disposal (ICASD), traveled through Europe during the summer of 1955 to promote trade, stopping at the Rome Trade Fair to visit an exhibit set up by the USDA Foreign Agricultural Service to interest foreign buyers in American goods. Despite the efforts of Benson, Clarence Francis, and American agricultural attaches around the world, however, even increased foreign sales did not eliminate American surpluses. By 1955, storing the surpluses was costing the CCC $700,000 dollars per day. Policymakers continued to seek new solutions to the problem of agricultural surpluses.[84]

Efforts to promote trade had revealed two major structural problems with the American surplus disposal efforts: the economies of friendly nations were not strong enough to absorb the surplus commodities without creating domestic economic instability; and, by placing communist nations off-limits, PL-480 had cut off some of the likeliest markets for these commodities. Far from an open and free world market, Benson and Francis and other policymakers confronted a world separated into at least two spheres by the Cold War. American foreign policy had for years tried to bolster the economies of friendly, non-communist nations. The Marshall Plan sought not just to stimulate foreign agricultural production but also to help Europe rebuild its roads, bridges, ports, and electrification and to promote manufacturing in Europe to establish the systems and infrastructure needed for the development of a world food system. Americans had therefore deliberately refrained from dumping food and farm commodities on foreign markets, a practice that Benson and others believed had helped create the surplus farm commodity problem in the first place. In the 1950s, Dulles and Clarence Randall, the chairman of the Council on Foreign Economic Policy, remained opposed to policies would have a negative economic impact on America's Cold War allies. Despite Benson's aggressive efforts to open up new markets for American goods, foreign-policy officials were willing to cede markets in friendly and non-aligned nations to accomplish their diplomatic aims. The policy debates divided administration officials, especially since the stance advocated by Dulles and Randall meant that the United States would, seemingly in per-petuity, need to accept considerable trade imbalances and financial costs in the name of fighting the Cold War.[85]

Some of Dulles's and the State Department's support of the ban was based on the belief that withholding American products from the Communist bloc nations would weaken their economies and hasten domestic unrest against the Soviets. In 1955, after persistent agricultural failures the Soviet Union, had asked to purchase large quantities of but-ter from the United States. Under PL-480, the request had to be turned down. In a 1955 report for the ICASD, Clarence Baughman, assistant vice president of the Federal Reserve Bank in Chicago, proposed revisions to American policy that included recommendations against dumping and the desirability of increasing East-West trade to reduce surpluses. While the report's public release in 1956 evoked little response, it did stimulate a lively debate within Eisenhower's Cabinet about the future of efforts to employ American food power and the need to reconcile domestic and foreign policy goals. Interestingly, in the 1956 debates, both Benson and Dulles opposed allowing trade with the Soviet Union, but Harold Stassen, former director of the short-lived Foreign Operations Administration, and then assistant to the president for disarmament, spoke in favor of it, pointing out that the restrictions only hampered the United States. Evidence from recent cases was marshaled to support policy change, including an instance in which Poland, unable to purchase wheat from the United States, had bought it from Canada, while Yugoslavia, likewise denied American wheat, had turned to the Soviet Union, contravening American efforts to separate Marshall Tito from the Soviet sphere of influ-ence. American trade policy was thus not successful in either advancing domestic efforts to reduce surpluses or bolstering American allies and partners to weaken the Communist bloc.[86]

Determined to address these failures, Eisenhower decided that policy change was needed. Based on the principle of what Eisenhower called "net advantage," the president argued that the United States should take actions that would provide it with the greatest benefit. Under such a principle, he argued, American stood to gain more from selling to communist nations than by refusing such sales. Benson supported the policy shift, provided it would not strengthen those nations economically. Administration policy-makers decided that, for more than a decade, Cold War polices had been harming American farmers and imposing costs of federal farm programs and farm-product storage on the American taxpayers. Not only were these polices distorting domestic markets, but the United States was also avoiding competing directly in the domestic markets of allies in order to boost their economy. The domestic farm problem was further exacerbated by the fact that the United States, in an effort to support allies, frequently imported foreign farm products that directly competed with American agricultural production.[87]

Having come to this conclusion, however, the Eisenhower administration made little headway convincing Congress to shift policies to help reduce surpluses or fully realize the offensive potential of food power. Continued attempts to implement PL-480 demonstrated to US officials that they faced a seemingly unsolvable dilemma. On the one hand, pursuing policies, both domestic and foreign, that advanced a free market required the United States to change Cold War polices that boosted the economies of friendly nations. It also forced the United States to confront the challenges of state-to-state trading systems, subsidies, protectionism, dumping of commodities, and the inconvertibility of currencies. On the other hand, continuing to place Cold War priorities ahead of need the to solve its domestic food and farm problems meant continued government involvement in agriculture and the high costs this entailed. Throughout the late 1950s, the Eisenhower administration pursued a middle way, continuing to accept these added costs as well to limit its overseas trade to advance its Cold War foreign policy goals, but also trying to slowly change domestic agricultural policy. However, in the face of such overriding foreign-policy concerns, Benson's controversial efforts to reduce surpluses by changing domestic farm policies had little chance of solving America's fundamental food and farm problems in the 1950s.[88]

As the problem of high surpluses and low farm prices continued, Benson became the target of blame. Even Republicans who were support-ive of the president worried that Benson's direct personal style and lack of knowledge of the political process inhibited his ability to accomplish the administration's larger goals. After his first exhaustive press confer-ence in 1953, Benson elaborated on his views in a speech to the Central Livestock Association Meeting in St. Paul, Minnesota, where he told an audience of about three thousand livestock and grain farmers, anxious about falling cattle prices, that the aim of government policy should be to give farmers sound assistance and help them stand on their own. Benson felt the speech was well received by the audience and by local press and officials in attendance. "The chairman of the meeting seemed delighted at the response. Hundreds of people had swarmed around the platform. It was a warm and satisfying reaction."[89] But the speech had played quite differently on the national stage. As Benson later recalled, "I flew back to Washington and the roof fell in."[90]

Despite the fact Benson's remarks closely followed the policy statement he had released six days earlier, the reaction from Democrats, and even some Republicans, such as Senator Milton Young of North Dakota, was vocal, animated, and cited as evidence that Benson and the administration wanted to do away with all price-support programs. Democratic Senator Burnet Maybank of South Carolina opined that the speech showed a lack of common sense and worried that, if it was "an indication of the policy thinking of the new Secretary, then God help the poor and working dirt farmers of this country."[91] The controversy raged in congressional cham-bers and newspapers for three weeks, and Benson worried that he had disappointed the president. Benson recalled that, on his next meeting with the president, he entered the oval office to find Eisenhower seated behind his desk. "He took off his glasses and looked at me sternly. It was a bad moment. And then his whole face lighted up as that brilliant smile leapt to his countenance. 'Ezra,' he said, 'I believe every word you said in St. Paul.' Now he began to chuckle. 'But I'm not sure you should have said it quite so soon.'"[92] This sort of support from the president would continue throughout Benson's turbulent tenure. In 1954, amid the controversy over price support policies, Eisenhower called Benson to the White House, where, "Old Soldier Eisenhower drew some lines on a piece of scratch paper to show Old Farmer Benson that, in military action, there are two ways to reach an objective—the direct way and by a zigzag approach. Advised Ike: try to understand the merits of the zigzag too."[93] Benson, who had been criticized for being stubborn and inflexible, admitted that Ike's advice had helped him learn the value of compromise. He relented on the level of price supports in order to get the principle of flexibility established as part of the Agricultural Act of 1954. Yet throughout his tenure in office, Benson's direct style and his self-confident, forthright manner of speaking and making policy allowed his critics to paint him as an uncaring advocate of the intensification of agriculture and an enemy of the small farmer.[94]

Though his push for flexible price supports would guide agricultural policy for the following two decades, the caricature of Benson as an unflinching champion of intensification and an enemy of the small farmer has been his legacy. When he appears in current discussions about food, he is most often associated with the phrase "get big or get out," his supposed advice to farmers to intensify the scale of their agricultural production to increase efficiencies of production and advantages of scale. Though this pithy advice is often attributed to Benson in the 1950s, it would also be attributed to Earl Butz, who served as assistant secretary of agriculture under Eisenhower and would return to serve as secretary of agriculture from 1971 to 1976 under both Nixon and Ford, when he would repeat the "get big" advice along with the added guidance to farmers that they must "adapt or die."[95]

But "get big" has stuck to Benson, in part because it seems to sum up, in retrospect, the critical domestic farming context of the 1950s—the move toward industrial agriculture and the way that government policies hurt small farmers. In 2013 when Kathleen Merrigan stepped down as the Deputy Secretary of the USDA, *Mother Jones* ran an article with the headline "The USDA's Sustainable Food Champion Steps Down" that contrasted Merrigan's advocacy of sustainable agriculture with the typical advice given by USDA. "For generations, the message from the US Department of Agriculture to the nation's farmers could be summed up in the famous piece of advice offered by Ezra Taft Benson, President Dwight Eisenhower's USDA chief: 'get big or get out.'"[96] Yet, while Benson was concerned about small farmers and about the way they were being disadvantaged by government policies, from his point of view—and that of most policymakers in the 1950s—the critical challenge they faced was reducing agricultural surpluses and bringing up farm incomes across the board.

Rather than a foe of small farmers, Benson was a foe of what he saw as undue government intervention in agriculture, of farmers producing not for markets and in response to consumer demand, but to sell crops to government programs that offered guaranteed prices. Throughout the 1950s, "the Agriculture Secretary was valiantly trying to explain the weakness of the price support system which had frozen production into uneconomic patterns by ignoring new consumer preferences and market demands."[97] In numerous press conferences and speeches to agriculture, food, and consumer groups across America, Benson sought to carefully describe his view that price supports, rather than a handout from government or a means to promote surpluses, should only be used as a means to stabilize food supplies and provide insurance against disaster. He was deeply concerned about farmers both large and small, but Benson was also aware of changing global dynamics in agriculture that included the recovery of agricultural production in Europe and Asia from postwar lows and changing consumer preferences for convenience foods and synthetic fibers in clothing. Benson, like Eisenhower, was deeply concerned about the farm problem. Mechanization, new technologies, and scientific advancements were having a profound effect on the productivity of American agriculture. Despite their efforts, Eisenhower, Benson and other policymakers who grappled with the farm problem did not find a satisfactory solution that met Cold War needs abroad that could also satisfy competing domestic constituencies at home. If ways could not be found to reduce production or deploy surpluses overseas, then perhaps, some policymakers and civil defense advocates reasoned, American food power could be utilized to help the nation prepare for the possibility of nuclear war.

4
—

What to Eat after an Atomic Bomb

Deploying Food Power Defensively

In 1960, Frank Pansch, a physician from Neenah, Wisconsin, prepared for a possible nuclear war by packing up tins of butterscotch, fancy dates, and cornflakes. Just ahead of a wave of interest in shelter building in the early 1960s, sparked by crises in Berlin and Cuba, Pansch and his family built an underground bomb shelter in their backyard. The L-shaped shelter was reached by descending a ladder, crawling through a narrow corridor past a second door and into an eight-by-ten-foot chamber made of poured concrete. The shelter included electricity; a phone line; a space heater; lighting; cooking equipment, including a coffee pot; and a portable toilet. Also included were medical and first aid supplies, as well as candles, flashlights, a radio, and a Geiger counter that could be used to measure radiation levels. The shelter was provisioned with food packed into sealed metal military-surplus containers and included Kellogg's Cornflakes, Flavor Kist saltines and chocolate chip cookies, Hawaiian Punch, Carnation powdered milk, Hills Bros. coffee, Del Monte raisins, and Sunsweet apricots, as well as the butterscotch candy, Vernell's Butter Mints, Heath candy bars, and cans of Hershey's Chocolate syrup. The family who purchased the house from Pansch's estate in 2010 discovered the shelter, relatively intact. Although it was partly filled with water, many of the foods stored in the sealed containers survived. The shelter provide a time capsule of the efforts of one American family to survive an atomic attack.[1]

Between the late 1940s and mid-1960s, as policymakers and the public became more concerned about the threat of nuclear war, the United States government developed a range of survival strategies—including mass evacuation plans, secret government shelters, and private citizen shelters. There is a rich and diverse literature on the development of civil defense efforts during the Cold War, but questions about food are often peripheral to those studies, which tend to focus on the national security and civil defense policy debates, the social and cultural aspects of the shelter debate, or design of shelters.[2] Some of the government shelters were complex facilities that required constant upkeep. Shelters envisioned for construction by private individuals were for the most part simple projects that required minimal maintenance, perhaps even serving a dual purpose as a hobby room or guest quarters.[3] But if constructing a shelter presented an assortment of economic and engineering challenges, so, too, did figuring out what food to put in it, including how to ensure that stored foods were fresh, safe, and palatable. This chapter looks at the various political and practical issues involved in the attempts to create a civil defense system built around shelters and helps to explain why, despite so much planning effort by the government and its encouragement of citizens to prepare for nuclear war, so few Americans actually built shelters.

Shelter provisioning activities required Americans, often housewives following government guidelines for "do-it yourself" citizen preparedness, to confront conflicting visions of food as a means to sustain and nourish life, provide emotional comfort, and ensure postnuclear survival. Questions about food revealed not only the full range of costs, problems, and possibilities of the efforts to prepare for life in a post-nuclear-war world, but ultimately raised questions about the ability of Americans to survive and achieve the good life that world. The chapter examines the place of food in civilian-defense planning debates to explore how the offensive use of agricultural abundance abroad had a counterpart in the defensive use of food at home. It considers the evolution of the government's civilian-protection planning and policies, including the debates about the need for and type of shelters necessary to protect America in the event of nuclear attack. It details how the approach that emerged—of an advisory government and the privately built citizen shelters—affected discussions of food, survival, and offensive strategy by initially encouraging stockpiling of civilian foods. It then explores alternative stockpiling strategies that were considered, including utilizing military rations and purpose-designed shelter foods, and considers efforts to apply shelter and stockpiling messages to farms and rural spaces.

CIVILIAN DEFENSE IN THE EARLY COLD WAR

From the late 1940s to early 1960s, federal government civil-defense strategies focused on promoting the voluntary construction and stocking of shelter spaces by families and communities while the federal government took on an educational, research, and advisory role. Debates about civilian protection, including questions about what sorts of foods to stockpile in shelters, were stimulated by changes in technology and military strategy that made civilians increasingly vulnerable to attack during wartime. World War II had laid bare the vulnerability of civilian populations to warfare's increased lethality. New kinds of weapons, such as nuclear weapons but also radiological, chemical, and biological weapons, greatly amplified the destructive capability of a single bomber, missile, or artillery round. As historian Jacob Darwin Hamblin notes, for wartime American generals, such as Curtis LeMay, in the brutal and persistent wars in both Europe and the Pacific, the goal of operations was not to win battles but to wage total war against an enemy by killing as many people as possible, including civilians.[4] Recognition of the need to protect civilian populations from attacks grew more acute in the face of the active programs of the United States and the Soviet Union to develop more lethal and deployable weapons.[5]

In the initial response to new threats and vulnerabilities, government planners and strategists settled on a do-it-yourself approach to civilian defense that relied on individuals. Early civilian-defense planning efforts, such as a 1947 report by the War Department's Civil Defense Board, identified civil defense as an area of civilian, rather than military, responsibility and advocated a strategy based on local implementation and voluntary, "self-help" activities.[6] In this regard, the United States had even more educative and preparatory work to do than its allies. America had reconstituted civilian defense efforts during World War II, but because of the continental United States' geographic isolation, Americans did not experience direct bombing raids and thus had little knowledge of the realities of the wartime shelter experiences of other nations.[7] The political climate shifted radically following the successful test of a nuclear weapon by the USSR in August 1949, which magnified the fears of communism's spread and of the possibility of an atomic attack.[8] Responding to calls from state and local officials seeking guidance on civil defense polices, Congress created the Federal Civil Defense Administration (FCDA) in 1951.[9] During the 1950s and 1960s, the name and governmental location of the agency responsible for civil defense would shift—including the creation of the Office of Civil and Defense Mobilization (OCDM) in 1958, superseding the FCDA, and the subsequent splitting of OCDM into the Office of Emergency Planning and the Office of Civil Defense (OCD) in 1961. Despite these moves, the federal government's general position that civil defense was primarily a state and local responsibility that should be handled through voluntary citizen efforts dominated policy proposals.[10]

While there was increasing awareness of the need for civilian defense, the costs to the government of building a civilian shelter system were prohibitive, and the Eisenhower administration initially focused its civil defense efforts away from costly proposals for the government to fund the construction of shelters. It instead focused on economic feasibility and shied away from major efforts, such as a massive military buildup or civil defense efforts involving federally funded shelter projects that might escalate Cold War tensions. Too, after the tests of thermonuclear bombs by the United States in 1952 and the Soviet Union in 1953, showed them to have much more powerful blast and heat effects than nuclear weapons, many experts began to question the viability of shelters.[11]

As shelters were de-emphasized, policymakers pursued measures that would have dual benefits: expanding the interstate highway system, for example, would have economic as well as defensive uses. But the primary civil-defense strategy concerned the evacuation of target areas, and its eff-ectiveness depended on having sufficient pre-attack warning and time to mobilize the civilian population.[12] By the mid-1950s, however, the grow-ing awareness of the dangers of radioactive fallout, which could travel long distances and spread radiation to areas far from the blast site, led to the recognition that the mass evacuation of cities was unworkable as a primary strategy of civilian defense. The possibility that radioactive fallout could contaminate areas well outside attack targets, potentially requiring extended stays in shelters reinvigorated efforts to encourage construction of shelters by private citizens. As policymakers began to think about shel-ters as places where people would have to stay weeks or even months, explicit discussions of how to construct and provision shelters for lengthy stays underground emerged.[13]

Studies conducted by the Eisenhower administration had shown that it would be prohibitively expensive for the government to take on the job of constructing a civilian shelter system. In 1957, the Security Resources Panel of the Science Advisory Committee, also known as the Gaither Committee, recommended a dramatic increase in active US defense forces, including making improvements in the bomber force and hardening of missile shelters. The committee also recognized that such steps would not reduce what they saw as the "extreme vulnerability of our people and our cities" and advocated for the construction of passive defense systems, such as a nationwide fallout shelter program which the committee felt to be "the only feasible protection for millions of people who will be increas-ingly exposed to the hazards of radiation."[14] A 1958 study sponsored and conducted by the Rand Corporation surveyed the possible forms that a system of national shelters could take. The report argued that such a sys-tem could alleviate some of the death and damage caused by a nuclear attack, but also that it could have a deterrent effect and provide greater flexibility for American foreign policy efforts because it would show enemies that the United States had the capacity to survive and recover from a nuclear attack.[15] The report examined a series of alternatives and estimated the possible costs of shelters designed to provide fallout and blast protection, ranging from improvised shelters made out of sandbags in existing buildings to a system of deep-rock shelters under New York City that could house four million people in tunnels 800 feet below the surface.[16] Other researchers considered some of the potential effects on shelter occupants, including isolation, stress, and anxiety, by examining analogs from experiences in submarines, polar expeditions, and at isolated radar bases.[17] They also weighed the impact of environmental conditions such as heat and humidity, which could increase the danger of certain kinds of health conditions, such as like respiratory distress, and also increase water requirements or discomfort of occupants in shelters.[18]

A further motivator of research and planning into shelters were assessments of civil defense actions taken by other countries. These included examination of the experiences of Great Britain during World War II that combined pre-attack evacuations of major cities with use of bomb shelters by remaining urban populations. These revealed the challenges in getting residents to consistently heed warnings and take shelter. Historical cases also revealed a problems with hygiene caused by the lack of running water and bathroom facilities in the subway tunnels that became bomb shelters.[19] Researchers looked as well at contemporary efforts. For instance, Sweden's shelter program called for pre-attack evacuation of densely populated urban areas and the construction of shelters for the remaining residents and for key workers in industries relevant to national security and war production that would provide some degree of protection against not only nuclear weapons, but also chemical and biological weapons. The Swedish model called for much more complex facilities—with sophisticated ventilation and heating and cooling systems—than the basement cinderblock and concrete shelters envisioned by American planners.[20]

Not surprisingly, planners and national security officials paid close attention to the Soviet Union's civil defense efforts.[21] Although sources in the Soviet Union reported on Soviet civil defense efforts, as of January 1958, State Department personnel in the American Embassy in Moscow had not actually observed any shelter building efforts, including in the excavation and building of large projects such as the construction of a major residential housing complex on the Lenin Hills.[22] Policymakers, nonetheless, worried that the United States was falling behind in preparedness. At a meeting of the National Security Council on March 21, 1958, CIA director Allen Dulles reported that it was the opinion of the intelligence community that the Soviet Union had built a network of shelters that could protect at a minimum between ten to fifteen million people, and that shelter construction efforts were ongoing.[23] A 1960 Rand Corporation assessment based on information obtained from Soviet and other sources described a Soviet civil defense effort that included mandatory training to produce approximately twenty million trained civil defense personnel and outlined the requirements for Soviet shelters, including the need for blast, radiation, and thermal protection.[24] Policymakers and planners thus worried that the lack of a civil defense strategy that included shelters placed the United States at a disadvantage in comparison to the Soviet Union.

Despite these reports, both the Eisenhower administration and Congress remained reluctant to shoulder the cost and responsibility for a nationwide system of civilian shelters. However, in the early 1950s, the government did begin building shelters for government officials. Facilities for military and executive branch officials included the Alternate Joint Communications Center in Raven Rock Mountain, Pennsylvania; the High Point Special Facility at Mount Weather near Berryville, Virginia; and the NORAD Cheyenne Mountain Complex near Colorado Springs, Colorado.[25] Other branches of government were also included. Arrangements were made, for example, to relocate the Supreme Court justices to the Grove Park Inn in Asheville, North Carolina.[26] Congress was to shelter in an elaborate facility constructed beneath the five-star Greenbrier esort outside White Sulphur Springs, West Virginia. The congressional bunker was protected by massive custom-built doors that could only be opened from the inside and included a six-month supply of food and water, a dining hall with false windows and painted country scenes to alleviate the sense of confinement that could come from a long stay underground, and large chambers in which the House and Senate could convene. The facility was maintained in secret by a small staff that kept the shelter well stocked and in working order until a reporter revealed the shelter's existence in 1992.[27]

Although policymaker and planners were willing to construct shelters to try to ensure the continuity of government operations, they were largely unwilling do the same for civilians. Proposals to build a national system of stocked shelters estimated the costs, depending on the sophistication of the facilities constructed, at between $2 billion and $25 billion per year, for ten or more years.[28] Congress was unwilling to appropriate these funds and only provided $65 million per year, on average, during Eisenhower's term in office.[29] Instead, as the 1950s wore on, the government continued to take an advisory role, encouraging citizens to build their own shelters and issuing guidelines about how to protect themselves from nuclear attacks. In 1958, the Eisenhower administration announced the National Plan for Civil Defense, which recognized shelters as part of national civil-defense policy alongside mass evacuation of target areas. The plan called for the government, still in its advisory role, to survey existing shelters built by citizens, accelerate research into shelter construction, develop prototype shelters, and a pledge to include fallout shelters in suitable new federal buildings.[30]

The federal government's primary role continued to be as educator and exemplar and the administration's new civil-defense policy the plan did not change the emphasis on voluntary construction of shelters by individuals and state and local authorities. As described by Gerald Gallagher, the director of research of the OCDM, the policy assigned "responsibility for the construction of shelters to the individual, be it the individual home owner, the individual industry, or the individual government. The policy stated flatly that there would be no massive federally-financed shelter construction program."[31] This message was reinforced by other civil-defense publications and speeches, such as one in November 1958 on the theme of "Operation You" to OCDM's Women's Advisory Committee (WAC), in which Leo Hoegh, director of the OCDM, asserted clearly that civilian defense was a "do-it-yourself" proposition and urged the two hundred representatives of the WAC to take steps to prepare their families.[32]

In accordance with this advisory and educational role, the government developed standards, plans, and recommendations for use by civilians and state and local governments for constructing their own shelters. In

1959, OCDM's *The Family Fallout Shelter*, presented a range of plans for shelters for possible construction by citizens, including basement concrete-block shelters, above-ground double-walled shelters, and underground concrete or pre-shaped metal shelters.[33] As historian Elaine Tyler May has described, the promotion of private, home-based shelters reflected prevailing attitudes of the home as a site of privacy and security from outside dangers, not to mention its role as the container for "visions of abundance and fulfillment."[34] In addition to relatively basic shelters, such as the one built in the 1960s by the Pansch family, more extravagant, professionally designed, private shelters were being built by celebrities such as Groucho Marx, Dinah Shore, and Pat Boone.[35] Even Americans who lived far from the potential big-city targets worried that fallout might drift and create problems. Eric Walker, dean of the College of Engineering at the Pennsylvania State College (Penn State), worried that fallout from a nuclear bomb dropped on Pittsburgh could reach the campus, in State College, and had a fallout shelter added to the house he built in 1952.[36]

After 1960, the Kennedy administration's emphasis on idea of "flexible response" which called for developing a range of conventional and nuclear military response options, as well as experiences during the Berlin Crisis of 1961 and the Cuban Missile Crisis of 1962, brought a shift in emphasis in shelter policies, and the Congress for the first time authorized significant funding for the development of shelter spaces. The Berlin Crisis precipitated congressional authorization of more than $200 million to identify, mark, and supply spaces that could serve as fallout shelters. Contemporaries saw this as a step in the right direction, but, as historian Kenneth Rose observes, this 1961 bump in funding "would prove to be the apex for civil defense" and federal investment in shelters.[37] Civil defense officials, who had struggled for years to secure funding, welcomed the allocation of funds though it was far below the "$20 billion to $250 billion (that is, $2 billion to $25 billion per year over a decade), depending on the scale attempted" that the 1958 Rand Corporaton study had estimated would be necessary for a robust shelter program.[38] Even events in Berlin and Cuba did not fundamentally alter the predominant view that civil defense was best undertaken voluntarily by families, businesses, and state and local governments.[39]

Nonetheless, government publications, newspaper articles, and popular magazines touted the advantages, beyond simply nuclear preparedness, of building a shelter. Hoegh noted that shelters "can serve a dual purpose— protection from tornadoes and other severe storms in addition to pro- tection from the fallout radiation of a nuclear bomb."[40] Historian Sarah Lichtman describes how some brochures sought to encourage shelter building by portraying them as an extension of the home's leisure space— the extra space could be used as a guest or hobby room—and a way to strengthen familial relationships since shelter construction provided an opportunity for father-son bonding and shelter provisioning, decorating, and housekeeping did the same for mothers and daughters.[41] Private shel- ters could be built to the needs and specifications of a family and stocked with items that fit family preferences alongside items vital to survival, including, critically, food. This tailoring of shelter spaces for families suited the federal government's goals of transferring civil defense responsibilities to individuals, but also raised a range of questions about what types and quantities of food citizens should be expected to stock in their shelters.

STOCKING THE SHELTER PANTRY

In addition to debates about whether, where, and what sorts of shelters should be built and who should be responsible for building them, govern- ment officials were confronted by questions about what should be put into shelters. While planners discussed the importance of providing activities to entertain and keep shelter occupants busy, perhaps through the inclu- sion of building materials like wood and tools or unassembled furniture kits that would enable shelter occupants to keep themselves busy by build- ing furniture for the shelter, a central topic of concern was the need for food and water.[42] During the 1950s, civil defense planners and officials from a range of organizations—including scientists from the USDA, home economists from FCDA, experts assembled by the National Research

Council, and systems analysts from the Rand Corporation—examined a range of questions related to how to stock shelters with sufficient food and other necessities. In addition to adequate nutrition, food was intended to help manage the psychological effects of nuclear attack and shelter occupancy by providing comfort and reminders of normal times, enhancing morale and fostering a sense of family or community cohesion through the sharing of meals. Food was also seen as critical to maintaining shelterees' health and vitality so that they could re-emerge fortified for the task of rebuilding the post-nuclear-war world. Planners struggled to reconcile these varied needs with changing views on the adequate nutritional needs for occupants and availability of foods for use in shelters.[43]

As noted earlier, as the understandings of the damage nuclear weapons could do evolved, the length of time that planners estimated Americans would need to spend in shelters increased from two to three days to two weeks or longer. Although experts noted that people could likely survive up to two weeks without food, provided they had sufficient water, most recognized that such conditions were not optimal. Robert Olson, a USDA chemist, wrote in 1960, "It is generally agreed that healthy persons can fast for two weeks of shelter existence without any undue suffering or adverse psychological effects as long as water is available. . . . On the other hand, it seems apparent, if shelters are to be manageable and beneficial to the entire population, that an adequate and palatable food supply is essential."[44] A 1963 planning guide for shelters noted that "shelterees receiving too little food may become pre-occupied and uncooperative. Anxiety may become widespread, and lack of food may have a detrimental effect on the ability of shelterees to perform critical shelter tasks."[45] There was a general consensus among planners that it would be best to have a minimal level of food supplies in place in the event an attack came suddenly.

Nonetheless, planners debated about who bore the responsibility for stocking shelters. During the Truman and Eisenhower administrations, officials followed the same do-it-yourself strategy for food as they did for shelters in general. This nonetheless left them with a range of questions to answer, such as what sorts of foods were best suited for the nutritional needs and environmental conditions of bomb shelters, in what quantities, and whether, beyond the food needed for survival during stays in shelters, larger stockpiles would be necessary to sustain people throughout the months and years of postattack recovery efforts? Policymakers identified three main food sources for shelters: commercially available civilian foods, military rations, and new foods developed to meet civil defense needs.[46] The latter two strategies focused on meeting specific calorie and and nutrient counts. In contrast, the use of commercially available food meant that experts and policymakers had to assess existing foods for their use as shelter provisions.

At a 1960 symposium held at the National Academy of Sciences in Washington, DC, the USDA's Robert Olson, speaking as a representative of OCDM Interdepartmental Ad Hoc Advisory Group on Research and Development for Food for Shelters, reported the four principal problems in determining the ideal shelter ration: "(a) stability, (b) palatability, (c) ease of serving, and (d) cost of food products."[47] Olson and other experts found that social issues complicated the solving of these problems. In determining how much and what kind of food to recommend, planners tried to account for not only the design and purpose of the shelter, but also its geographic location, the economic means of the people who would shelter there, the social relationships of the shelterees, and the cultural and psychological roles that food could play for people under duress. For instance, in a small family shelter, if the family in question was not well off, then cost might become a factor in selecting the foods to store. For larger shelters, a central question was whether to plan and hope that people would bring food with them from their personal stockpiles or whether it was necessary to stock the shelters ahead of time.[48] A further set of questions involved food preparation and the availability of cooking or dining facilities that might determine whether food needed to be packaged for individuals or small groups or whether it could be stored in bulk for large group feedings. Cooking equipment, even just for boiling water, could increase the range of foods available to shelterees and provide more palatable hot foods that could also boost morale. Yet cooking also raised issue of energy supplies and generated the additional heat and moisture, requiring more sophisticated cooling and ventilation systems.[49]

A major challenge to be addressed in developing food stockpiles related to palatability and food safety. This meant confronting the perishability of most regular foods, even those that consumers typically thought of as nonperishable. Although foods such as canned and jarred goods seemed to be able to be stored for long periods of time, studies, during the 1940s and 1950s, of the stability of commercially available foods indicated that they were typically best if consumed within two years of production which limited their utility for use in long-term stockpiles without requiring frequent rotation of stored foods.[50] Food experts detailed the various forms of decay that could make the food that people were likely to stock in shelters unpalatable or unsafe. For example, tin cans were subject to internal corrosion. The viability of canned goods depended on the food contained in cans (fruits and vegetables spoiled sooner than corn or fish). Dry foods such as cereals and crackers were typically packaged in flexible materials like paper and foil that were vulnerable to holes, tears, and insect or rodent damage.[51] While this might not matter in grocery stores or even in home use, problems of spoilage, breakage, and weak packaging could prove to be critical in a shelter situation.

The discussions of food perishability were complicated by questions about how to maintain shelter food supplies. Would food be periodically inspected, used, and refreshed, or was the goal to identify a set of foods that could be placed in a shelter for a given period of time and then discarded and replaced? The former strategy had the advantage of stocking family or community shelters with foods that were normally used and could be rotated out on a given schedule. For larger or community shelters, rotational strategies might make good sense if shelter management could be integrated with restaurant or commissary operations. Rotational stockpiling also offered some cost advantages for individual family shelters; although there were initial start-up costs to purchase additional foods the costs of maintaining the stockpile would be recovered through gradual use and replacement. Managing the rotation of foods could become a longer-term problem in family shelters, or even in business operations, as the initial enthusiasm for the task of maintaining the stockpile waned. The second strategy, of placing supplies in shelters and then replacing them at or near the end of their shelf life, required less vigilance and upkeep but also entailed repeated large costs to purchase foods.[52]

The use of what planners termed the "grocery store ration" offered advantages of immediate availability, the capability to select items to provide a varied and nutritious diet, and the ability of shelter owners to choose items based on their personal needs, tastes, and preferences. As with shelter construction in general, the ways the government promoted the stockpiling of civilian foods changed as experts began to better understand the effects of nuclear attack. For instance, early educational efforts were shaped by reports of experiences at Hiroshima and Nagasaki that suggested that blast, heat, and, to a much lesser extent, radioactivity were the chief dangers of atomic weapons. *Survival under Atomic Attack: The Official U.S. Government Booklet*, published in 1950, mainly focused on strategies for addressing the problems caused by heat and fire. The tone is generally upbeat, recommending, for instance, that homeowners prepare for possible attack by practicing "fireproof housekeeping" by, for example, not allowing combustible trash to pile up.[53] After an atomic explosion, the booklet advised, Americans should throw out all their unpackaged foods, since dust from ground bursts (or mist from underwater bursts) could settle on open food; but it offered reassurance that if the attack were an airburst, then the food in the house would be safe to use.[54] Though it recommended washing canned and bottled foods to remove radioactive dust, the only general advice on stockpiling was to have canned goods in the house.[55]

Eschewing the lightly reassuring tone of *Survival under Atomic Attack*, mid-1950s civil defense efforts sought to calm anxieties about nuclear attacks by reminding Americans that their ancestors had faced and overcome adversities as well. Perhaps the best example of this is the 1955 "Grandma's Pantry Was Ready" campaign, which used images of a tidy kitchen with a wood burning stove to promote the virtues of the grocery store strategy of stockpiling foods.[56] The campaign involved a series of informational pamphlets and displays and was a collaborative effort between FCDA, the National Grocers' Association, and the National Dietetic Association. It promoted preparedness by appealing to images of frontier self-sufficiency. Educational pamphlets warned housewives that in the event of a nuclear attack, water and sewer systems might be non-functional, garbage collection could be interrupted, and that it would be hard for suppliers to make deliveries of food and fresh milk. Pamphlets asked housewives to consider the question: "Is your 'pantry' ready in event of emergency?" If not, then the solution was to stockpile food as a part of everyday shopping activities. Because of the campaign's focus on food, it provides much greater detail than other materials about the type and amount of foods that would be best for stockpiling efforts.[57]

Campaign materials were reprinted widely and featured at fairs and women's meetings throughout the mid- to late 1950s. An April 1955 food column by Lucy Reeves from Mason City, Iowa, asked readers, "How prepared are you? Not for when unexpected friends drop in, but when unexpected bombs drop in. . . . Even if you don't like to think about it, it's not a bad idea."[58] Reeves asked whether her readers remembered " 'Grandma's Pantry' with its shelves loaded with food ready for any emergency, whether it be unexpected company or roads blocked for days by a winter's storm?"[59] Stocking the pantry was thus presented in the nostalgic frame of frontier preparedness, and readers were warned that the perils of possible enemy attack necessitated the re-creation of a pantry in the shelter areas of modern homes (thus gently reminding readers that they should, of course, have such a shelter area).

While pamphlets and newspaper articles encouraged selecting foods and amounts based on personal or family needs, they also provided shopping lists, ready to be clipped. A 1955 column in the *Post-Standard* in Syracuse, New York, suggested stockpiling 14 to 15 ounces of canned milk, 12 ounces of canned meats, and 12 ounces of canned soups and vegetables daily, per person, as well as canned fruit and other items, such as flour, yeast, salt, cookies and crackers, and special foods for babies and pets.[60] Columnists reminded housewives that preparedness required continued diligence, exhorting them to regularly check and rotate their shelter pantry stock. One columnist urged readers to check stockpiles monthly and to rotate out bottled water every six weeks.[61] While the initial phase of the campaign began in 1955, its message was continued through the late 1950s. In March 1958, for instance, the wife of the civil defense director of Saline County, Illinois, used Grandma's Pantry, as well as a display set up by a local grocery store, as her theme in a speech on civil defense at a community high school.[62] Grandma's Pantry even proved to be adaptable to changing civil defense instructions. By 1958, a three-part series of articles on civilian defense in the *Sentinel-Sun* in Santa Cruz, California, cautioned readers to prepare for a seven-day, rather than a three-day stay in a shelter.[63] Maintaing such preparedness—were housewives to carry it out—would have made preparation for nuclear war a regular part of their shopping and housekeeping duties, and normalizing nuclear war in their homemaking strategies.[64]

Grocery store and grocer's associations also picked up on the messages of the "Grandma's Pantry" campaign by weaving civil defense warnings into their weekly ad circulars. In 1955, the Easter weekend advertisement for IGA Grocery Stores in Lewiston, Maine, included a section with the headline "Grandma's Pantry Was Ready!" reminding shoppers that civil defense agencies advised "the housewife to stockpile 3 days' of reserve food supply for the members of her family, in case of an emergency, either war-caused or from wind, water or fire." The ad also included the pitch to use not just any foods, but to "Stock Your Shelves with IGA Quality Foods Today!"[65] Preparedness thus positioned images of homey self-sufficiency that hearkened back to frontier self-reliance alongside gentle encouragement of brand loyalty. Further, portraying nuclear war as a catastrophe on a par with power outages and bad storms that would require only a three- or seven-day stay in a home shelter demonstrates some of the difficulties planners and government officials faced in determining what tone to take in motivating preparedness without provoking alarm.

NUTRITION FOR ATOMIC SURVIVAL

Encouraging individuals to stock their shelters with commercially available food was the most common strategy promoted by the government. But policymakers also explored the use of military rations and the development of new high-calorie, low-spoilage foods. Both would have to be developed and largely provided by the government or by government-funded sources. These strategies took little account of the emotional or psychological role of food; they were not designed for taste and comfort, but strictly to achieve the utilitarian goals of nutrition, performativity, and durability. Planners assessed the lowest caloric requirements for survival and applied nutritional science to find the cheapest, hardiest options.

Some planners believed that the use of military-style rations could overcome concerns about the relatively short, two-year shelf life of civilian foods. By the mid-1950s, a range of rations had been developed for use by military forces. During World War II, the US Armed Forces developed more than twenty different type of rations for use in different settings around the world, including individually packaged daily rations (K rations); an individual ration that consisted of canned, precooked food (C rations); and even an emergency chocolate ration bar (D bars).[66] While military rations offered the advantages of ready availability, easily scaled up production, palatability, and nutritional adequacy, they also had some shortcomings, chief among which was their high cost. A 1958 Rand study estimated that military rations would cost almost twice as much per person as some sort of purpose-designed shelter ration.[67] The difficulty of securing funding for civil defense efforts kept planners ever mindful of the need to find ways to keep the costs of shelter foods, as well as of shelter programs as a whole, as low as possible.

Additionally, the individual or unit sized portions of military meals was a problem for the planners of community-scale shelters. Some worried that individually packaged rations might encourage hoarding or fighting over who got which parts of ration packages. On the other hand, individual packaging might limit any incident of food poisoning to the individuals who consumed the unsafe rations. Understandably, concerns about food poisoning were high; planners envisioned groups of people in confined spaces with limited opportunities for medical treatment, hygiene, and air exchange. The military-style rations, such as B rations, that were intended for use in group settings typically needed to be heated to be pleasant to eat.[68] While hot foods and beverages were more appealing, improving inhabitants' moods, and better for marking the day and night cycle inside shelters, as noted earlier, cooking required both equipment and an energy source. The resulting heat as well as cooling and ventilation problems could also speed up the decomposition of foods and other items packaged in metal.[69]

As an alternative to both civilian and military foods, officials sought to develop low-cost, long shelf-life foods specifically intended for use in shelters. The ideal product that planners envisioned was a multipurpose compressed cereal bar that could be eaten as a stand-alone product, used as a carrier for foods like jams and peanut butter, served in milk or water as a hot or cold cereal, or served with soup or sauce as a dinner. They eventually, following the guidance of experts, settled on a shelter ration that included crackers, biscuits, bulgur wafers, and a carbohydrate supplement (hard candy). The rations were made by a variety of companies that were under contract to civil defense. The Kroger, Co. of Columbus, Ohio, for example, made All-Purpose Survival Biscuits.[70] These biscuits were produced by a number of companies nationwide, under different names— in Nebraska they were called Nebraskits.[71] Some private companies also got involved. General Mills sold a product called Multi-Purpose Food (or MPF), a powdered, protein-rich food that had originally been developed for emergency use at the end of World War II.[72]

Shelter rations thus represented the ultimate embodiment of nutritional science—conceptualizing food as containing component parts that could be compared, disassembled, and reassembled to provide optimal nutrition. In this modern, scientific view, foods could be divorced from cultural and even ecological contexts and deployed to meet political needs, such as the eradication of hunger or advancement of national security. The butterscotches and Vernell's Butter Mints in the Pansch family shelter might evoke, for those living underground for weeks on end, a favorite childhood treat, providing a psychological and emotional boost. Yet to the early Cold War civil defense planners who wrote the Department of Defense's *Shelter Management Textbook*, candy was simply a carbohydrate supplement intended to add variety to the survival diet.[73]

Purpose-designed shelter rations ensured that nutritional requirements would be met and provided a diet that would be palatable (but not necessarily pleasurable) to eat, and addressed the concerns of experts that the vagaries of individual taste or happenstance stockpiling efforts based on shopping behaviors might not provide shelterees with optimal diets. Purpose-designed shelter foods could also be rationed out in the precise amounts needed. For example, one shelter-management handbook contained tables that listed standard amounts of crackers, wafers, and carbohydrate supplements that could be distributed throughout a typical day, either in five to six equal servings or three larger servings at normal meal times, with two smaller snack servings between meals. Shelter rations also allowed experts to calculate the ideal food to water ratio required in shelters and reduced the amount of water that would be needed to be stored since foods could be chosen for the ability to provide nutrition but not kick off thirst responses by containing high levels of substances such as salt. Finally, developing civil defense foods simplified supply chains and civil defense logistics by providing clear guidance on optimal diets for shelterees and fixed set of options for meeting those needs.[74]

Planners turned to the food and nutritional sciences to develop products that would be edible and generally acceptable to most shelterees, but not so palatable that shelterees were tempted to eat them all at once rather than follow the prescribed feeding plans. In 1960, Hoegh assured members of Congress that civil defense foods would be acceptable to the American people, describing one such food as "palatable. It is a cross between good Iowa corn and soybeans," and opined that it was far better than the military's ration D bar. "It tastes much better than the candy bar they used to give us. You know those hard chocolate bars that broke my teeth."[75] Finding the right balance between palatability and utility was essential for foods that were engineered to be consumed only in the direst circumstances.

In fact, government food planners had long recognized that lack of palatability could be an asset in designing foods for survival situations. For example, when representatives from the US Army Quartermaster met with employees of the Hershey Chocolate Company in 1937 to discuss the creation of the ration D-bar, they indicated that a standard chocolate bar was too tempting and that the survival ration sought by the Army was one that a soldier would eat only when he was on the verge of starvation; thus it should taste "just a little better than a boiled potato."[76] Shelter rations that provided optimal nutrition and were palatable but not enjoyable ensured that shelterees would be much less likely to eat for pleasure or out of boredom, ensuring that food reserves would last the duration.

The amount of food to stock remained an ongoing issue of debate. In the late 1950s, planning estimates established as a goal a shelter ration program that could provide a typical diet of 2,000 calories per occupant per day, for a two-week period.[77] Over time, this amount was considerably reduced— by half in 1963, with recognition that "work output is not impaired by limiting food intake to less than 1,000 calories per day."[78] By 1967, the target amount was set at 10,000 calories per shelter space for a two-week period, approximately 700 calories per person per day.[79] In part, the lower calorie requirements could be justified by reduced levels of physical activity; the change also helped lower the amount of required drinking water. Some civil defense authorities even touted the potential health and weight-loss benefits of a stay in a shelter. In 1960, Hoegh reported to Congress about one shelter study in which General Mills put a man in a shelter for two weeks with water, vitamin C tablets, and a two-week supply of their Multi-Purpose Food. "He went in with a flabby 213 pounds and came out a very healthy specimen at 198 pounds 2 weeks later. A physical examination revealed he was in better shape than when he went in" and reassured Congress that such foods could sustain Americans in shelters.[80]

There was a bit of marketing involved in reducing the daily calorie requirements for shelters: reducing the amount of food per shelteree to be supplied by the federal government increased the number of shelters that could be said to have been stocked. In the early 1960s, the Defense Civil Preparedness Agency purchased 165,000 tons of shelter foods, which were placed in approximately 100,000 fallout shelters between 1962 and 1970.[81] Reducing provision requirements from 2,000 to 700 calories per day stretched the procured supplies much further. Yet even the use of lower daily caloric standards and creation of purpose-designed civil defense foods could only stretch the total amount of food supplies to a decade or so. Thus, provisioning shelters represented not just a one-time cost but required continual appropriations to allow stockpiles to be refreshed and rotated. By the late 1960s, with national attention focused on the escalating war in Vietnam and domestic turbulence generated by antiwar and social movements, neither the president nor Congress wanted to make such ongoing financial commitments. Funding for shelter stockpiling efforts ended in 1969.[82]

FOOD, FARMS, AND FALLOUT

In addition to determining shelter-food types and quantities for urban and suburban areas, officials considered the special needs of farms and rural areas. Government publications directed at farmers contained the same advice on creating and stocking a shelter, practicing fire-safe housekeeping, and developing sanitation facilities on shelter spaces. Yet these planning guides also recognized that, in many ways, families on farms faced a more complex problem in that they could not as easily depend on local governments or employers, and that "farmers and their families must necessarily undertake a much larger part of the protection of themselves and their means of livelihood."[83] Guides tailored to rural settings included such relevant to topics as warnings that "a spring or deep well may be useless if the pump depends on public power supplies," information about the impact of fallout on different types of vegetables and livestock (e.g., eggs would be safe to eat even if chickens had been exposed to small amounts of radioactivity, but peas would need to be shelled before eating), and reminders to provide covered and sheltered food and water for animals.[84]

Civilian defense efforts raised useful questions about the role of rural spaces and their residents as the state planned for attacks in the nuclear age. Critically, policymakers were uncertain whether rural areas should primarily be considered hinterlands that supplied food and materials to urban and suburban areas, or as spaces on the frontlines of nuclear war.[85] In the former view, rural areas would likely be seen by the enemy as low-value targets and could thus be counted on to serve as evacuation zones for urban and suburban refugees, as well as sites where farming, ranching, and food production could resume following an initial post-bomb hiatus. In the latter view, rural areas were largely seen empty spaces, where high-value targets, such as military bases and missile silos, could be located to reduce the possibility of attacks on high-population urban and suburban areas. American policy pursued both views of rural areas simultaneously. Passive defense policies focused on the importance of rural areas as evacuation zones and productive spaces, while active defense policies focused on the value of rural spaces to counter the increasing precision and lethality of nuclear weapons by dispersing American war-fighting capabilities across broad geographic areas.[86]

Pursuing this contradictory strategy of preparing and utilizing rural areas for nuclear war meant that rural areas were simultaneously defensive and productive. On the defensive side, civil defense plans designated rural spaces as relocation areas for particular urban areas. For example, as mentioned earlier, the five-star Greenbrier resort was the location of a secret, well-stocked shelter for Congress. At the same time, Greenbrier County, West Virginia, was the designated relocation site for civilian evacuees from Fairfax County, Virginia, on the outskirts of Washington, DC. At the Greenbrier, members of Congress would shelter in a bunker with a six-month supply of food; however, no provisions of food, shelter, or medical care for the civilian evacuees of Fairfax County were made, other than the hope that they would bring their own food, medicine, and supplies or a hope that they would be cared and provided for by rural residents.[87]

The emphasis on rural areas as productive spaces was manifested in materials that outlined the responsibility of farmers and food production to develop and stock shelter spaces, as well as return to work as soon as possible following an attack. For example, the USDA's 1958 brochure, *Defense against Radioactive Fallout on the Farm*, clearly stated that the obligations of farmers went above and beyond those of ordinary citizens. If America were attacked, farmers were told, then, "you, the American farmer, would be counted on to supply the food and fiber needed to keep the economy going."[88] A key theme in these materials was the need to protect human capital and, with it, agricultural know-how. Farmers were advised, in the event of an attack, to protect themselves, their families, and their neighbors, ahead of crops, livestock, and land.[89]

Though it was considered a secondary problem, the need to protect animals and crops was still crucial—particularly with respect to what it would take to resume food production. A further set of publications thus addressed the special problems of protecting livestock from the effects of blast, fire, and nuclear radiation, and included designs for livestock shelters. For example, Plan No. 5950 from the USDA's Cooperative Farm Building Plan Exchange, entitled a "Bunker-type Fallout Shelter ... FOR BEEF CATTLE," published in 1964, described how to build a basic emergency shelter for beef cattle that could be adapted for use by sheep, hogs, or poultry. If properly built, it provided a radioactive-protection factor of about 90.[90] In addition to glossy brochure-style publications, USDA partnered with state extension agencies to provide complete, detailed blueprints and working drawings that adapted the basic concepts of shelter design for specific geographical and ecological settings.[91] Shelters for livestock, especially for dairy cattle, presented challenges for planners as farmers would need to access dairy cattle to milk in order to keep cattle healthy and prodictive.[92]

In all sectors, the quick return to normal production was the goal. In 1962, the USDA issued recommendations for how to protect the facilities and equipment of the food industry, including the trained personnel required to operate the facilities. The guide included tips on preparing for an attack as well as information about cooperating with the government during immediate postattack and economic stabilization efforts.[93] Writing in 1962, secretary of agriculture Orville Freeman warned food producers that the complex network connecting the farms that produced the food precursors of food processors distributors would be a prime target of possible attacks.[94] Beyond simply encouraging planning to ensure the continuity of operations following an attack, Freeman argued that preparedness could help forestall such attacks entirely: "The better we understand the dangers and train ourselves to do those things which will add to our capability for survival, the greater deterrent we create against a possible enemy's belief that he could destroy our food industry."[95] Preparations for nuclear attacks on farms and in food production facilities were thus also seen as important aspects of strategic deterrence efforts.

This deterrent function received explicit attention from officials and researchers. Having adequate stock of food could demonstrate that America could survive nuclear attack and that its citizens were prepared for recovery after a nuclear attack. For example, a Rand Corporation study from 1958 posited "surviving food inventories, after either a 50-city or a 150-city attack, would be sufficient for at least survival."[96] Other studies, such as one by RAND's Joseph Carrier, suggested that recovery efforts could be greatly enhanced by maintaining three-month stockpiles of transitional foods in shelters and perhaps a longer-range stockpile in mines and caves, of at least a several years' supply of vitamins and foods. These plans would allow the rotation of foods grown and produced after a nuclear war, which might be contaminated with radioactivity, with foods and food precursors stockpiled before the war to ensure that people receive as little radioactivity as possible from contaminated food supplies.[97]

However, all these plans to devote significant portions of American food stocks to shelters and civil defense stockpiles ran counter to the ongoing effort to reduce agricultural surpluses. The large-scale accumulation of defensive supplies of food and commodities, perhaps packed into deep mines or complex shelter systems, competed with prevailing policy efforts by the Eisenhower administartion to deploy food offensively through international humanitarian aid and by actively seeking new markets for American agricultural products. As a result, all the planning and proposals came to naught. The costs entailed, combined with Congress's general unwillingness to appropriate funds for civilian shelter programs, much less large-scale, nationwide, long-range stockpiling efforts, prevented enactment of the proposed plans.

The food that took its place on the (mostly imagined) shelves of American bomb shelters sat at the center of strategies, hopes, and plans as a variety of actors attempted to envision how Americans would survive and recover in the face of devastation. Amid discussions of mass evacuation plans and shelter construction efforts, food was an essential element of American plans to address the threat of nuclear war. More importantly, however, addressing the multiple challenges inherent in using American food defensively helped contribute to a growing sense among planners and the American people that recovering from or even surviving a nuclear war was not possible. Beyond the issues of whether and what sorts of shelters to build was a complex set of food problems, including identifying the proper foods to use in shelters, deciding who was responsible for stocking shelters and managing shelter food stockpiles, determining nutritional and dietary needs for shelter situations, and confronting questions about the status of rural areas and the impact of nuclear attacks on agriculture and food production.

In choosing not to act on the government's recommendations, Americans showed their unwillingness to bear the burden of making a likely futile attempt to prepare for the nuclear threat, illustrating the gap between the high-level efforts to integrate food into national security policy and the ways that American society and the food system were actually developing. Both the high costs of sheltering programs and worries about increasing the authority of the federal government proved to be major obstacles to the development of a robust nonmilitary defense network centered on shelters. The question of who was responsible for civil defense was also a critical component of the shelter debates. Presidents and congresses may have been content to identify civil defense as a responsibility best left to individuals and local communities, but Americans felt the opposite. A 1960 Gallup poll revealed that only 21 percent of Americans had ever given any thought to building a home shelter, and fewer than 3 percent of Americans reported that they had actually built one.[98] However, "when asked in 1960 if they 'would favor or oppose a law which would require every community to build public bomb shelters,' 72 percent of Americans said they would favor such a law."[99] This gap demonstrates that Americans did not share the government's opinions about the value of do-it-yourself security.

But questions of cost and responsibility were not the only factors that prevented shelter development. As debates progressed during the 1950s and early 1960s, many Americans looked closely at shelter discussions and seemed to wonder how, exactly, planners envisioned American society in a postnuclear world. Debates about constructing shelters, hoarding food stockpiles, and even the need to use violence to protect one's shelter and supplies from neighbors or strangers who had not taken steps to prepare contributed to the belief that nuclear war was not an event to be survived but one to be avoided.[100] Certainly, Americans conceded, some people might survive a nuclear war. But in the images of retreating underground to wait and hope that blast effects, heat, or radiation levels did not exceed survival thresholds of shelter spaces, as well as the thought of living on rationed supplies of Nebraskits and carbohydrate supplements, Americans began to doubt that the postnuclear society would bear much resemblance to prewar America.[101]

By the mid-1960s, studies showing that even limited nuclear exchanges would have significant biological effects on seeds, soil, and animal species and made it clear that restarting food production in the United States in a postnuclear world would be far more complex a challenge than simply just having farmers and livestock emerge from their two-week stay in shelters and get back to work.[102] Many Americans became convinced that a nuclear war would not be a simple crisis that could be weathered by turning to a few days of food stocked up in Grandma's Pantry, but a catastrophe that would threaten the very survival of American society and core American values.

For the early Cold War planners, questions of overstocking shelter pantries were part of a debate about the shape of national security. Should civil defense be a component of a national security strategy? And, if so, whose responsibility was it? If government should provide support, what amount of support was appropriate and would prevent the rise of a garrison state?[103] Policymakers and planners saw the potential in deploying food as a defensive element of national power to improve the ability of Americans to survive and recover from nuclear war. For decades, in the face of a threat that many people had begun to feel it was impossible to prepare for, the government continued making building and provisioning shelters a central part of its deployment of food power. Yet, the American people made day-to-day choices that differed from the government recommendations, based on their own perceptions of threats, vulnerabilities, and priorities.

A changing landscape of security challenges that blurred the distinctions between soldiers and civilians, frontline and homefront, and wartime and peacetime, confronted American leaders with a new set of obligations. The increasing complexity of the nuclear weapon threat fueled the the public's sense that science and technology, let alone shelters, could not sufficiently counter it. Science and technology, combined with American agricultural abundance and advances in food processing, had found ways to turn corn and soy into nutritional, mildly palatable bulwarks against future catastrophe. But few Americans ultimately had the stomach for the future envisioned by the planners. Deliberations in the 1950s and early 1960s showed that, even though Americans could contemplate creating some sort of resilient network of shelters, food supplies, food-production areas, and food-production facilities, which could be relinked following a nuclear war to enable postattack recovery, American food power could more productively be used to reduce international tensions and the possibility that nuclear war would ever take place.

Food for Peace and the War on Hunger

Food Power in the 1960s

In the 1960 presidential race, Senator John F. Kennedy and Vice President Richard Nixon unveiled a dueling proposals based on contrary visions of how to deal with the issue of America's agricultural surplus. Both candidates agreed that continued surpluses were an issue that needed to be addressed. But for Kennedy, surpluses also showed how government policy could effectively rationalize agricultural production while using food to influence the Cold War strategic landscape. For Nixon, they represented excess and needed to be eliminated through detailed policy plans that would extricate the government from its involvement in agriculture. As American concerns about Cold War competition intensified, the candidates' positions on the farm problem to a certain degree got swept up in foreign policy issues. Over the course of the coming decade, this would lead to significant outlays of American food aid both at home and abroad. During the election, however, the candidates stayed focused on the domestic aspects of their farm plans they felt were key to securing the farm vote.

The candidates presented those plans to that core constituency at the National Plowing Contest in Sioux Falls, South Dakota, in September 1960. Speaking on September 23, Kennedy revealed the details of his farm program in a speech to more than twenty thousand farmers, who had braved the rain and mud to listen. He reminded his audience that Republicans had failed to fulfill their 1952 and 1956 pledges to help farmers achieve full parity of income. Farm incomes had, instead, declined 20 percent since 1952. The Republicans' farm policy, he said, had resulted not only in lower incomes but also in higher surpluses. Kennedy also called attention to the many undernourished people in America—some four million Americans who received meager government assistance in the form of surplus food packages containing grain, rice, and, as of that summer, lard. Kennedy promised a new approach to the farm problem—supply management—aimed at achieving "full parity of income for American farmers." It was undergirded by the view that agricultural abundance was not a problem but a blessing. America's surplus agricultural production was one of its strengths, Kennedy noted, an area in which the United States was clearly outpacing the Soviet Union.[1]

The following day, Nixon spoke about his farm program to a slightly smaller crowd, who had braved even deeper mud than the day before (so deep that Nixon's car had to be towed onto the festival grounds by a tractor). The speech was Nixon's second major address on farm policy, following one given in Iowa the week before. In the Iowa speech, he had described "Operation Consume," a four-part, four-year program to eliminate surpluses. First, it would expand overseas deployment of surplus commodities through the food for peace program. Second, it would create a domestic food reserve, creating stockpiles at strategic locations throughout the country that would be refreshed and renewed periodically and could be used in the event of enemy attack. Third, it would establish a barter system to expand acerage reserve and land conservation programs by "paying" farmers with stored surplus crops that could be sold or fed to livestock. Fourth, Nixon's plan proposed establishing a new program to convert excess grain into low-cost protein foods, such as powdered milk, eggs, canned chicken, and beef, which could be distributed to those in need at home and abroad.[2]

In the South Dakota speech, Nixon described "Operation Safeguard," his plan to reduce production by temporarily increasing the size of the acerage reserve programs in a way that would still allow farmers flexibility in the event of increased future demand. Nixon explained that effective price supports would move the country toward a system of agriculture that was free of all government controls, something he knew, from the many letters from them he received, that farmers wanted. Nixon said he agreed in principle with that goal, but cautioned that achieving it would require a transition period, during which it would be necessary to continue to protect farm income while agricultural production and consumption were brought into balance. Operation Safeguard called for temporarily reducing acreage allotments for surplus crops, such as wheat, and adding fallowed acres into the conservation reserve program. To help farmers deal with the rising costs of machinery and inputs, which were increasing faster than farm income, he proposed implementing rural development programs to help provide new sources of livelihood for farmers unable to continue making a living in agriculture.[3]

Observers at the time were unable to tell which program was better received. Nixon eventually won the farm belt in the November election, though the number of issues on the table make it hard to isolate this factor. Nevertheless, Nixon's plans were more graciously received in farm country. The *New York Times* reported that "a sampling of farmers showed opinion divided as to whether we could put over" a program like Kennedy's.[4] Assessing Nixon's farm program, Iowa Congressman Charles B. Hoeven, the senior Republican member of the House Agricultural Committee, said it was "the key to the door which has locked the farm belt out of America's prosperity."[5] In practice, both plans offered, at least in the short run, similar strategies for easing surpluses through the expanded deployment of foods overseas and at home and intensified government management of agricultural production to better align supply with demand. In the long-term, the two approaches differed markedly. Although he was careful never to mention the politically unpopular Ezra Taft Benson, Nixon had generally adopted the goal favored by Benson—that is, to get the government out of agriculture and restore a free market as quickly as possible. Kennedy's plan, meanwhile, envisioned a continuing positive government role in helping farmers manage production. Kennedy's ideas about "supply management," had been developed by Willard Cochrane, one of the senator's farm advisers and a professor of agricultural economics at the University of Minnesota.[6]

Following Kennedy's victory in November, as America embarked on what Kennedy was calling the New Frontier, the country still confronted the complex and seemingly intractable farm problem that had dogged American expansion across the old frontier.[7] What was the best way to harmonize agricultural supply and demand, ensure rural prosperity and low food prices for consumers, and use the country's full spectrum of capabilities to check the Soviet threat? When we ask the question this way, it becomes clear that a major challenge of the farm problem lay in its encompassing multiple, sometimes contradictory, goals. Reducing surpluses required foreseeing trends in domestic consumption while also strategizing what amount of food could be deployed into overseas markets and humanitarian assistance.

This chapter discusses the efforts to deal with the farm problem during the Kennedy and Johnson administrations. It first discusses the new policies that Presidents Kennedy and Johnson developed to manage or reduce surpluses. Food power as a kind of strategic policymaking came to its maturity in this decade, and the persistent farm surpluses of the postwar years slowly began to decline. But, both administrations found that surpluses could not be addressed simply by changing farm policies, such as by expanding programs to divert lands out of production. Instead, they tried deploy food power both at home, through enhanced domestic aid programs such as food stamps and free school lunches, and abroad, by increasing international sales—including to the Soviet Union—and increasing international food aid. Formal government efforts were augmented by increasing efforts by both government and the nonprofit sector to boost food production in strategic countries. In the 1960s, the use of food power made American food a presence in the day-to-day lives of people around the world. While a clear, overarching strategy for the use of American food power did not emerge, the policies of the decade expanded the scope of the postwar food system by adding the need of many nations for humanitarian assistance to rationales for food-aid programs and by greatly increasing technical assistance to countries abroad to fuel an American vision of a peaceful world of prosperous nations untied through trade.

FOOD POWER AT HOME IN THE 1960S

As Eisenhower and Benson had found in the 1950s, solving the farm problem was a complex challenge, especially once the dominant issue of surpluses became subsumed in a rapidly changing food landscape in a turbulent political landscape. Between 1960 and 1968, the American government would become even more deeply involved in the nation's farms, creating a permanent domestic nutrition-assistance program and escalating the Food for Peace program, which established food aid as an enduring and visible core of American policy at home and abroad.

In the 1960s, the Soviet Union's need to make large-scale purchases of grain from the United States and its allies was interpreted domestically as a clear demonstration of the superiority of free-world agricultural systems over Soviet-style agriculture. A broader set of groups and interests began participating in American food politics. The shift in legislative terminology from "farm bills" to "food and agriculture acts" represented the recognition that food politics was no longer simply the domain of farmers but also involved an increasingly diverse set of actors, concerned with a broad range of issues related to the characteristics and values of food and their implications for social justice, animal welfare, and the environment.[8] While farmers still retained a great deal of power and influence over food policy, during the 1960s, American consumers would take a more active role in food politics. The farm problem confronting President Kennedy thus involved an even more complex set of challenges than those Eisenhower and Benson had been unable to solve, more complex even than the program Kennedy had detailed during his campaign could effectively address.

Supply management required even more government restrictions on production and higher price supports, reversing the previous administration's focus on reducing government control. Choosing his point person on food issues was thus especially critical for Kennedy. Unlike Eisenhower, Kennedy did not have roots in farm country and was, by his own admission, largely uninterested in agricultural affairs. Kennedy's failure to win the farm belt, and his narrow victory in the election would make it even harder for the administration to implement its plans.[9] Kennedy chose Orville Freeman, a former three-term governor of Minnesota, to be his secretary of agriculture. Freeman was close to Senator Hubert Humphrey and had also worked with Willard Cochrane, who was appointed the director of agriculture economics. Kennedy's farm advisers revived acreage controls and also considered tightening production controls, establishing limits on on even smaller units, such as pound or bushel quotas. As noted in chapter 3, one of the problems with acreage controls was that farmers tended to increase their yields per acre by concentrating production on their best land; at the same time, they sought to boost productivity by mechanizing and using fertilizer and higher-yield seed varieties.[10] Conservation reserve efforts had also failed to reduce production because farmers typically entered their least productive land into the programs. Establishing production quotas based on pounds or bushels, as the supply-management policies sought to do, was thus an effort to limit productivity based on how much farmers actually produced.[11]

Freeman, supported by Kennedy, asked Congress to cede the authority for the management of commodity programs to the Department of Agriculture. In an omnibus bill submitted to Congress in March 1961, the administration proposed that instead of asking Congress to develop commodity programs, the secretary of agriculture would be empowered to develop commodity-management policy. The secretary would then organize committees to recommend policy, selecting members from candidates nominated by the farmer committees administering commodity programs. Once a committee recommended a set of production-control measures such as acerage control programs, the secretary would draft a proposal to submit to Congress. If Congress did not veto the plan within sixty days, and if the president approved it, the plan would then be submitted to the farmers producing the commodity in a referendum that required a two-thirds vote of approval from farmers before it became law.[12]

The plan was supported by the National Farmer's Union and the Grange, but opposed by the much larger Farm Bureau. And despite the Democratic majority in Congress, conservative Southern Democrats and Republicans joined together to oppose the bill. Notwithstanding repeated efforts to get Freeman to compromise on some of the bill's provisions, he was unwilling to budge on any of the key points. Congress, meanwhile, was unwilling to surrender its power to develop farm legislation. It rejected the plan, dealing a major blow to the administration. A second bill, presented to Congress in spring 1962, to place mandatory production limits on wheat, dairy products, and feed grains also met with sustained resistance in Congress. It eventually passed, but only the provisions related to wheat remained in the bill, although in heavily modified form. When it was submitted to a referendum vote by farmers, however, in May 1963, wheat farmers voted overwhelmingly against the changes represented by the administration's program. It was the first time in US history that wheat farmers had rejected a government program.[13]

Although it was unable to put in place mandatory controls, the Kennedy administration was able to implement new voluntary programs to reduce surpluses. By early 1961, lack of production controls and low prices meant that the amount of stored corn and other feed grains, such as sorghum, had reached over eighty million tons, and an estimated additional increase of ten million tons was likely by the end of 1961, an amount that would require securing additional storage facilities. Under the Emergency Feed Grains Bill, which Congress passed in March 1961 (in the House, by a margin of only seven votes), Freeman was authorized to take steps to reduce the stored surpluses. The administration raised price supports, for example, from $1.06 to $1.20 per bushel, and farmers could receive even higher supports if they agreed to divert acreage from production into conservation programs. Further acreage reductions would result in additional cash or in-kind payments from the government's own stores of crops, thus further reducing surpluses. The program was voluntary, but if farmers did not participate then their crops would be sold at market prices that were likely to be heavily depressed by Secretary Freeman's efforts to reduce surpluses by dumping stored commodities on the market. The program was successful, reducing production in 1961 by 11 percent below 1960 levels, leading to a total reduction of 280 million bushels of feed grains in storage, the first substantive reduction since 1952. The policy proved to be highly popular with farmers and also helped boost net farm incomes by $1 billion. The main objection to the policy was its cost; the government paid $786 million for land diversion, only some of which was recouped through the reduced storage costs. Still, despite its initial opposition, Congress voted to extend feed grains program into 1962, and even passed a wheat program modeled on the feed grains program. The voluntary programs were able to boost total farm income while also reducing the surpluses of wheat and corn, the two major commodities, but this came at steadily increasing cost.[14] And ironically, the popularity of the voluntary program made it more difficult for the administration to implement mandatory controls.

Policymakers in the Kennedy administration also tried to address the imbalance of supply and demand by increasing consumption of key commodities. One of the cleavages that had emerged in the debates over the 1961 omnibus bill and the Emergency Feed Grains Bill was between Democrats from the South, who tended to ally with Republicans on farm issues, and Democrats from the North, who were becoming increasingly concerned with issues relevant to their urban and suburban constituencies, such as urban poverty and hunger. Now, however, the interests of both were served by the government's proposal to buy up surplus grain that could then be used in new nutritional-assistance programs. It seemed like a win-win situation, and it was, so long as there continued to be sufficient agricultural surpluses, so that the government's purchases did not affect consumer prices.[15]

The intertwining of these seemingly disparate goals—propping up farm incomes and keeping food prices low—occurred in 1964 when Congress passed new legislation supporting wheat and cotton prices at levels that were supported by farmers and supported in by congressional Republicans, and both Southern and Northern Democrats. In return for their support, urban Democrats received backing from other legislators to establish the United States' first permanent nutrition-assistance program. The USDA had administered a relatively small nutrition food-stamp program beginning in 1939, but abandoned it in 1943. Legislators began pushing the idea of a permanent nutrition-assistance program in the 1950s, though Benson and other Eisenhower administration officials resisted these efforts. In 1959, Public Law 86-341 had authorized the creation of a food-stamp program, but Eisenhower did not implement it.[16]

Kennedy had supported legislation to establish nutrition-assistance programs when he was in the Senate, and immediately upon taking office as president, he began talking steps to do so. His first Executive Order, EO 10914, issued on January 21, 1961, called for expanded food distribution to needy Americans.[17] In February 1961, Kennedy announced that the USDA would begin a pilot food-stamp program. Unlike its predecessor from 1939, Kennedy's pilot program did not require that foods come from surplus commodities. The new program was designed by a four-person team and directed by Isabelle Kelley. The first Americans to purchase the new food stamps were Mr. and Mrs. Alderson Muncy of Paynesville, West Virginia, who bought food stamps for their fifteen-person household, on May 29, 1961. In their first transaction, they bought a can of pork and beans from Henderson's Supermarket. By January of 1964, the pilot program had expanded from the initial eight test areas to forty-three areas in twenty-two states, with 380,000 participants.[18]

After overcoming opposition from some Southern Democrats and Midwestern Republicans, who objected to the program's cost and to what they worried was government overreach, a permanent program was established in 1964 via H.R. 10222, sponsored by Democratic congresswoman Leonor K. Sullivan of Missouri. Sullivan was a long-time advocate for government nutrition assistance, and she had been working since 1954 to pass food-stamp legislation. The bill enjoyed the support of the president and many Democratic members of Congress; nevertheless, both houses debated whether the emphasis in the government's programs should be solely on providing food assistance or also take into account the needs of farmers. Proponents appealed to lawmakers' concerns about their agricultural constituencies and argued that domestic nutrition assistance would help the country deal with agricultural surpluses and put extra money in farmers' pockets. These arguments failed to win over the naysayers, however. Instead, the bill was passed by supporters who argued for the importance of the health and welfare aspects of nutrition needs. The passage of the bill, and the decision to make nutrition assistance part of the mission of the USDA, was a striking commentary on the shifting food landscape of the 1960s. Democratic congressman Benjamin Rosenthal of New York, for example, argued that the USDA must become more concerned about problems of health and nutrition that impacted all Americans and not simply focused on boosting farm income.[19]

Once enacted, the scope of the program continued to expand, and more Americans began using food stamps to supplement their food budgets. The appropriation for the first year of the program was $75 million, and the USDA estimated that the program would eventually expand to four million Americans, at a cost of $360 million a year. But the program was so popular that the first million Americans had enrolled by March 1966; six million had enrolled by May 1970, and ten million by February 1971. Families could use the stamps to purchase any food except alcoholic beverages—the initial House version of the bill would also have prohibited soft drinks and prepared frozen meals, which were considered luxury foods at the time. Along with free-lunch programs in schools, needy Americans gained a much more nutritional range of foods than had been provided by the packages of grain, rice, and lard Kennedy had seen when campaigning in West Virginia in 1960.[20]

Upon taking office, President Lyndon Johnson sought to build on the gains made by the Kennedy administration, while de-emphasizing conflicts over farm polices by embedding agriculture and food in broader social reform questions. Mindful of failure of high-profile farm-policy reform efforts during both the Eisenhower and Kennedy administrations, the Johnson administration avoided controversial measures, such as government marketing quotas and acreage controls, in favor of voluntary programs. In the 1964 presidential election, farm policy was not the prominent issue it had been during the 1960 campaign, but it remained a subject of discussion. Johnson released a farm policy paper describing three sets of programs designed to improve farmers' income; increase consumer demand for agricultural products, including by expanding the food-stamp and Food for Peace programs; and boost the standard of living of rural Americans.[21] Agricultural policy in the mid- to late-1960s continued to support prices and payments to farmers who diverted acreage from production into conservation programs.

Johnson, along with his vice president, Hubert Humphrey of Minnesota, understood the importance of agricultural programs. During Johnson's long tenure as Senate majority leader, however, he had witnessed first-hand the unsuccessful efforts by the Eisenhower administration to reform farm policy. Humphrey, too, had been involved in agricultural policy in the Senate, and was an early leader in the effort to expand the use of surpluses for foreign assistance, which culminated in the 1954 Agricultural Trade Development and Assistance Act (PL-480). Thus, rather than tackle the morass of agricultural policy and farm income issues, Johnson preferred to focus his energies on broad-based efforts to address poverty in America, through the set of initiatives he labeled the "Great Society." Johnson saw rural poverty and the welfare of farmers as part of broader issues of hunger, health, and poverty in America, a position also consistent with the views of Senator Robert F. Kennedy of New York and Senator George McGovern of South Dakota. By the late 1960s, farm policy discussions regularly broached a topic that had been unspeakable in previous decades: an acceptance of the reality that postwar changes in agriculture such as mechanization and intensification meant that small, low-income farmers could not be helped much by traditional government agricultural programs. Policy discussions among Democrats and Republicans began to focus, not on aiding such farmers by setting agricultural policies, but on helping them make a transition from farming to other forms of employment. Johnson was, however, deeply interested in one aspect of American agriculture: using its bounty abroad in order to advance American security and national interests.[22]

THE WAR ON HUNGER: DEPLOYING
FOOD POWER OVERSEAS

As the debate over farm policy in the 1960 presidential campaigns had made clear, both parties could agree that there was a role for American food in American foreign affairs. Even though candidates Kennedy and Nixon steered clear of the making foreign food assistance a central talking point in their campaigns, they did not ignore the subject completely. In a speech on September 22 at the Corn Palace in Mitchell, South Dakota, Kennedy had said, "I think the farmers can bring more credit, more lasting goodwill, more chance for freedom, more chance for peace, than almost any other group of Americans in the next ten years, if we recognize that food is strength, and food is peace, and food is freedom, and food is a helping hand to people around the world whose good will and friendship we want."[23] At the National Plowing Contest in Sioux Falls, South Dakota, the same day, Kennedy also proposed the idea of the United States distributing surpluses directly overseas or giving them to the United Nations to distribute.[24] Nixon also endorsed increasing foreign food aid, but went further than Kennedy and proposed creating a new multilateral body to distribute surplus food. The idea was really Eisenhower's who, after being stymied by Congress in his efforts to create an expanded American foreign food-assistance program, presented the UN General Assembly a proposal in September 1960 to create a multilateral Food for Peace program. Although the proposal was criticized by the Soviet Union as being driven by election politics, it was adopted by the General Assembly on October 27, 1960. This resolution set in motion the process of establishing a branch of the United Nations to provide emergency food assistance that would culminate in the creation of the World Food Program in 1961.[25]

During Eisenhower's second term, the administration's overseas food-aid programs were increasingly criticized by policymakers who argued their true focus was on solving domestic issues rather than serving the country's foreign policy needs. Following the 1954 passage of PL-480, the United States' foreign food assistance had increased dramatically. By the early 1960s, more than eighteen million tons of food aid was being disbursed annually, and the PL-480 programs represented the costliest American foreign policy undertaking since the Marshall Plan.[26] But, critics argued, such programs were designed more to reduce American surpluses than to assist needy people in friendly nations, and thus neglected emerging fronts in the Cold War, such as Poland. For example, in 1958, Senator Humphrey, at the request of Allen J. Ellender, Democratic senator from Louisiana and chair of the Senate Committee on Agriculture and Forestry, undertook a study on the operations of PL-480. The year-long study included ten days of public hearings, and its findings were released in the report *Food and Fiber as a Force for Freedom* in April 1958.[27] The report criticized the narrow goal of surplus disposal and argued for a much broader program of assistance, "A breakthrough in the conquest of hunger could be more significant in the cold war than the conquest of outer space."[28] Humphrey's report also identified administrative problems among the groups responsible for implementing PL-480, and cited the need for clear leadership. Humphrey introduced a bill in April 1959 (S. 1711) to revise PL-480 to emphasize humanitarian aspects of food aid and address administrative problems through the creation of a new government position, Peace Food Administrator, to be appointed by the White House with the status of special assistant to the president, who would oversee all PL-480 related activities.[29]

Humphrey's proposals were not initially well received by Congress or by officials in the Eisenhower administration, though by January 1959, Eisenhower himself was also urging the development of a broader Food for Peace plan.[30] In September of 1959, Congress passed a two-year extension of the 1954 act (PL 86–341) that made minor changes to the structure of assistance efforts but did not adopt many of Humphrey's most far-reaching proposals, such as the ideas for a food-reserve program or a food-for-development grant program.[31] Eisenhower did appoint Don Paarlberg, special assistant to the president for economic affairs, to be the Food for Peace coordinator in 1960. In addition to his World Food Program proposal, Eisenhower supported other efforts to enhance US foreign assistance. In May 1959, Benson convened a Food for Peace conference in Washington, DC, to better coordinate America's wheat exports with those of Argentina, Australia, Canada, and France—which, along with the United States, were the worlds' top wheat-exporting nations.[32] Despite these measures, however, it remained clear that Eisenhower continued to approach food assistance primarily as a means to reduce domestic agricultural surpluses.[33]

Kennedy's election had brought a significant change in the structure and status of food diplomacy programs in the American government, including efforts to get the public involved. On October 31, 1960, he had pledged that if he were elected, he would create a committee of distinguished citizens to make recommendations for transforming Food for Peace from a surplus disposal operation into a surplus use operation, and from a slogan "into a truly effective long-range use of our food abundance to build lasting foundations for durable peace and progress."[34] He announced that he had formed a committee to make recommendations on the topic to the new administration in early 1961. The committee was headed by Murray D. Lincoln, the president of CARE and president of Nationwide Mutual Insurance Companies, and also included Senator Humphrey, Donald Murphy, George W. Forell, William Benton, and Mrs. Mary Lasker.[35] The committee submitted its report to the president-elect on January 19, 1961, which endorsed many of the proposals from Humphrey's 1959 Food for Peace bill, including the creation of a national food reserve and development of national health and education programs.[36] Once he took office, Kennedy followed through on his campaign promise to increase public involvement in food diplomacy, and on May 6, 1961 created the American Food for Peace Council to help implement the committee's reccomendations. The Council would advise the Food for Peace director, develop public information on world hunger, and enlist support for the efforts to alleviate hunger. Kennedy named James A. Michener and Mrs. Raymond Clapper co-chairs of the council; other members included the opera singer Marian Anderson, actors Yul Brenner and Danny Kaye, former adviser to Kennedy and President Truman Clark M. Clifford, and former representative Clifford Hope of Kansas, among others.[37] Kennedy also invited a number of organizations to send representatives. Ultimately, the council would have two hundred members and hold conferences at the state and regional levels to underscore the importance of reducing surpluses and addressing global food needs.[38]

Three days after his first Executive Order 1041 expanded distribution of a greater variety and quality of foods to needy families, Kennedy issued Executive Order 10915, which redefined the responsibilities of the director of the Food for Peace program.[39] In his first State of the Union message, delivered just ten days after his inauguration, Kennedy recommended immediately dispatching a Food for Peace mission Latin America "to explore ways in which our vast food abundance can be used to help end hunger and malnutrition in certain areas of suffering in our own hemisphere." Kennedy also announced his intention to further expand the Food for Peace Program, asserting that America's "abundance must be used more effectively to relieve hunger and help economic growth in all corners of the globe. And I have asked the Director of this Program to recommend additional ways in which these surpluses can advance the interests of world peace–including the establishment of world food reserves."[40] Through his words and actions, Kennedy signaled that American food assistance was being transformed into polices designed to do more than just alleviate American agricultural surpluses. Kennedy also took immediate action to promote the use of American agricultural abundance for humanitarian ends. Food assistance to nations such as South Vietnam, Korea, and Taiwan in the early 1960s demonstrated the ways in which American abundance could support nations, and especially governments, that were amenable to America's goals. In particular, food-aid shipments allowed America to exceed the dollar caps put on foreign assistance to South Vietnam at the Geneva Conference in 1954.[41]

In March 1961, Kennedy wrote to Congress about the need to shift the focus of American food aid from surplus disposal toward constructive uses of food at home and abroad.[42] Kennedy's interest in the Food for Peace program was more clearly explained by presidential adviser Ted Sorensen in an address to the American Food for Peace Council in January 1962. Sorensen said that better determining how much food was needed at home and abroad was critical to Kennedy's supply-management approach to agricultural policy. Changes to the Food for Peace program, he argued, would also help the president fulfill pledges to improve American foreign-aid programs, and be part of a strategy to build strong, stable, and free nations that could assist in building the institutions of peace. While Kennedy stressed reasons other than surplus management for his policy decisions, Sorensen's address was a reminder that reduction of surpluses continued to be a prominent driver of American deployment of food abroad.[43]

Kennedy appointed former Democratic congressman George McGovern as the first director of the Office of Food for Peace. In February of 1961, McGovern and other administration officials undertook the mission to Latin America Kennedy promised in his State of the Union message, with a charge from Kennedy "to explore the manner in which our food abundance can be used to help end hunger and malnutrition in every area of suffering throughout the hemisphere."[44] McGovern reported that, while there was a need to use American surpluses to feed hungry people, "food can be no more than one of the building blocks" of peace and development and he advised that "any long-range program for feeding the hungry should be linked with incentives for self help and with orderly progress in economic development."[45] Following the mission, the United States established food programs in Latin American schools and developed programs that provided food to people participating in agricultural and construction projects in Africa and Latin America.[46] These kinds of efforts—integrating food aid into broader social reconstruction efforts—would characterize McGovern's Food for Peace work. Though not a farmer himself, McGovern had been born and raised in a small rural community in South Dakota, where he had witnessed the effects of the decline of farm incomes and of rural poverty. As he helped to build the Democratic Party in his staunchly Republican home state, McGovern became a fierce critic of the Eisenhower administration's agricultural policies. He was especially vexed by the paradox that US surpluses were growing and the government was spending more on crop storage even as levels of hunger and poverty were also growing, both at home and abroad.[47]

Believing that aid could not be a substitute for expanding the capabilities of nations to boost their own agricultural and economic productivity,

McGovern advocated that grants of food aid be integrated with other forms of assistance.[48] McGovern was supportive of Kennedy's efforts to expand and unify United States foreign-assistance efforts. The Foreign Assistance Act of 1961 created the Agency for International Development (AID) and allowed Kennedy, via with Executive Order 10973, to reorganize and centralize the distribution of funds and technical assistance to foreign nations.[49] McGovern also encouraged efforts to create a multilateral food-distribution program and to expand the role of the FAO. He wrote to Kennedy that world needs were such that a multilateral approach was needed to supplement the actions of countries like the United States. Though McGovern resigned his position in 1962, his work at the Office of Food for Peace helped to establish food as a critical component of American foreign assistance efforts, an approach that echoes through contemporary programs such as government's Feed the Future initiative.[50] The expansion of United States' foreign-assistance programs in the 1960s was part of a larger shift in thinking, in which surpluses were not simply to be disposed of or avoided through good policy but could be used in beneficial ways to address nutritional needs and promote economic development in friendly foreign countries.[51]

FOOD POWER AND THE COLD WAR

An opening for a more direct use of food power in Soviet-American relations was provided by a Soviet food crisis in the 1960s. Following his ascension to the post of First Secretary of the Communist Party in 1953, Nikita Khrushchev made reforming Soviet agricultural production a top priority. Initiatives such as the Virgin Lands Campaign sought to open up new land for grain production in Kazakhstan, the Caucasus, and western Siberia.[52] During the 1950s, people in the Soviet Union subsisted on a diet of root vegetables such as sugar beets, peas, and thin soups. Grains, especially corn, were used to feed cattle and hogs. For Khrushchev, improving the standard of living of people in the Soviet Union by providing more milk and meat was an important arena of competition with the capitalist world.[53] According to Khrushchev, "If we catch up with the United States in per capita production of meat, butter and milk, we will fire the most powerful torpedo against the foundations of capitalism."[54] The cultivation of additional lands and good weather in the late 1950s had resulted in good crops in 1954, 1956, and 1958.[55]

These production gains gave Khrushchev the confidence to predict in 1957 that the USSR would surpass the United States in the per capita production of meat and milk by the start of the 1960s. Yet smaller harvests after 1958 revealed deep troubles within the Soviet agricultural system, including a failure to implement proper farming practices for the country's semi-arid regions and an overconfidence that good crop years would compensate for poor harvests. Reduced grain production had necessitated the culling of livestock herds, which resulted in the reduced availability of milk and meat for Soviet citizens. The situation was especially galling because Khrushchev was eager to show that, at long last, communism was improving the people's daily lives. The Soviet agricultural failures created an opening for American policymakers, when, facing unrest and dissent at home, Soviet officials turned outward for food supplies.[56]

By early 1963, American intelligence agencies were reporting that Soviet estimates of agricultural performance had been overstated. In a memorandum, dated January 10, 1963, to McGeorge Bundy, President Kennedy's national security adviser, Ray Cline, deputy director (intelligence) of the Central Intelligence Agency (CIA), reported that "in 1962 consumer dissatisfaction in the Soviet Union over food supplies and prices not only was a significant cause of some general unrest but in a few places was a factor which sparked civilian rioting." He continued, "We believe that unless Khrushchev takes strong measures, such as drawing down heavily on state reserves and curtailing exports, there may well be further instances of civil disorder in the coming months."[57] That summer, during a tour of the Soviet Union by American agricultural officials, Secretary Freeman had a frank exchange with Premier Khrushchev about the state of Soviet agriculture (in which the premier admitted that there was a need to improve production) and told Khrushchev that the Soviet Union could improve its agricultural productivity by shifting investments. Khrushchev responded, "Now we are going to decrease money for rockets, we have enough rockets. We are going to (spend more money on) (divert this money to) agriculture."[58] Despite Khrushchev's rhetorical effort to change the subject, shifting the point of comparison from agricultural failures to Soviet success in building a nuclear arsenal, he was ultimately unable to improve Soviet agricultural production or food availability.[59]

By the fall of 1963, Soviet officials were forced to seek food on the global market. In September, the Soviet Union contracted to purchase of a large quantity of wheat from Canada.[60] At an October 1 meeting, the National Security Council discussed the possibility of selling American wheat to the Soviet Union and considered how to circumvent challenges to the sale, such as the 1961 Latta amendment, which restricted sales of agricultural commodities to "friendly nations." It was decided that the amendment applied to general trade agreememts, not to a one-time sale that, members hoped, could be portrayed as a failure of communism. Strategically, the council hoped the sales would draw down Soviet monetary reserves and ensure stability in US-Soviet relations during the months it would take for the wheat to be delivered.[61] By October 8, it was public knowledge that Soviet officials had approached the United States to purchase four million tons of American wheat.[62] On October 9, President Kennedy announced that he had approved the sale of $250 million of wheat to the Soviet Union and another $60 million in sales to the Soviet-bloc countries Czechoslovakia, Bulgaria, and Hungary.[63]

The Soviet grain purchases—from the United States as well as many Western countries—were massive, but they did little to quell the country's internal unrest. Assessing the crisis, Freeman estimated that the Soviet Union's grain production was down fifteen million tons from recent years. He predicted that the sales to the Soviet Union and other communist nations might mean that the United States would export 1 billion bushels of wheat in 1963.[64] After some debate in Congress over requirements to ship a certain percentage of grain on US-flagged vessels, the terms of the deal were approved. On January 21, the first shipment of wheat left northeastern North Dakota, loaded into 103 boxcars bound for Norfolk, Virginia.[65] Eventually, the Soviet Union would purchase approximately

$140 million in US grain, not only wheat but also fifty thousand metric tons of rice worth $78.5 million. This was in addition to more than $500 million of wheat the Soviet government purchased from Canada, Australia, Argentina, and Western Europe. Grain sellers expected that future purchases would be necessary given Soviet agricultural conditions.[66] Yet the purchased food did little to improve the agricultural situation in the Soviet Union. This, together with his perceived weakness during the Cuban missile crisis, eventually led to Khrushchev's downfall and replacement by Leonid Brezhnev as first secretary and Alexei Kosygin as the Soviet premier.[67]

The sales to the USSR presaged new foreign policy applications for food aid. Such applications were widely deployed by the Johnson administration, based on what became known as its "short-tether policy," that is, making very short-term promises of foreign aid that could be used as a bargaining chip in US international negotiations in other areas affecting the national interests. The short-tether policy was initially designed to encourage recipient nations, such as India and Vietnam, to invest in boosting their own agricultural production, but it was also consciously used as an instrument designed to broaden international support for America's foreign policies. Johnson's presidency was characterized by the deepening of America's involvement in Vietnam and efforts to prevent Communist expansion abroad; his foreign policy was sustained by the notion that the United States should not simply give handouts to its allies but should take active steps to improve their political stability and economic development. At home, Johnson advanced his sweeping program to improve the health and welfare of America's poorest people.[68] Johnson saw the Great Society and his foreign policy goals as linked.[69]

In part, Johnson's concern about hunger and poverty stemmed from his personal experiences teaching poor children in Texas. He would later recall that he was motivated to confront hunger because, "I knew what hunger meant. I had seen its effects early in life—on the faces of children, pupils who came to my school day after day without food in their stomachs."[70] Like Kennedy, Johnson did not see surpluses as a problem to be avoided, but as abundance that gave the United States a tool that could be used to promote security and freedom. In his 1964 statement on farm policy, Johnson announced his intention to expand the Food for Peace program, stating, "The Food for Peace program is good international policy and it is good economic policy. People who are hungry are weak allies of freedom."[71] Johnson continued to emphasize the humanitarian and foreign policy aspects of food assistance.[72]

The 1966 passage of Food for Peace Act (PL-98-808) provided Johnson with a major new tool for using food to advance freedom. The act was the most significant revision to American food-aid policy since the passage of the original Agricultural Trade Development and Assistance Act of 1954. In March 1966, Johnson appealed to Congress to join him in helping "the United States lead the world in a war against hunger" by passing a new statue that provided $3.3 billion in funding per year for five years.[73] Johnson sought to revise PL-480 to make self-help a core objective of food-aid programs, remove the requirement to use only surplus foods for foreign aid, and expand the size and scale of food-aid shipments. Besides expanding the aid programs, Johnson's goal was to make foreign policy goals, not the disposal of surpluses, the primary motivator of American food-aid practices. In part, this shift was motivated by the fact that surpluses were declining. The proposals also emphasized the importance of self-help, an idea that was a cornerstone of Johnson's foreign assistance efforts. In keeping with his belief in domestic self-help, Johnson was guided by a general principle that countries would have to do their part to address their own food problems.[74]

While Johnson's proposals were not accepted in their entirety, his ideas did heavily shape the final law. Proposals were also introduced by both the House and the Senate. The House Agriculture Committee integrated the various proposals into a single bill (H.R. 14-929), which, after two rounds of consideration by a conference committee, was passed by both houses on October 21, 1966. The most far-reaching change was the elimination of the requirement only surpluses could be used to provide food aid. Johnson cited the declining need to reduce surpluses when he signed the Food for Peace Act on November 12: "We have rationalized our domestic agriculture to eliminate unneeded surpluses. During the past few months, we have acted to expand wheat and feed grain production. Half of our 60 million acre cropland reserve will be returned to production."[75] By the late 1960s, administration officials had taken steps to return fallowed land to cropland.[76]

The Food for Peace Act of 1966, though it provided far less funding than Johnson had hoped for, did shift the focus of American policy to expanding international trade, combating hunger and malnutrition, and promoting the foreign policy of the United States. The new law did place some new limits on food aid, such restricting the Food for Peace shipments to commodities that the recipient countries could not grow themselves or obtain with their own resources. In his statement at the signing ceremony, Johnson had also emphasized self-help, declaring, "grants will be made only where the country receiving the grant demonstrates its own willingness to help win its own war on hunger."[77] Countries were required to show progress in achieving production self-sufficiency. The law also directed the president to transition out of the policy of allowing payment in foreign currencies toward payment in US dollars or other convertible currencies, and set a target date for completion of 1971. PL-98-808 also took away the secretary of agriculture's authority to designate recipient countries and reorganize aid programs. Title I of PL-98-808 allowed for sales in both foreign currencies and dollars. Revisions to Title II allowed for a foreign donation program that had not been authorized by the previous Titles II and III. A new Title III provided authorization for transactions made by bartering while Title IV laid out general provisions and definitions of the law and gave the secretary of agriculture the authority to decide the "agriculture commodities and quantities thereof available for disposition."[78] Instead of the five-year extension Johnson had asked for, PL 98-808 instead extended the 1954 act through the end of 1968, and provided only $2.5 billion per year for two years.[79]

Johnson's clearest use of American food power came in his efforts to keep India close. In the mid-1960s, India experienced a reduction of food production, due to lower than expected monsoon rainfall, and appealed to the United States for food assistance. In the meantime, war between India and Pakistan broke out in 1965 and, in response, Johnson developed a new strategy of using food as a leverage to influence short- and long-term outcomes on the ground. Rather than agree to the longer-term, multiyear contracts allowed under PL-480, Johnson instructed Freeman to enter into only short-term month-to-month contracts; this came to be known as the short-tether policy[80] As historian Kristen Ahlberg writes, "a combination of altruism and self-interest, the short tether scheme linked U.S. food shipments to the willingness of the Indian Government to implement and perfect American-style economic and agricultural reforms."[81] Subsequently, the short-tether policy was also used with Egypt, Ghana, Columbia, and Brazil, among other countries.[82]

If Johnson and other policymakers used American food aid to catalyze larger changes in the agricultural and economic systems of nations they were supporting, this policy in was in part, a recognition that as surpluses dwindled in America, Johnson, unlike any president since Truman, faced the possibility that sending large amounts of food overseas might affect food prices and availability at home. But Johnson also sought to link American food aid to the technological advancements that were changing the face of agriculture. Boosters felt these developments could not only bring nations into America's postwar food system but could also open up new markets for American seeds, fertilizers, and agricultural machinery.

AMERICAN FOOD POWER AND THE GREEN REVOLUTION

One of the most important developments in the postwar American food system was initially not the result of government action. The "Green Revolution" is the name given to a set of technological and methodological developments that improved agricultural yields in many developing countries. Although these methods would later become a key part of government's strategy for addressing food insecurity, private foundations were the initial drivers of these efforts. Prominent among these was the Rockefeller Foundation. After World War II, a number of trends—mechanization, rural electrification, advances in plant and animal breeding, and developments in synthetic chemical pesticides and fertilizers and medicines—led to rapid improvements in agricultural productivity. Beginning in the early 1940s, scientists at the Rockefeller Foundation began developing new strains of high-yield staple crops, chiefly wheat, rice, and corn (maize), that they hoped would alleviate some of the problems of insecurity and instability in poor nations that lacked sufficient food. By the 1960s and 1970s, a set of technologies and agricultural methods had been developed that resulted in significant increases in crops yields around the world. For example, in the period 1961–63, the combined yield of wheat from ninety-three developing countries was 868 kilograms per hectare (kg/ha), rising in 1969–71 to 1,153 kg/ha and in 1979–81 to 1,637 kg/ha. Corn yields increased from 1,818 kg/ha in 1961–63 to 2,653 kg/ha by 1979–81.[83]

These gains were made possible by the development of crop strains that responded well to the use of chemical fertilizers and irrigation water, were resistant to pests, and were compatible with mechanical harvesting. Especially critical to the success of the Green Revolution was the development of dwarf varieties of wheat and rice, shorter plants with stronger stems that could hold up heavy heads of grain. Along with new varieties of plants, the Green Revolution involved the expanded use of chemical fertilizers and pesticides; irrigation made possible by fossil-fuel-powered pumps that allowed access to much deeper supplies of groundwater; and new machinery that made preparing fields, planting, maintaining, and harvesting crops easier and faster. Taking advantage of these inputs, from new seeds to fertilizers, required capital and knowledge. The largest beneficiaries tended to be large, highly capitalized farmers who could afford those costs and had the expertise to put them to good use.[84]

The hope behind the Green Revolution was not simply to improve food availability or to boost the largest, most successful farmers, but rather to raise the productivity and improve the livelihoods of small peasant farmers. As with many agricultural policy efforts in the United States, it would prove easier to improve food production than to solve the complex set of problems related to ensuring farmer's prosperity. The research by Rockefeller Foundation in the 1940s had been guided by the foundation's belief in supporting programs that improved the people's well-being.[85] Other nations were doing similar research in the 1940s, primarily in the industrialized economies of America, Western Europe, and Japan. Nonindustrialized nations had little capacity to undertake such experimentation. Industrialization brought mechanization, but it also reduced the number of workers needed to produce food and created incentives for rapidly industrializing nations to look for ways to improve food production in order to keep growing urban populations well fed with reasonably priced food.[86]

Rockefeller scientists drew on previous research that had left an impressive legacy of achievements. Agricultural research in Japan, for instance, began in the 1880s, and by 1925, after the repeated crossbreeding of Japanese and American wheat, had produced Norin 10, the first semidwarf variety of wheat. Efforts in the United States focused on developing higher-yield varieties of corn with greater resistance to disease. In the early 1920s, Henry Cantwell Wallace, editor of *Wallaces Farmer* and secretary of agriculture for presidents Harding and Coolidge, supported research into hybrid corn by the Bureau of Plant Investigations. His son, Henry A. Wallace, who succeeded his father as editor of *Wallaces Farmer* and would serve as secretary of agriculture, secretary of commerce, and vice president to Franklin D. Roosevelt, formed the first company to sell hybrid seed, the High-Bred Corn Company, in 1925. The corn promised to increase yields by 10 percent to 15 percent. Farmers were initially slow to adopt a new and expensive seed they had to buy every year (instead of just holding over some of their crop to use for planting the next year), but by 1949, more than three-quarters of farmers in the corn belt were using hybrid seeds.[87]

By 1941, when the Rockefeller Foundation began its research efforts to improve staple crops in Mexico, it had already had some success with corn. In the Mexico program, the foundation also tried a new approach; instead of hiring local staff as it had done in the 1930s in China, it began bringing in American experts to teach and oversee the agricultural experiments.[88]

Interest among foundation officials in a program in Mexico dated to the early 1930s when John A. Ferrell, the foundation's regional director for public health, began discussions with Josephus Daniels, the US ambassador to Mexico, but tensions between the United States and Mexico prevented the talks from moving ahead. In 1940, when vice-president-elect Wallace attended the inauguration of new Mexican president, Manuel Avila Camacho, he had a chance to talk with Daniels about the opportunity to improve the lives of poor rural Mexicans. Upon his return to the United States, Wallace met with foundation officials, including Ferrell and foundation president Raymond B. Fosdick, to encourage them to think about programs that could, for example, improve the productivity of dietary staples like corn and beans. The meeting came at an opportune time for the foundation since many of its operations in Europe and China had been disrupted by the onset of the Second World War.[89]

After an extensive survey mission to Mexico in 1941, the foundation worked with the Mexican government to establish an operational research program, the Mexican Agricultural Program (MAP), in 1943. Unlike previous foundation programs in foreign countries that disbursed grants to scientists who would then conduct research, the Mexico program involved employing American experts to directly undertake research. The initial scientific staff consisted of J. George Harrar as director, as well as corn breeders Edwin J. Wellhausen and Lewis A. Roberts, soil scientist William E. Colwell, and plant pathologist Norman E. Borlaug. The foundation's involvement in Mexico came at a time when American relations with Mexico were improving, and the United States had an interest in ensuring that the new Mexican administration did not turn too far toward fascism or socialism. The foundation's efforts thus advanced its own goals, but also served American foreign policy interests.[90]

The foundation's Mexico operations, and the methods and technologies developed by foundation scientists, became the cornerstone of a new approach to using food power. It demonstrated that America could advance national interests and protect national security not only by deploying American food overseas, but also by working to boost the agricultural productivity of friendly foreign nations. In 1946, Chester C. Davis, chairman of the Truman's President's Famine Emergency Committee, endorsed this approach, arguing that a program of intelligently directed and integrated international cooperation could improve world food production by providing capital, modern tools, and machines, and transferring

American "farming know-how" to other countries.[91] Davis maintained that the problems in world food production stemmed not from lack of natural resources but from poor farming methods, primitive transportation systems, and inefficient crop-production systems, and he stressed that no matter how much American food production could increase, it would not be sufficient to feed the entire world. Truman endorsed Davis's ideas in his 1949 inaugural address. Outlining his Point Four Program, Truman emphasized that providing technical assistance to help nations develop was a critical addition to the provision food, fuel, and materials under the Marshall Plan.[92] During the 1950s, technical assistance remained a critical component of American modernization efforts to help catalyze economic development in countries where the United States sought to contain Soviet power.[93]

By the late 1960s, the Rockefeller Foundation's work was having considerable impact not just in Mexico but around the world. High-yield varieties of wheat developed at the foundation-operated International Maize and Wheat Improvement Center of Mexico increased Mexican yields by almost a factor of four, from eleven to forty bushels per acre. Norman Borlaug led a a team of scientists from seventeen nations who were involved in breeding the wheat varieties. In 1970, he was awarded the Nobel Peace Prize "for his great contribution toward creating a new world situation with regard to nutrition."[94] High-yield wheat varieties boosted production in other nations, including Pakistan, which planted 600,000 acres of high-yield wheat in 1967 and 3.5 million acres in 1968, and Turkey, where total wheat production in 1968 was one-third higher than in 1965, thanks to the new seeds. After its success with wheat, the Rockefeller Foundation turned to rice, partnering with the Ford Foundation to establish the International Rice Research Institute (IRRI) in the Philippines to develop high-yield varieties of this important staple crop. In the 1960s, rice was eaten by more people in the world than any other grain, making up most of the diet for over 90 percent of the 1.5 billion inhabitants of Asia. By the late 1960s, IRRI scientists had sucessfully crossed a tall variety of rice from the Philippines with a short variety from Taiwan to produce IR-8, a stiff, short variety that was especially durable. IR-8 offered the additional advantage of maturing quickly and raised the possibility that farmers could plant and harvest two or three plantings per year, each with yields four to six times greater than to the yields of traditional varieties.[95]

But the impact of the Green Revolution went beyond simply developing new varieties of crops. It was, in the words of historian John R. McNeill, "a technical and managerial package exported from the First World to the Third."[96] In a March 1968 speech to the Society for International Development, William Gaud, the administrator of the Agency for International Development, assessed the impact of the new model of agriculture and commented, "Record yields, harvests of unprecedented size and crops now in the ground demonstrate that throughout much the developing world—and particularly in Asia—we are on the verge of an agricultural revolution."[97] Gaud went on to give a name to these efforts, "It is not a violent Red Revolution like that of the Soviets, nor is it a White Revolution like that of the Shah of Iran. I call it the Green Revolution."[98] Developing high-yield seed varieties was critical to the alternative vision of the world offered by the Green Revolution, but the seeds would not grow themselves. Support from governments was needed. Through AID, the United States provided more than $260 million in loans to such countries as Pakistan, India, Brazil, Chile, Morocco, Indonesia, and Laos to enable them to buy the fertilizer needed to produce the higher yields. The exporting of what McNeill identifies as a "a technical and managerial package" however, did not simply happen, and support from the US government was critical to the expanded use of the Green Revolution's technologies and methods in countries around the world.[99]

In addition to boosting yields, exporting technologies and social practices based on the American model of agriculture that depended on capital intensive inputs such as machinery and synthetic checmical fertilizers were controversial. Critics objected to the replacement of existing systems of agriculture with a new model that increased environmental impact. Green Revolution technologies lowered genetic diversity; required the use of fertilizers and other products derived from petrochemicals; increased soil salinization because of the more intensive irrigation methods; increased likelihood of pest outbreaks from monocropping; reduced populations of beneficial insects, such as spiders and dragonflies, killed off by broad-spectrum pesticides. There were also criticisms of the social effects of the Green Revolution, which deepened inequality by supporting larger farmers and, as a result, displacing smaller agricultural producers. Easing out smaller, now-marginal producers exacerbated the problems of rural poverty and hunger even as technologies were improving overall agricultural productivity worldwide. These effects in the developing world mirrored those in the United States, where benefits of these advancements tended to accrue to larger, better-capitalized farmers, who could invest in new seeds, inputs and machines.[100]

Still, the increased food production did, for a time, keep concerns about hunger and overpopulation at bay. But, assessing the results of the Green Revolution in 1970, Borlaug cautioned, "All we've really done is buy time, maybe 20 or 30 years. . . . We have instilled hope where there was despair. But every time the clock ticks there are 2.2 more new mouths to feed. That ticking keeps eroding away what progress we've been able to make."[101] In addition to the concern that productivity gains would not keep up with human population increases, voiced by Robert F. Kennedy, and others benefits of new technologies were not shared equally. Hunger and poverty persisted amid abundance and prosperity, even in the United States. That producing more food had not solved all problems is something that would become clearer during the world food crisis in the 1970s.[102]

The persistence of large agricultural surpluses in the United States into the 1960s had presented Presidents Kennedy and Johnson with both a problem and an opportunity. Over the course of the decade, both administrations developed a broader policy toward America's agricultural abundance that sought to address not just the problem of how to increase rural prosperity and lower food costs for consumers, but also how to improve the nutrition, health, and welfare of the most needy people in America and around the world. The motivation behind assistance programs, however, was not purely altruistic. Both Kennedy and Johnson linked improvements in food availability and nutrition to their visions of a modern and prosperous America. Kennedy's New Frontier and Johnson's Great Society, both sought to realize the dream of full economic security envisioned by President Franklin D. Roosevelt's New Deal. Abroad, the Kennedy and Johnson administrations developed a new, offensive food-power doctrine, deploying it in aggressive efforts to counter communism, and using food strategically to make key nations such as India dependent on American food aid and technical assistance. The embrace of the Green Revolution by American leaders and policymakers demonstrates that in addition to food, hunger, poverty, and communism could be tackled with American know-how, its advanced technological and managerial techniques. It also demonstrated the diffuse mechanisms available for use of American food power, including not only official government programs such as food aid, but also through the activities of private foundations.

In the wake of key flashpoints such as the Berlin Crisis and the Cuban Missile Crisis, which had highlighted the dangers and unsurvivability of nuclear war, food power provided Kennedy and Johnson with a flexible tool that could be used to accomplish American foreign policy objectives. Food power was all the more useful as it could be deployed under the guise of humanitarian assistance and economic development instead of more aggressive foreign policy strategies such as covert operations or military action. Food power was a form of soft power that could be used to encourage, rather than forcibly coerce, the actions of competitors, such as the Soviet Union, and nonaligned nations such as India.[103]

The problem with the Kennedy's and Johnson's stepped-up domestic and overseas food-assistance programs was that they were dependent on maintaining massive agricultural surpluses. Those surpluses would be maintained throughout the 1960s, though they were slowly being reduced. By the early 1970s, however, the food supplies of poor and dependent populations were, more than ever, tied into the expanding American food system and to international markets that were growing based on the intervention of American funding and know-how.

The World Food Crisis and the End of the Postwar Food System

In November 1974, global leaders gathered in Rome for the World Food Conference, a meeting held as the world was experiencing the first large-scale food crisis since the end of World War II. Beginning in 1972, reduced harvests, increased demand by a growing world population, and growing consumer affluence along with domestic agricultural policies that had finally succeeded in taming America's large surpluses had all converged to set the stage for the crisis. Global grain reserves of had fallen from a high of ninety-five days' worth in 1961 to just twenty-six days in 1974, the lowest level in more than two decades. *Time* reported in November 1974 that nearly a half billion people suffered from some form of hunger; ten thousand people were dying each week in Africa, Asia, and Latin America; and in India alone, thirty million people were facing starvation.[1]

Years of record harvests throughout the 1950s and 1960s in the United States and other parts of the world had created a sense that gains in agricultural productivity had eradicated the perpetual human plague of famine. American policymakers no longer faced the problem of how to boost agricultural productivity; instead they struggled with how to manage the disruptive effects and potential benefits of agricultural abundance. By the early 1970s, the Green Revolution had created the hope that developing countries would soon experience agricultural revolutions of their own and become self-sufficient in food production, and perhaps even food exporters in their own right. How to produce enough food to feed all the world's people seemed to many policymakers, even amid growing concerns in the late 1960s about global population increases, to be a problem solved. Then a rapid series of political, economic, environmental, and demographic shifts created both short-term and long-term problems on both the supply and demand sides of world food supplies to create a major global food crisis.

American economic and agricultural policy decisions were one set of factors contributing to the 1970s food crisis. As we have seen in previous chapters, since the end of World War II, American farmers had been producing more food and food precursors, such as feed grains. Maintaining large stocks of surplus grain sparked concerns at home about overproduction and the costs of crop storage, and a great deal of attention was focused during the 1960s and 1970s on reducing or eliminating surpluses. Programs such as diversion of acreage into conservation reserves and selling or providing food aid to needy people overseas did reduce surpluses, and increased global demand furthered the job, greatly reducing total American surpluses by the early 1970s. Then, between 1970 and 1972, in order to fully eliminate the cost of surplus storage, the United States adopted policies that reduced production from 15 percent to 10 percent of global grain production. Policymakers also continued to reduce stocks of stored grain through disbursement strategies such as food stamps and relief programs at home and Food for Peace efforts abroad. Policymakers did not seem to realize that these surpluses and grain stocks were part of what was stabilizing global grain prices and providing critical sources of cheap grain in many parts of the world. At the same time, American policy under the Nixon administration shifted the majority of food aid toward foreign policy goals, especially the war in Vietnam, rather than the use of American food for humanitarian relief needs, which further increased food needs in many countries.[2] The elimination of large surpluses that could be used for food assistance would bring volatility into global food markets and, eventually, spell the end of the postwar food system.[3]

A rapid reduction in grain reserves in the early 1970s, and the decision, as policymakers struggled with the resulting spikes in grain prices, not to establish global grain reserves in response, brought to an end a period of relative stability in global wheat prices. After World War II, wheat had emerged as a cheap, storable, and transportable source of nutrients world-wide. Because of the large amounts of wheat, along with other crops, in storage during the 1950s and 1960s any fluctuations in production caused by short-term policies or bad weather had resulted in only minor fluc-tuations in price. For example, in eleven of the twelve crop years between 1960 and 1971, wheat prices stayed within a relatively stable band of $59 to $65 per ton. Prices of corn and other surplus grains followed a simi-lar pattern. The depletion of grain reserves removed this buffer between events and prices. Of major grain-importing countries, only India took steps to increase stocks in response to policy shifts in America and other grain-producing nations.

As a result, in addition to agricultural polices designed to reduce pro-duction and prevent the accumulation of surpluses, a series of shocks, or severe, unexpected events, in the early 1970s, contributed to a food crisis between 1972 and 1974. The causes of this world food crisis were more complex than simply bad harvests; they fall into three broad cat-egories: American agricultural and economic policies that eliminated domestic grain surpluses, a set of both supply side and demand side shocks affecting food supplies, and a series of longer-term pressures on world food supplies. The result was not just price spikes that discomfited the American middle class and caused hunger and famine throughout the world—it was the end of the postwar food system. This ushered in a period that we are still living in today in which a complex world food network has brought seemingly continual concerns about food security, safety and sustainability.[4]

This chapter traces the transformation of the postwar food system into an unwieldy network in which no single actor played a stabilizing role. The first in the chain of events that eventually led to the world food crisis of the early 1970s was the disinvestment in American grain reserves, beginning with the authorization of massive grain sales to the Soviets in 1972. The resulting spike in domestic grain prices was a harbinger of more shocks to come, as a series of unrelated local and global trends, from reductions in Peruvian fishmeal to an increasingly affluent and growing global population, converged to further reduce global food supplies. Two years into the crisis, policymakers had to confront the possibility that the conditions were not temporary, but a new permanent reality. Discussions of a renewed investment in global food reserves and other global initiatives to stabilize food supplies followed, but what these discussions revealed most clearly was that what replaced the postwar food system was no system at all, but a loose and ever-shifting global network of producers, manufacturers, marketers, and consumers. This network was, and remains, difficult to stabilize in the face of famine, food-safety scares, environmental concerns, and the many other challenges that confront the global food supply.

THE GREAT GRAIN ROBBERY

The first of the unexpected events that led to the destruction of the postwar food system was the 1971 decision by President Nixon to regularize exports from the United States to communist countries. In the 1960s, one-time grain sales to the USSR had required clearance from the Department of Commerce and that a percentage of all the grain sold had to be carried to its destination by American-flagged vessels. The shipping provision in particular proved to be a sticking point because it increased the transportation costs and also created shipping bottlenecks when US-flagged vessels were not available. In the early 1970s, American policymakers again considered the potential benefits of opening up regular trade channels with communist countries. On July 8, 1972, the United States announced an agreement to sell grain to the Soviet Union at subsidized prices by providing up to $750 million of credit to the Soviet government over a three-year period. American farmers and grain dealers would profit from these sales, and the Nixon administration also hoped the agreement would assist in its efforts to establish a Soviet-American trade maritime accord;

it also wanted to settle the issue of outstanding payments for World War II Lend Lease aid.[5] The deal called for the Soviet Union to purchase 433 million bushels of American wheat for about $700 million dollars. It also agreed to purchase 246 million bushels of corn and 37 million bushels of soybeans, which brought the total sale to $1.1 billion, the largest sale of food in American history.[6] A condition of the deal was that the United States ship the grain before the 1973 planting season. The 433 bushels of wheat purchased by the Soviet Union was a considerable amount of global food supplies and represented one-third of American wheat production in an average year. The sale used up half of the stocks of wheat stored by grain dealers in the United States. This meant that to replenish its stores, America needed at least an average wheat crop in 1973. Global grain stocks were further depleted when the Soviet Union also purchased large amounts of wheat from Canada.[7]

The decision to sell grain to the Soviet Union was influenced by the government's desire to further reduce stored surplus crops and market projections that showed the United States had sufficient grain to meet normal purchase demands, as well as by larger geopolitical issues. Given the continued poor performance of Soviet agriculture, American policymakers felt that food could perhaps be a bargaining chip, used to influence Soviet policy in other areas of vital concern, especially with regard to the war in Vietnam. In April 1972, while he was in Moscow meeting with Soviet officials to secretly negotiate grain sales, Earl Butz, Nixon's secretary of agriculture, received a cable from the US national security adviser, Henry Kissinger, conveying Nixon's instructions to delay the negotiations so that they would not disrupt the Moscow Summit scheduled for the following month.[8] This cable followed another communication to Butz, from presidential aid Peter Flanigan, reinforcing the president's wish to use grain sales to pressure the Soviet Union to support positions favorable to the United States in Vietnam. For its part, the Soviet Union was taking a hard line on the terms of the deal. The negotitions were therefore not resolved in April and were instead delayed until a May visit to Washington by Russian Minister of Foreign Trade Nikolai Patolichev.[9] In July, when an agreement was finally reached, Kissinger spoke with the

Soviet ambassador to the United States, Anatoly Dobrynin, to coordinate the timing of the announcement of the deal.[10]

It had been clear by late summer that Soviet agriculture had suffered significant setbacks. Severe droughts in 1972 had affected many parts of the Soviet Union, especially the grain-growing areas in Kazakhstan and Siberia. Not just wheat but also potatoes, a staple of the Russian diet, were affected. Winter had not yet arrived, but there were already reports that Russians were hoarding food and fears that the situation could worsen.[11] In addition to its wheat and soybean purchases from the United States, the Soviet Union purchased wheat and barley from Canada and France and made requests to purchase additional wheat from West Germany and Romania.[12] American commentators at the time saw in the Soviet food vulnerability a potential to use wield American food power. For example, the *Evening Standard*, in Uniontown, Pennsylvania, speculated that the grain sale was perhaps one reason the Soviets had not protested the mining of Haiphong harbor, North Vietnam's major port, earlier in the year. Communism had been unable to solve the Soviet agricultural problems, the *Standard* wrote, going on to lament that "the United States missed a chance to extract major concessions from the Kremlin, such as putting more pressure on North Vietnam to make peace."[13] In December 1972, amid the second round of strategic arms limitation talks in Geneva, the *Standard-Speaker* in Hazelton, Pennsylvania, suggested that "if the Soviet Harvest continues to deteriorate and dependence grows on the United States grain supplies, the need can drive the Soviet's closer to an agreement."[14] The Soviet Union seemed unaware that its need for continued grain imports might be seen as a vulnerability to be exploited by the United States.

But if it seemed in 1972 that the United States had scored a great victory for free-nation agricultural systems over communist-controlled systems, by 1973 it was becoming clear that the Soviets had gotten the better part of the deal. The Soviets had driven hard bargains and received very favorable prices and credit terms on the loans it had taken from the United States to finance the sales. They had also secured major concessions in how the grain would be transported; the United States had even been willing to grant a waiver that allowed Soviet ships to not only carry the grain but also to stop in Cuba.[15] This represented a significant exception to US policy toward Cuba, but American officials were so eager to sign a deal that they decided to worry later about details and precedent.[16] Kissinger and other key officials quietly reached out to labor unions to try and avoid protests related to the shipping of goods financed by the government on non-US-flagged vessels. Officials also developed a strategy that would obscure the financing structure with the hope that at some point in the future Congress would enact legislation to address the issue of financing the deal. However, secretary of commerce Peter Peterson advised Kissinger that the administration should not "parade this through Congress now," lest it run into the problems and questions that had had plagued Kennedy's grain sale in 1963.[17] The administration was also worried that the sale would become a political issue in the 1972 presidential election. White House officials tried to prevent Democratic nominee George McGovern from scuttling the deal or using it to gain support in the election. In September 1972, for example, Charles Colson sent presidential assistant Pat Buchanan a memo with talking points for Butz to use to paint McGovern as desperate to deflect attention from agricultural failures by previous Democratic administrations by trying to scuttle a grain deal that was good for farmers, labor unions, and the country.[18]

The administration's worries about the political and economic impacts of the grain sale turned out to have been justified, as food prices had increased considerably by the fall. In July 1972, the export price for wheat was $1.68 per bushel; by August 1972, it had risen to $2.40 per bushel, and it would keep increasing, up to $4.45 per bushel by August of 1973. The stability of wheat prices over the preceding decades had led to the belief among policymakers and economists that the current high prices were not sustainable, and the spike was seen as a temporary reaction. This led the United States to keep the subsidized export price for wheat at $1.63 per bushel through September 1972. As a result, the cost of domestic farm subsidies in the United States more than tripled, from the $67 million projected for 1973 to $300 million. The announcement of the Soviet grain sale also caused a rise in the domestic prices of wheat, corn, sorghum, soybeans, and livestock. The domestic price of wheat almost tripled between August 1972 and August 1973, while price of corn and soybeans more than doubled. Increases in the cost of feed grains were passed on to consumers in the form of higher prices for meat, such as a 150 percent increase in the price of chickens by August 1973.[19]

Almost immediately, the popular press linked the price increases to the subsidized grain sale. In October 1972, the *Evening Standard* wrote, "Some people are beginning to call the great grain deal between the United States and the U.S.S.R. the Great Grain Robbery."[20] In August 1973, *Time* declared, "Consumers have a particularly good reason for anger: the deal contributed to a grain shortage in the U.S., driving up prices for bread, meat, poultry, and dairy products."[21] Beyond the effect on American consumers, the deal had created tension between the Nixon administration and farmers, many of whom had sold their wheat for $1.35 a bushel just weeks before the deal was announced and prices had jumped more than thirty cents a bushel. The deal also impacted shipping in the United States as the railroads, truckers, and other transportation sources had to scramble to transport the grain within the deal's short time frame. This disrupted the shipping of other goods into 1973 and resulted in shortages of key materials for manufacturing and businesses across the United States. But if the link between the Soviet sale and rising prices was clear by 1973, in the late summer and fall of 1972 policymakers and economists were still struggling to understand the situation.[22]

In the summer of 1972, there had been few indicators of any shortages that would lead to price rises, certainly not the 140 percent increase in the export price of wheat, or the 165 percent for corn and 210 percent for soybeans that had occurred by the following summer. The domestic price increases on bread and flour-based products and a more than 40 percent annual increase in the US consumer price index for meat, poultry, and fish were equally unprecedented and unexpected. Prices had been stable, despite previous large-scale sales, albeit none were quite as large as the 1972 sale. A review by General Accounting Office (GAO) in 1973 found little evidence that would have led anyone at the time to think that the 1972 sale would be any different. Nevertheless, the GAO review did find that the

Agriculture Department had exhibited "weakness in managing the sale" for allowing $4.3 billion in subsidy costs to accumulate between the onset of the sale in July and the suspension of government subsidies to the export price in September.[23] Part of the problem, the GAO review concluded, lay in the structure of private grain sales. Typically, the USDA committed to a subsidy level, and then private grain dealers entered into agreements with buyers. Only after the sale had been concluded did exporters have to tell USDA how much it cost; thus even in September, when USDA set the subsidy rates for export sales to zero amid concern about mounting costs, it was still unaware of the magnitude of deals made since the bargain had been struck. While better management might have reduced the costs to the American government, the speed and scale of the total sale meant that by the time price increases began, grain had already begun to be shipped. Only after that did critical factors that contributed to price increases come to light.[24]

By the fall of 1973, administration officials had soured on the deal amid increasing public and congressional outcry. Price rises continued, with consumers facing noticeable upticks in their supermarket bills. In August 1973, three nationwide baking companies announced price increases of one to four cents for a loaf of bread, which was selling at the time for 46 or 47 cents a loaf in New York City, already a 4 percent to 5 percent rise over the previous year's price.[25] In fact, a loaf of bread cost more in the United States than in Russia, a situation that led treasury secretary George Shultz to admit that the United States had been "burned" on the grain deal with the Soviet Union. He vowed that such an event would not happen again.[26] In 1972, the *New York Times* had hailed the deal as an event of great significance that demonstrated, "The United States and the Soviet Union—like the United States and the Chinese People's Republic—are giving public demonstration of their willingness to have businesslike relations and to reach mutually beneficial agreements."[27] Yet a year later, the *Times* characterized the sale as a "little Watergate," complete with a Senate investigation into what administration officials knew and when they knew it. Senators were especially determined to find out why $300 million of federal subsidies were paid to support an artificially low export price for wheat and how a small team of Soviet grain buyers could "move into a New York hotel suite and buy up 11 million tons of wheat—a quarter of the United States crop—from half a dozen grain companies without anyone, including officials from the Department of Agriculture, knowing what they were up to or worrying about the prospective effects on the costs of the nation's food."[28] In congressional hearings, Senator Henry M. "Scoop" Jackson, a Democrat from Washington State, called the grain sale "a monumental blunder born in Government secrecy and bureaucratic negligence."[29] The GAO and the FBI investigated allegations of corruption and conflicts of interest by administration officials who had overseen the deal while maneuvering for jobs with major grain-selling firms; investigators found no evidence of corruption, but plenty of evidence of bungling and mismanagement, with taxpayers ultimately having to cover the costs of the deal.[30]

Things went from bad to worse in September 1973, when it was reported that, having exhausted its wheat surpluses through a combination of the Nixon administration's efforts to reduce production and the Soviet sale, the United States was unable to meet a request from India for grain to help alleviate a food shortage. India instead turned to the Soviet Union, which provided more than four million tons of grain—including more than two million tons purchased from the United States the year before—in order to promote Moscow's "aspirations to develop friendly Soviet-India relations."[31] For the first time since the end of World War II, American food power was exhausted; the nation was unable to send food to an ally in need. The failure was especially critical given the long-standing American efforts to woo India away from Soviet influence. It was worse, of course, that India not only received food from the Soviet Union, but that it was food bought from the United States using loans provided by the federal government that cost the country hundreds of millions of dollars in export subsidies. In a misguided effort to solve the farm problem at home, the Nixon administration had ended up heavily subsidizing the Soviet Union's successful deployment of food power to further its own interests. Had the already embattled Nixon not chosen to resign in August 1974, it is likely that the controversy would have continued to grow in significance. Butz responded by developing a new reporting system for crop sales so that the USDA received better, faster information. Perhaps the most significant policy outcome of the sale was the decision by Butz, following the advice of the President's Cost of Living Council, to end all conservation diversion programs and put sixty million acres of fallowed cropland into production in 1974. He encouraged full production by exhorting farmers to "plow fencerow to fencerow" so that the United States' food arsenal would never again be empty, and it would be able to once again yield "agripower" to enhance American national security.[32] The need to increase production was emphasized by the announcement in the fall of 1973 that Canada had entered into an agreement to sell up to 224 million bushels of wheat to China, a sale worth more than $1 billion, in a move that was expected to boost prices beyond the record level of $5.60 per bushel.[33] American policymakers hoped boosting production would lead in coming years to reductions in shortages and high prices. In the short term though, people in America and nations around the world faced record high food prices.[34]

SHOCKS TO THE FOOD SYSTEM

The grain sale to the Soviet Union was not the only cause of disruption to the postwar food system. The sudden entry of so many new consumers into the world's food markets in the early 1970s represented a major demand-side shock to world food systems, as consumers in Russia, China, and other communist nations began competing with consumers in the United States, Europe, Africa, Asia, and Latin America. This converged with supply-side shocks to have an amplified effect on the global supply of food. For example, a dramatic reduction in the production of fishmeal from Peru, an important source of protein for animal feed, contributed to rising feed and livestock prices around the world. So, too, did the decision by many American hog farmers to cease hog production following heavy losses in 1971 and the efforts by beef producers to expand their herds by adding heifers—a move that would boost long-term beef supply, but in the short run restricted it. Individually, each of these shifts might have been manageable, but some were already intertwined with the grain crisis, while others simply piled on to already rising prices. The total effect was shock after shock to the food system.[35]

Global food production was also heavily impacted by a series of extreme weather events, including harsh winters, droughts, and tropical cyclones, that impacted production in Argentina, Australia, India, and Peru. Expectations for demand in 1972 suggested a need to increase food production by twenty-five million tons. Instead, world food production of wheat, rice, and coarse grains such as corn, rye, and barley fell by thirty-two million tons, producing a sudden, fifty-seven-million-ton gap in global food supplies.[36] Dramatic reductions in the production of wheat, rice, corn, and peanuts in many parts of the world had increased demand for American wheat, soybeans, corn, and other feed grains. This increased demand, based on concerns about the food supply in many parts of the world, converged with the increased demand from new global market consumers to result in a massive increase in demand for more food from the United States at precisely the moment when the country had taken steps to limit overproduction and reduce surpluses. What might have been an opportunity to increase export sales instead resulted in concern about the food insufficiencies, a concern that was only heightened by smaller-than-expected harvests in 1972 due to bad weather in the United States. Even the convergence of so many output shocks in a short period of time however, does not explain the dramatic rise in world food prices that occurred in the early 1970s. A similar series of events in the 1960s for instance, did not produce noticeable impacts on world food prices. Important contributing factors to the crisis of the 1970s came from longer-term factors including population growth and changing food consumption patterns based on increasing affluence.[37]

The tension between food supply and population growth has a long history; the most common starting point for modern concerns are the writings of Thomas Malthus. Malthus worried that differing rates of increase in human population and food supply meant that famines were inevitable. He argued that because "population, when unchecked, goes on doubling itself every twenty-five years, or increases in a geometrical ratio ... the means of subsistence ... could not possibly be made to increase faster than in an arithmetical ratio."[38] Though Malthus's numbers were proved wrong—after all, the incredible surpluses of the mid-century demonstrated that food supplies could sometimes increase at faster rates than population—his writings marked the first of recurring concerns about potential catastrophic outcomes of an imbalance of food supply and human population in the modern era. A new period of concern began in the mid-1960s, triggered by two years of monsoon failures and poor harvests in Asia that required aid shipments and sparked concern about widespread famine. Asia's population was was increasing at the same time. In the early 1970s, the world population was growing at a rate of 75 million people per year, or 200,000 per day. Reduced food supplies thus occurred at a time when population growth was a high-profile, somewhat alarmist, issue.[39]

Population growth rates focused attention on the politically charged question of population control. In 1974, *Time* reported, "The apparent inability, or unwillingness, of most poor countries to restrain their profligacy has embittered many agricultural economists."[40] Perhaps no voice was more prominent in this debate than that of Nobel Peace Prize–winner Norman Borlaug, who said that benefits to food production from high-yield seeds had been meant to give underdeveloped nations room to take steps to curb population growth. Instead, he lamented in 1974, "Our efforts to buy time have been frittered away because political leaders in developing nations have refused to come to grips with the population monster."[41] Characterizing food problems as resulting from the failure of developing countries to curb their behavior would become a common narrative in coming years.[42] Public awareness of population issues was stoked by such works as Paul Ehrlich's book *The Population Bomb* (1968) and Harry Harrison's novel *Make Room! Make Room!* (1969). Harrison's book gained a much wider audience when it was adapted into the 1973 film *Soylent Green* in which the main character, played by Charlton Heston, discovers that in a future of overcrowded and overpopulated cities, the only solution to hunger is to make food out of people.[43] As concerns about overpopulation were rising, questions arose about whether the improved yields from the Green Revolution could be sustained. The problem was even more critical in Africa, especially the North African countires of Egypt, Algeria, and Morroco, where there had been no Green Revolution and a greater percentage of the food supplies came from imported grain. These worries coalesced in the early 1970s.[44]

Demand for food was driven not simply by the growing number of people on the planet, but also by changing diets as many of those people became more affluent. Between 1930 and 1970, as much as one-third of the increased demand for grain came from consumers in wealthier countries.[45] As people moved up the income ladder, their diets contained more milk and dairy products and "convenience" packaged and prepared foods, symbols of their changing social status. Dietary changes from increased affluence began having effects in developing countries, where achieving independence from colonial rule brought hopes for improved standards of living. At the same time, strong economic growth in developed countries during the 1950s and 1960s fueled demand for more resource- and feed-intensive products, such as meat and milk. In 1974, *Time* reported, "Affluence, as well as population, eats into the world's food supply. As standards of living in the developing nations rise, their citizens . . . increasingly eat their foods in forms that enormously burden the earth's agriculture."[46]

Dietary changes gave rise to new questions about optimal diets and how to equitably distribute the world's food supply. In the early 1970s, the average person in a developing country consumed about four hundred pounds of grain each year, while the average American consumed two thousand pounds of grain, mostly in the form of grain-fed beef, pork, and chicken. As Harvard nutritionist Jean Mayer noted in 1974, "The same amount of food that is feeding 210 million Americans would feed 1.5 billion Chinese on an average Chinese diet."[47] A preference for diets heavy in meat had become the norm in many industrialized countries, not just America. Unlike in 1963, when the Soviet Union had slaughtered cattle to reduce grain needs, a major driver behind the massive purchase of grain from the United States in 1972 was to avoid having to mass cull animals and also to enable the continuation of Soviet meat production and consumption. Questions about the ethics of eating meat, as well as concerns in the post–*Silent Spring* era about the environmental effects of industrial agriculture and the industrial food system, did spark small-scale efforts by counterculture groups and health-conscious consumers, to advocate eating natural, organic, or vegetarian diets.[48] In the 1960s and 1970s, however, this did little to change the predominant dietary trends.[49]

Even the effects of increased population and consumption do not fully explain the rise in prices in the early 1970s. A further critical set of explanatory factors comes from additional political and economic events: first, the 1971 decision by Nixon to withdraw from the Bretton Woods system and, second, the oil crisis of 1973–74. Spending on the Vietnam war and Johnson's Great Society programs had increased the supply of dollars outside the United States and increased the pressure on foreign governments to revalue their currencies, making foreign goods more expensive for Americans. The United States faced a considerable problem because the foreign holdings of American dollars exceeded the supply of gold held by the United States, which by 1971 had been reduced to half of the 1960 level. The United States was also running a considerable trade deficit and, for the first time in history, was experiencing high unemployment, a recession, and sizable inflation all at the same time. Nixon had intended to announce a new economic policy after Labor Day, but his hand was forced on August 12, when Great Britain demanded that the United States guarantee its holdings of $750 million dollars. Nixon summoned his key economic advisers to Camp David for a secret meeting on economic policy. John Connally, Nixon's secretary of commerce, unveiled the administration's plan and worked to bring all of Nixon's advisers on board.[50]

What became known as the "Nixon shock" occurred on Sunday, August 15, when the president issued Executive Order 11615, freezing all prices, rents, wages, and salaries for ninety days, establishing the Cost of Living Council, and delegating to it all powers conferred on the president by the Economic Stabilization Act of 1970.[51] Wholesale agricultural commodities and raw foods were exempted from the price freeze to make allowances for food prices that varied seasonally. Food was subjected to the price freeze once it was processed, when cucumbers were made into pickles, for example, or packaged into cartons, like milk, "unless you drink it right by the cow," as

Nixon's consumer affairs adviser Virginia Knauer explained.[52] In addition to the executive order freezing wages and prices, Nixon instructed the secretary of the treasury to withdraw the United States from the the Bretton Woods system and end the direct convertibility of the United States dollar to gold.[53] Nixon also announced an across-the-board 10 percent import surcharge to make American products more competitive against the currency fluctuations that were expected in the wake of the announcement. Nixon, advised by Connally, hoped to use the import surcharge to pressure other nations to negotiate favorable exchange rates with the United States. His advisers argued that he must explain the moves to America before the markets opened on Monday, and the president agreed (though he worried that a Sunday evening primetime address would preempt the popular television show *Bonanza* and potentially alienate its viewers).[54] In the address, Nixon explained that his sudden actions were part of an effort to create a new prosperity without war. "Prosperity without war requires action on three fronts: We must create more and better jobs; we must stop the rise in the cost of living; we must protect the dollar from the attacks of international money speculators."[55] Nixon blamed currency speculators and unfair exchange rates for the problems facing the United States and argued that his policies were necessary to stabilize the economy, reduce inflation, and minimize unemployment.[56]

Before the announcement, Nixon had wondered whether headlines would credit him with changing his mind or acting boldly. The press responded in the latter fashion, with the *New York Times* declaring, "We applaud the scope and daring of his effort to bring inflation under control and get the economy off and running."[57] The day after the announcement, the Dow Jones Industrial Average rose almost thirty-three points, the largest single-day rise in history. The new economic policy did allow administration officials to negotiate a favorable revaluation of currency exchange rates, and the 90-day price freeze helped to stabilize inflation, allowing Nixon to win re-election in November 1972. The price controls, however, proved hard to remove and extended well beyond the initial ninety-day term. Inflation also proved harder to tame in the following months. By 1974, when Nixon resigned, it had risen to 11 percent and would continue to rise, to 14 percent by 1980, causing problems for Presidents Ford and

Carter. In the near term, the removal of the United States from the gold-exchange standard—which pegged the value of the US dollar to the price of gold, and pegged all other currencies to the US dollar—meant that the value of the dollar would begin to fluctuate. As a result, the value of the dollar declined, increasing the dollar price of grain by as much as 15 percent. A broader realignment of currency values globally also allowed increased commodity purchases from the United States. As the value of the American dollar sank relative to other currencies, American food and commodity products became an even better value on world markets, something that made purchasing food from the United States even more attractive for foreign consumers, but also drove up the costs of food produced domestically in those nations. An even greater consequence of Nixon's actions was the triggering of a series of destabilizing events in global oil markets.[58]

The final factor contributing to the world food crisis in the 1970s was the OPEC oil crisis of 1973–74. After Nixon's announced his new economic policy, OPEC announced that since oil had been priced in dollars, and since the devaluation of the American currency meant that producers were losing income, oil would be priced against gold rather than dollars going forward. As with food prices, oil prices had been relatively stable since World War II, rising on average less than 2 percent a year between 1947 and 1967. Oil prices became more volatile in the late 1960s; but it was another political event that sparked the oil crisis. On October 17, 1973, OPEC announced that it would no longer ship oil to nations that supported Israel against the coalition led by Syria and Egypt in the ongoing Yom Kippur War.[59] The embargo was in effect from October 1973 until March of 1974 and targeted the United States, Canada, the United Kingdom, the Netherlands, and Japan. The effects of the embargo were dramatic, causing the price of oil to increase fourfold, from $3 to $12 a barrel. Nixon responded by asking Americans to lower their thermostats and Congress to impose daylight savings time for two years and set a national speed limit to encourage conservation, and he announced programs, such as Project Independence, to boost domestic energy production.[60] In the United States, consumers felt the crisis through rising prices and disrupted supplies of gasoline that gave Americans their first experience with waiting in long lines to purchase essential consumer goods.[61]

Though the long lines at the gas station would be one of the enduring images of the domestic effects of the crisis, its effects on the food system were even more significant, because by the 1970s global food systems had become heavily intertwined with global energy systems. Oil was needed to run machinery and transport food. It also provided raw materials for many essential food-system inputs, such as fertilizers. In the United States and other affected countries, rising oil prices translated directly into rising fuel prices, and led to inflation. These impacts spread well beyond the developed nations. The United States and Canada had become the breadbaskets of the world with their large and dependable harvests. Elevated production costs of key food producers translated into elevated food prices for consumers in many nations around the world. The effects of rising prices especially harmed non-oil-producing developing nations, because they could not offset the higher food prices with higher returns from oil production. Producers in developing countries were also hit hard by rising costs of key agricultural inputs. For example, between 1972 and 1974, the world price of nitrogen fertilizer more than doubled, from 11 cents to 25 cents per pound.[62] The farmers most affected were those who had been the most successful adopters of the high-yield seed varieties and the Green Revolution agricultural techniques. These producers depended on inputs like fertilizer in order to produce yields that not only provided more food, but also allowed sufficient return to cover the greater capital required by such methods. Small farmers in developing countries were even more vulnerable to rising fertilizer prices because they typically bought their inputs in small quantities from distributors at the end of long supply chains. The impact was considerable, as high prices led to shortages of fuel and fertilizer in India that caused the wheat harvest in 1974 to fall seven million tons short of what had been expected at planting.[63]

Higher costs for transportation and food also had an impact on broader elements of foreign policy, such as American strategy and food-aid flows. In November 1973, Butz indicated that the United States was contemplating a food embargo to respond to the oil embargo. In a news conference at the

Rome headquarters of the FAO, Butz noted that "there is a feeling that the United States should stop food shipments" to the Middle East but said that the United States was hesitant to do so, especially since the US grain shipments to the region were relatively small, and the expected excellent harvests in the Soviet Union meant that Russia could easily make up shortfall.[64] The situation demonstrated the drawbacks of using food as an element of national power. The United States instead chose to use its political influence to broker an end to the Arab-Israeli war that had provoked the embargo. The embargo also impacted foreign policy by reducing the effectiveness of food aid. By 1974, the cost of food aid had almost doubled. Higher prices, combined with lower amounts of aid meant that food-aid flows from the United States in 1974 were less than half of what they had been in the late 1960s. American distribution of food aid was thus reduced at a time when many nations around the world most needed food assistance. [65]

THE WORLD FOOD CRISIS AND
INTERNATIONAL RESPONSES

The world food crisis was not simply a sudden and unexpected crisis resulting from a convergence of causal factors unlikely to recur—it was the end of the postwar food system. Following the disruptions caused by World War II, there had been a period of relative stability and predictability in world food affairs. Even events such as the Soviet grain crisis in 1963 had caused only minor disruptions in global food markets. Surpluses of easily storable and transportable foods like wheat and food precursors like animal feed allowed the United States, along with its allies Canada and Australia, to deploy food power to advance domestic interests and protect national security. As policymakers had realized amid the debates in the 1950s over defensively using food power to prepare for nuclear war, food power was much more useful when it was offensively deployed as a component of foreign policy. American food power also provided policymakers with critical public examples, in the 1960s and 1970s, of the clear superiority of free-market over command-economy agricultural systems.

Large surpluses, however, rather than being seen as investments in maintaining a strategic national food reserve that could be used to ensure stability and prosperity, had become a problem to be done away with. While policymakers, especially in the early 1950s, had struggled with suddenly confronting large and seemingly inexhaustible surpluses of agricultural products, by the early 1970s, the productivity gains of the modern agricultural revolution were beginning to slow down. At the same time, growing demand and political events were injecting instability into global energy markets. Increasing uncertainty about the costs of fuel and fertilizer, early concerns about increased disruptions from environmental and climate changes, as well as projections of growing food demand due to population growth and increased purchasing power all indicated an increased need to understand the changing food security landscape.

Policymakers at the time did not have the benefit of a full understanding of all of the trends producing the global food crisis. But they did recognize that prices were rising, people were hungry, and action was necessary. Of critical concern was the nutritional adequacy of food supplies. The shortages of the early 1970s underscored this as millions survived the crisis but on nutritionally inadequate diets. Many people around the world, especially most impoverished, were subsisting on diets that did not meet their daily nutritional needs. In 1974, a report by the United Nations estimated that two-thirds of the populations of the developing world lived in countries in which domestic demand rose faster than food output.[66] Despite narratives about overpopulation and the lack of progress on development, improvements in food production in the developing nations had kept pace with those in developed countries. The main difference lay in the differing pace of the increased demand; developing countries were growing at 3.5 percent a year; the developed countries, at only 2.5 percent a year. The result of this imbalance between supply and demand meant that, while many countries had been able to keep pace with demand increases for many parts of their populations, the world's poorest people were increasingly suffering from malnutrition.[67] The progress that had been made in achieving economic development goals during the previous two decades meant that in many nations there had been a decline in the percentage of people suffering from undernourishment. The increase in the total size of the global population, however, meant that the absolute number of hungry people was higher than at any time in recent history. Thus the world food crisis did have the effect of increasing public understanding that hunger was often caused by poor diets typically resulting from extreme poverty, and it focused attention on the problem of the nutritional adequacy of people's diets.[68]

In examining contemporary events and forecasts of future trends, policymakers and food officials were confronted with the possibility that the events of 1972–74 were not an anomaly; rather, they were the beginning of a new period of instability in the world food system. In a comparison of various projections of growing food supply and demand, the United Nations concluded that during the remainder of the 1970s and the 1980s, conservative estimates of increased demand projected a growth rate of 2.4 percent (2 percent of which would be from population growth, and 0.4 percent from increased purchasing power). Based on these estimates, in 1985 there would be 800 million people in the world with diets that did not provide them with sufficient food energy. Good harvests in 1973 and 1974 had helped to alleviate some of the immediate concerns about food deficiencies. Nonetheless, a half million people worldwide were estimated to have died during the crisis, due to high food prices, food shortages, and inadequate systems for emergency food distribution. Millions more suffered from malnutrition that reduced their health and productivity, and could affect their physical and mental development as well as their susceptibility to disease in years to come.[69]

Amid this recognition of the great changes taking place in the global food system, advocates of convening a major international meeting on food saw an opportunity to embed food problems in a broader range of international issues. The idea of holding a world food conference had first been publicly proposed Henry Kissinger September 1973, to provide a forum in which nations could collectively address the growing threats to the world food supply.[70] The idea had originated with Sartaj Aziz, a Pakistani economist and the head of FAO's Commodities and Trade Division, who suggested the idea to Senator Hubert Humphrey. Humphrey then sent a memo to Kissinger and other administration officials suggesting that Kissinger propose the idea. Kissinger's nomination as secretary of state had encountered a great deal of opposition in the Senate, and it was reported that Humphrey agreed to withdraw his objections to Kissinger's nomination if he agreed to support the idea of an international conference hosted by the United Nations. There were multiple advantages in having the UN hold the conference. Primarily, it would keep the issue under the purview of the State Department, which had been much more amenable to taking an international position on the crisis than the Department of Agriculture. Since Russia was a member of the United Nations, but not the FAO, having the UN host the meeting ensured that any agreement reached would include the USSR. Once Kissinger propsed the idea of a conference in September, preparations for the conference were undertaken by a committee led by FAO staff directed by Aziz and funded by the Ford and Rockefeller Foundations.[71]

By the time official delegates, from 131 nations—as well as observers from 26 United Nations organizations, 25 intergovernmental organizations, and more than 161 nongovernmental organizations—gathered in Rome in November 1974, a set of five core issues had been identified. First, the highest priority was given to efforts to increase food production in developing countries. Second was the need to develop policies and programs to feed the hungry and improve nutrtion in all countries, especially those that would ensure sufficient food for vulnerable populations in developing countries. Third was to make food security a global priority, which could be strengthened through such strategies as information sharing, developing early warning systems for food crises, creating of international food reserves, and developing of more effective food-aid systems. The fourth was improving international trading systems to promote market development and price stabilization. The fifth was to develop new arrangements and institutions that would be responsible for implementing the conference recommendations, perhaps through the creation of a new world food authority. The full conference was convened to endorse the world food strategy developed in meetings prior to the conference, develop plans for its implementation, and identify resources to support the strategy.[72]

As with previous efforts to create a World Food Board, the conference did not endorse the grand strategy and support the proposed creation of a World Food Authority, though it did take important steps to address world food problems. Delegates adopted the "Universal Declaration on the Eradication of Hunger and Malnutrition," which proclaimed that "every man, woman and child has the inalienable right to be free from hunger and malnutrition in order to develop fully and maintain their physical and mental faculties."[73] The declaration went on to note that sufficient technology, resources, and organization existed to eradicate hunger, and affirmed that it was the common aim of all countries to help achieve this goal. The conference adopted twenty other nonbinding resolutions related to food production and food aid, and also defined and outlined steps to improve food security. The Rome meeting helped to focus global attention on world food problems and also added energy and vision to the efforts of existing institutions, such as the FAO, the World Food Programme, and the United Nations Environment Programme. It also led to the emergence of new institutions to help govern the global food system, including the International Fund for Agricultural Development, to help finance food security efforts; enhanced research activities by the International Food Policy Research Institute and the Consultative Group on International Agricultural Research; and the Global Information and Early Warning System on Food and Agriculture, a worldwide early-warning system for food problems.[74] The conference also considered creating a world food reserve as a bulwark against future instability.

The primary underlying shock that led to the world food crisis in the early 1970s was the elimination of surpluses of food that could be deployed in times of need. It is somewhat ironic, then, that it was Nixon, who as a candidate in 1960 had advocated the creation of strategic national food stockpiles, who as president had eliminated large surpluses and introduced uncertainty and volatility into global food markets. In the 1970s, there was not, however, a popular consensus on the value of eliminating surpluses. In 1974, when pondering the effects of the world food crisis, *Time* noted that Americans must ask whether they have "a moral obligation to feed those who are starving."[75] For many, the answer was yes.

Yet popular opinion ran in the other direction, too, among those who were concerned about the cost to taxpayers. Perhaps for this reason, few leaders made the case for maintaining food reserves an essential element of United States national security, on par with the considerable costs of maintaining conventional and nuclear military forces. In the Rome discussion of world reserves, beyond having taxpayers in developed nations fund stockpiles, strategies were discussed to shift costs from countries that produced and held food supplies onto the countries and consumers who would benefit from use of food reserves in emergency situations. If these were refreshed at times of high production, they might even represent an investment for nations, which might even able to stockpile grains and sell them at times of higher prices and global need. The reduction of surplus stockpiles, however, had combined with a major drought during the summer of 1974 to leave the United States with the problem of insufficient food supplies at a time when many nations, and many Americans, such as the American Freedom from Hunger Foundation—a bipartisan group of church leaders, voluntary agencies, and congressional leaders—were advocating an increase in global food aid. National reserves thus proved vulnerable to localized natural disasters and shifts in national policy.[76]

Given the problems with relying on national stockpiles, one of the topics under consideration at the World Food Summit in Rome was the creation of an international food reserve system. President Gerald Ford endorsed the idea in his first major foreign policy speech to the UN General Assembly. On September 18, 1974, he stated that in order to "ensure the survival of millions of our fellow men does not depend on the vagaries of the weather, the United States is prepared to join in a worldwide effort to negotiate, establish and maintain an international system of food reserves."[77] Ford presented an idea for an internationally held and managed system of food reserves and promised a detailed proposal at November conference. Not all administration officials supported the idea of reserves. Butz, for example, endorsed the idea of grain and food reserves, but felt that companies rather than countries should take a major role in building and maintaining them. Further, while Butz understood the need for the international exchange of information on production, supplies, and trade of food, he wanted each nation to develop its own reserves and to manage them for their national interest rather than surrender authority to an international governing body. The State Department was initially more flexible, favoring an international reserve in principle. Ford's speech in September laid out a middle course; he was willing to participate in international negotiations on food reserves, but also indicated a need for nations to maintain control over the portion of reserves allocated to them.[78]

In his speech before the Rome Conference, Kissinger further clarified the US position: it would support the creation of an international system of reserves provided each nation was able to choose its own method for managing the reserves. In both 1974 and 1975, the House and Senate passed measures supporting the reserve. Following the World Food Conference, the discussion was taken up by the International Wheat Council (IWC). The United States developed and presented a proposal, at a meeting of the council in September 1975, for establishing a wheat reserve, with the possibility of extending it to include coarse grains like corn, oats, and other feed grains. The proposal was supported by Australia and Canada, but received sharp questioning from representatives of the European Economic Community and an unfriendly response from the Soviet Union, who saw the plan as favoring US interests. Ultimately, IWC members' concerns about financing and management meant that the American proposal was not adopted.[79] Some nations, such as African countries that had been deeply impacted by the food crisis, did develop individual reserves, but these were plagued by problems of poor oversight and financial problems, and almost all national reserves were dismantled by the 1990s.[80] The idea of an international system of food reserves that could help stabilize world food prices and respond to emergencies fell victim to the same reluctance to surrender national control that had scuttled the much more ambitious plan for the World Food Board proposed by Boyd Orr after World War II.[81] Even following the world's worst food crisis since the beginning of the postwar period, the link between food, national security, prosperity was still too strong for states to be comfortable ceding even limited sovereignty over their food supplies to an international organization.[82]

Nonetheless, the causes and magnitude of the world food crisis, as well as the steps taken to resolve it, pointed to the beginning of a new era in world food relations. Between 1945 and 1975, a postwar food system had slowly emerged against the backdrop of the Cold War, a modern agricultural revolution that would transform food production in developed and developing nations, and the development of policy tools to enable the United States to harness agricultural abundance to national priorities. Stalin's refusal to allow Communist nations to participate in the Marshall Plan meant that the communist world was largely absent from both this evolving postwar food system and the broader international system emerging under the Bretton Woods Institutions. The result was a postwar food system based on capitalist market principles and heavily wedded to American desires for interdependence, stability, and security. Of course, American actions were not the only ones that mattered; as the postwar world food system was heavily affected by events in Europe, Asia and the Soviet sphere as well as by actions of companies, philanthropic foundations, and nongovernmental organizations. But American efforts were central, and in many cases generative, to the global system and its outcomes. Time and again during the postwar era, the United States used food to advance national security and national interests, whether through bilateral aid agreements, the Marshall Plan in the 1940s, PL-480 in the 1950s, or Food for Peace in the 1960s. Aid, of course was not given for purely moral and humanitarian reasons, but tied to American perceptions of needs and interests in a fluid Cold War strategic environment. American leaders and policymakers struggled to weigh competing domestic and foreign policy interests amid times of great social, technological, and economic change. American policy was not always clear or consistent, but food was a strong core running through its efforts to navigate a changing security landscape.

The 1970s food crisis marked the clearest debate about the use of American food power between those who favored cooperative and humanitarian approaches and those who saw it as an implement of coercion. The sense that food should be used to promote international cooperation and humanitarian aims was championed by Senators Hubert

Humphrey and George McGovern, and in Kissinger's original call for a World Food Conference. In his September 1973 statement to the United Nations, Kissinger underlined the global nature of the challenge: "No one country can cope with this problem."[83] From this perspective, solutions to world food problems could only be arrived at through international agreements that would be beneficial to all nations, even if some nations, such as the United States, tended to benefit more. On the other side of the argument were those like Butz who saw food as a weapon, a form of power that could be used to achieve American national objectives.[84] In 1973, Butz floated the idea of using a food embargo as America's response to the oil embargo.[85] White House officials rejected the idea, with one remarking anonymously to *BusinessWeek*, "Can you imagine the repercussions of the U.S. trying to play God with food?" Echoing this sentiment, a State Department official commented that food power was "power over people who are hungry—people we don't want to push around anyway."[86] Later in the decade, some Americans urged the deployment of the food weapon through an embargo of sales of food to Iran in an effort to force a resolution of the 1979 Iranian hostage crisis.[87] Certainly, food could be used to American advantage and to support American interests, but because of its disproportionate effect on the powerless and the ability of targeted nations to seek out other sources of food, it had to be used very carefully lest it end up undermining American values and goals.

Discussions in the 1970s about the uses of food power thus clearly established some limits on the degree to which most American officials were comfortable using food power. An oil embargo might cause disruption and hardship to people and economies, but food embargos would certainly cause rapid and harsh effects, and if the experiences of the early 1970s were any guide, such effects would be felt disproportionately by women and children and the poorest, most marginalized groups in society. To American policymakers, food power was a difficult weapon to use against the decision-makers and elites in societies. It was also an imprecise one, subject to unexpected consequences and carrying a heavy possibility of blowback against states that tried to employ it. This lesson was learned by President Carter in 1979, when he withheld food sales to the Soviet Union to punish it for invading Afghanistan and instead ended up closing off a major market for American food exports, which contributed to the American farm crisis in the early 1980s. The intrinsic and necessary nature of food and the universal human revulsion to starvation made the explicit coercive use of food power unattractive.[88]

The World Food Conference, and the food crisis of the 1970s, can be seen as the beginning of a new global food network. However, unlike the postwar food system, which was characterized by steadily increasing global food production, relatively stable food prices, and the significant guiding factor of the American use of food power, the postcrisis food network that was emerging would be a truly global one. This new network engaged America as a key actor, but also had increasing roles for the European Community, the Soviet Union, and other Communist-bloc nations, as well as economies in developing nations. International institutions played important roles in the new system, while emerging economic ideas of neoliberalism shifted the goals and terms of international aid flows. Global capital flows and multinational corporations would also play a much broader role in the global food network than in previous periods. Rather than a return to the relative stability of the precrisis period, the world food crisis that occurred between 1972 and 1974 represents an inflection in world food regimes, one that, in the words of sociologist Harriet Friedmann, "initiated a period of instability from which we have not yet recovered."[89] Perhaps the most important feature of this inflection, however, was not that it gave rise to a new, postcrisis global food system, but that it led to the emergence of a new world food network, one that connects people and places around the world through food.

Conclusion

The Past, Present, and Future of World Food Problems

The postwar food system that developed after World War II was strongly shaped by the American efforts to manage its unprecedented agricultural abundance. From the late 1940s to the early 1970s, surpluses of food and food precursors supported American national security and national interests at home and abroad. These food stockpiles were a flexible tool used by presidents and policymakers to promote peace and prosperity by ensuring the availability of food and stability in food prices. Through the upheaval of postwar recovery, severe weather events such as the harsh winters in the 1940s and droughts in the 1960s, and dramatic changes in consumption patterns, American food power helped allies and even competitors cope with disasters and shortfalls. Though surpluses were perceived of as a problem to be done away with at home, they became a vital element of America's Cold War strategy to contain and productively engage with the Soviet Union and other communist countries. America's unwillingness and inability to continue to provide an abundance of food, combined with a converging series of unexpected events in the early 1970s, brought an end to the postwar food system.

In the wake of the world food crisis of 1972–74, and the failure of world leaders to agree on a new world food system, a new pattern in global food relations emerged: the world food network. This food network was distinct from the postwar food system. Networks, made up of nodes and hubs, have a pattern of organization that is different from the planned and controlled operations of a system. Since the 1970s, the world food network has taken shape as an amalgamation of local, regional, national, and transnational food systems. Some of the key actors in the postwar world food system—such as the United States, the Soviet Union, the European Community, and United Nations organizations such as the FAO—remain critically important hubs in the new world food network. The decades after the mid-1970s, however, also saw the emergence of other kinds of actors—such as transnational corporations, new kinds of international finance flows, and technologically empowered nongovernmental organizations—that also helped to determine the network's structure. The world food network links food chains at multiple scales in a complex and rapidly shifting web of food relations that provides the world's growing number of people with food on a day-to-day basis. Foods of many varieties—industrial food; processed food; local food; organic food; genetically modified food; cheap food; luxury food; artisanal food; seasonal food; seasonless food, such as fresh vegetables and tropical fruits that are available year round in stores across the planet; old food, such as like heirloom wheat, quinoa, and other ancient grains; new foods such as coconut water, almond milk, and cricket protein-based energy bars—travel through this world food network from producers to consumers.

One of the distinguishing features of the world food network is that it is far less responsive to the actions of states, especially states that seek a dominant and controlling position in the network, such as the United States. There are many actors and outcomes are shaped by many variables. Policymakers, scholars, businesspeople, and consumers are all still trying to understand this pattern in food relations, even as it changes, disconnects, and reconnects to form new links through a changing assortment of hubs and nodes. At the same time that people ponder the future of food in a world of old problems, such as population growth and the unequal distribution of food, the food network is confronted with challenges of climate change and transnational threats such as terrorism, pandemics, and cybercrime, all empowered by global information and transportation networks.[1]

This constantly changing global food landscape is similar in many ways to the shifting global security landscape that historian Edward Meade Earl predicted in the 1930s. His ideas influenced the organization of the US national security community, setting it up to respond not just to to a specific threat, but to a changing and evolving range of threats to be identified by such organizations as the Department of Defense, National Security Council, and the Central Intelligence Agency.[2] Earl underscored the notion that the global security landscape was unlikely to settle into a stable and predictable pattern.[3] The same is likely true of the global food network. Rather than trying to reclaim the brief stability of the postwar period, we should recognize that in a world of population growth, shifting demographics, and environmental and climate change, the global food landscape will likely always be shifting. This book's exploration of the American engagement with the postwar food system offers two assertions that can be helpful in understanding the world food network and in trying to develop strategies for the United States and other nations, as well as individuals and communities, to use in addressing world food problems.

The first is that the United States was most successful using food power softly. Although food power exists on a spectrum, from coercive uses to diplomatic and humanitarian uses, the history of the two and a half decades after World War II suggest that it was the softer end of the spectrum that most helped the nation to achieving its strategic goals.[4] From the postwar Marshall Plan to Food for Peace in the 1960s, American initiatives to provide food for humanitarian or diplomatic purposes were more in accordance with both core American values and evolving norms of international relations that expanded the wartime goal of freedom from want into a postwar understanding of food as a human right.[5] When American leaders and policymakers sought to use food to achieve specific political aims, such as Johnson's short-tether policy in India in the 1960s or the hope that the 1972 grain sales to the Soviet Union could be used to shape Russian policy on Vietnam, they found that coercive ends were much more difficult to achieve. In addition to not being effective, such efforts undercut the core goals of foreign policy. One of the best examples of this is the Soviet grain sale, which instead of being seen as an example of the failure of Soviet agricultural reforms, actually ended up costing the United States, both economically and in terms of political legitimacy. This was in part because Communist negotiators swindled capitalist American buyers and in part because poor oversight by government officials allowed massive sales of wheat at subsidized prices before the scope of the sale was be fully understood. Furthermore, possessing American grain allowed the Soviet Union to deploy food power of its own by providing humanitarian food aid to India that the United States, having exhausted its own supplies, was unable to deliver. Soviet outreach deepened Soviet-Indo relations, precisely the outcome that American policymakers had hoped to avoid.

The notion that food has to be deployed carefully and in accordance with American values and international norms has dominated recent policymaking. Examples of this include President George W. Bush's decision in 2013 to allow USAID (United States Agency for International Development) officials to purchase a portion of the total amount of food aid supplied by the United States from national or regional markets rather than limiting aid to only food that is produced in the U.S., a move designed to provide aid more rapidly and to avoid undercutting local and regional agricultural producers.[6] Another example is the Obama administration's Feed the Future initiative, developed in response to the global food price crisis of 2007–8, which seeks to address global food security needs through partnering with other countries to help them improve their agricultural production and the nutritional status of their people.[7] Food power, when exercised coercively, is, as one State Department Official cautioned in the 1970s, power over hungry people.[8] American leaders and policymakers from Herbert Hoover to John F. Kennedy recognized that food power works best when used in humanitarian and diplomatic ways. Deployed properly, food power can be an effective element of America's efforts to promote peace, stability, and prosperity.

The second assertion is that food reserves gave policymakers options. In the postwar food system, large surpluses of food and food precursors such as feed grains, provided stability in prices and food availability. In the early 1970s, when the exhaustion of American surpluses coincided with increased demand, higher prices, and lower-than-expected production, policymakers lost the ability to immediately deploy food to stabilize prices and address humanitarian needs. The arsenal that had empowered the Marshall Plan, bilateral aid to nations in need, and various incarnations of the Food for Peace program was empty, just when America and the world needed it most. American officials had developed a food strategy that, if analogized to the military, was like beginning to train soldiers and build tanks and airplanes only after a security threat had developed.

At the end of World War II, policymakers at home and abroad recognized the key link between insufficient food and global insecurity. In the postwar years, they made considerable and continuous investments to maintain standing conventional and nuclear military forces, while also developing entire industries and infrastructure, from aerospace to higher education, to ensure national security. In contrast, the middle decades of the twentieth century saw sporadic and sometimes contradictory efforts to understand, develop, and maintain mechanisms for the deployment of American food power. As America and its leaders moved beyond the war, the surplus production became, not an asset, but a problem to be done away with. While models of just-in-time production and delivery have come to dominate in a globalizing, interconnected world that prizes certain forms of efficiency and profitability as key outcomes, agriculture and food production are a poor fit with an industrial model that seeks to harmonize food supply and demand.[9] The maintenance of American food reserves was not without cost to farmers, consumers, and American taxpayers, but perhaps, in looking back, such costs were useful outlays against uncertainty in a complex and changing world.

In the face of a shifting landscape of global security, environmental, and economic challenges, it is perhaps prudent to once again consider the role that food reserves could play in promoting peace and prosperity. The failure of efforts to establish a world reserve system following the 1970s food crisis, and the slow decline of national reserves, meant the world had fewer options in 2007–8, when it once again confronted a global food crisis.[10] Establishing a system of reserves would be a complex and difficult task, one requiring leadership and an international willingness to find a balance between ensuring state sovereignty and providing a global public good. Neither past failures nor assessments of the difficulty should deter consideration of an idea that grows more necessary as future impacts of global climate change on agriculture and food production become more certain. Forecasting the future is always a tricky business; however, a range of recent assessments have concluded that future impacts and shocks on agriculture and food production from climate change and variability are highly probable.[11] Combined with ongoing population growth, demographic changes, and linkages between global food, energy, and water networks, simply hoping that food production will keep up with demand seems a dangerous bet to make.

There are a number of reasons to think seriously about the idea of food reserves. The long time lag between increased need and increased food production is a strong reason to develop a global food reserve capability that could respond to short-term emergencies as well as longer-term needs. Waiting for another global food crisis to galvanize public and media interest does not allow the time that will be necessary to overcome the issues of state sovereignty, the growing propensity of governments to not want to invest in public goods, and debates over the role of governments versus nongovernmental or private sector, actors that have historically stood in the way of such efforts.[12]

Moreover, in the absence of domestic and international actions toward establishing food reserves, a little-known, but increasingly visible number of Americans are taking steps to prepare themselves and their families for coming uncertainty by stocking their own private food reserves in their garages and basements.[13] Perhaps such private "prepper" efforts will be seen as the early twenty-first century equivalent of the 1950s fallout shelters that were not built and pantry shelves that were not stocked. But these efforts illustrate the continued resonance of connections between food and security. The experience of shelter provisioning demonstrated that a national strategy reliant on do-it-yourself preparedness led to results that were uneven and less than optimal. Americans should thus be

hesitant about policy responses that address potential crisis and instability not by developing a managed and coordinated food reserve system,
but by returning to the self-help messages of 1950s-era civil defense campaigns. These messages recur every September in the campaigns that urge
Americans to celebrate National Preparedness Month by building their
own disaster kits.[14]

In a world food network of increasingly tenuous and far-flung connections, food reserves, in the form of stored crops or easily storable foods,
would be a deployable resource. That resource could be utilized in the
event of regional, national, or international need and would help provide
resilience against unexpected shocks or negative events. Amid the complex terrain of global political, social, and economic problems, there is an
unfortunate pattern whereby food gains attention during some crisis, and
then fades into the background until a new crisis arises. This occurred in
the years after World War II and during the 1970s; more recently, food
again rose to the top of global concerns during the price crisis in 2007–8.
Amid a rapid rise in global food prices, policymakers once again worried
about link between high food prices; the instability in more than forty
nations; the rise of populist movements, such as the Arab Spring; and the
wider instability in the Middle East.[15] Food is too critical a component in
global peace and prosperity to be left to the heightened but short-lived
attention it receives during a crisis. In a crisis, commitments to develop a
different sort of food network can be made, but the cultivation of such a
network will take years and likely even decades. Yet the development of
a more resilient and sustainable network is necessary if the global community is to face the uncertainties of the coming decades without famine,
food shortages, and rising food prices becoming a reality in many parts of
the world.

Food, even in a time of the new threats of global terrorism and cybercrime, remains one of the cornerstones of the security, well-being, and
flourishing of nations, communities, and individuals. The rise and fall
of the world food system this book has traced demonstrates that food—
however inadvertently—has been a focus of national security in the past,
and in ways that affected global affairs, improved America's standing in the

world, and reduced global hunger and deprivation. Moreover, it illustrates that even with greater flexibility in the food network, food is unlikely to ever be a solved problem. Instead, it should be seen as a landscape of challenges that each generation must take up again for themselves, to consider anew how to best fulfill their food needs and wants.[16] The lesson of the postwar world food system is that food matters to national and global security. We now have to figure out how to make our awareness of that fact shape uses of food power that lead to a more secure, more sustainable, and more just world.

NOTES

INTRODUCTION

1. "Why We Eat Better: Industrial Advances in U.S. Open the Way to Rich, Varied Diet," *Better Living* 5 (November–December 1951), 2–3.
2. "Why We Eat Better," 2–8.
3. Steven T. Sheehan, "Better Citizens through *Better Living*: Consumer Culture and Corporate Capital in Employee Communications and Public Relations at Du Pont Chemical 1945-1960," *Iowa Journal of Cultural Studies* 12, no. 13 (Spring and Fall 2010): 55–77; Kari Frederickson, *Cold War Dixie: Militarization and Modernization in the American South* (Athens: University of Georgia Press, 2013), 128–130; Carroll Pursell, *Technology in Postwar America: A History* (New York: Columbia University Press, 2013), 100–101. For a contemporary look at what families in America and around the world eat, see Peter Menzel and Faith D'Aluisio, *Hungry Planet: What the World Eats* (Berkeley, CA: Material World Books, 2005).
4. Franklin Delano Roosevelt, "Message to Congress 1941," January 6, 1941, 21, accessed May 1, 2016, http://www.fdrlibrary.marist.edu/pdfs/ffreadingcopy.pdf. The Four Freedoms also served as a backdrop to the discussions at the Atlantic Conference between President Roosevelt and Prime Minister Churchill in August 1941. See, for example, *Foreign Relations of the United States Diplomatic Papers*, 1941, vol. I, General, the Soviet Union, eds. E. R. Perkins and Gustave A. Nuermberger (Washington, DC: Government Printing Office, 1958), 341–373 accessed May 1, 2016, http://digital.library.wisc.edu/1711.dl/FRUS.FRUS1941v01.
5. "U.S. Food Power: Ultimate Weapon in World Politics," *BusinessWeek*, December 15, 1975, 54–60; "Power in US Food Harvests," *The Guardian*, January 7, 1976, 2.
6. Hugh Sidney, "More Powerful Than Atom Bombs," *Time*, January 12, 1976, 15.
7. Ibid.
8. Congressional Research Service, *Use of U.S. Food Resources for Diplomatic Purposes: An Examination of the Issues* (Washington, DC: Government Printing Office, 1977), 1.
9. Quoted in "U.S. Food Power: Ultimate Weapon," 54–60.
10. "Butz Hints U.S. Weighed Food Embargo on Arabs," *New York Times*, November 14, 1973.

11. Robert Paarlberg, "The Failure of Food Power," *Policy Studies Journal* 6, no. 4 (1978): 537–542.

12. United Nations, "The Universal Declaration of Human Rights," 1948, accessed May 1, 2016, http://www.un.org/en/documents/udhr/.

13. Peter Wallensteen, "Scarce Goods as Political Weapons: The Case of Food," *Journal of Peace Research* 13, no. 4 (1976): 277–298; Congressional Research Service, *Use of Food Resources*; Jack LeCuyer, "Food as a Component of National Defense Strategy," *Parameters: Journal of the US Army War College* 7, no. 4 (1977): 56–70; Robert Paarlberg, "Food, Oil and Coercive Resource Power," *International Security* 3, no. 2 (Fall 1978): 3–19. On soft power, see Joseph Nye, *Bound to Lead: The Changing Nature of American Power* (New York: Basic Books, 1990).

14. Mitchel B. Wallerstein, *Food for War, Food for Peace: United States Food Aid in a Global Context* (Cambridge, MA: MIT Press, 1980), 180–225; Richard L. Armitage and Joseph S. Nye Jr., *CSIS Commission on Smart Power: A Smarter, More Secure America* (Washington, DC: Center for Strategic and International Studies, 2007), accessed May 1, 2016, http://csis.org/files/media/csis/pubs/071106_csissmartpow-erreport.pdf.

15. USDA, *Guide to Civil Defense Management in the Food Industry*, Agriculture Handbook no. 254 (Washington, DC: Government Printing Office, 1963), i.

16. On the history of food security, see D. John Shaw, *World Food Security: A History since 1945* (New York: Palgrave Macmillan, 2007). For historical perspectives of the importance of food to security, see Geoffrey Parker, *Global Crisis: War, Climate Change and Catastrophe in the Seventeenth Century* (New Haven, CT: Yale University Press, 2013), chapter 3; Evan D. Fraser and Andrew Rimas, *Empires of Food: Feast, Famine, and the Rise and Fall of Civilizations* (New York: Free Press, 2010).

17. Harriet Friedmann, "The Political Economy of Food: A Global Crisis," *New Left Review* 197 (1993): 29–57.

18. Friedmann, "Political Economy of Food"; "The World Food Crisis," *Time*, November 11, 1974, 94; Derek Heady and Shenggen Fen, *Reflections on the Global Food Crisis: How Did It Happen? How Has It Hurt? And How Can We Prevent the Next One?* (Washington, DC: International Food Policy Research Institute, 2010).

19. Foresight, *The Future of Food and Farming: Challenges and Choices for Global Sustainability* (London: Government Office for Science, 2011), 10.

20. On contemporary world food problems, see Eric Schlosser, *Fast Food Nation: The Dark Side of the All-American Meal* (Boston: Houghton Mifflin, 2001); Marion Nestle, *Food Politics: How the Food Industry Influences Nutrition and Health* (Berkeley: University of California Press, 2002); Michael Pollan, *The Omnivore's Dilemma: A Natural History of Four Meals* (New York: Penguin, 2006); Harvey Blatt, *America's Food: What You Don't Know about What You Eat* (Cambridge, MA: MIT Press, 2008); Barbara Kingsolver, Camille Kingsolver, and Steven L. Hopp, *Animal, Vegetable, Miracle* (New York: HarperCollins, 2009); Jennifer Clapp and Doris Fuchs, *Corporate Power in Global Agrifood Governance* (Cambridge, MA: MIT Press, 2009); James McWilliams, *Just Food: Where Locavores Get It Wrong and How We Can Truly Eat Responsibly* (New York: Little, Brown , 2009); Jennifer Clapp, *Hunger in the Balance: The New Politics of International Food Aid* (Ithaca, NY:

Cornell University Press, 2012); Raj Patel, *Stuffed and Starved: The Hidden Battle for the World Food System* (Brooklyn, NY: Melville House, 2012); Howard G. Buffett, *Forty Chances: Finding Hope in a Hungry World* (New York: Simon and Schuster, 2013).

21. US Food and Drug Administration, *Pathway to Global Product Safety and Quality* (Washington, DC: Government Printing Office, 2011), 1.

22. Charles Elton, *Animal Ecology* (1927; Chicago: University of Chicago Press, 2001), 50–70.

23. Institute of Medicine and National Research Council, *A Framework for Assessing Effects of the Food System* (Washington, DC: National Academies Press, 2015), 31. On definitions of a food system, see also J. D. Kinsey, "The New Food Economy: Consumers, Farms, Pharms, and Science," *American Journal of Agricultural Economics* 83, no. 5 (2001): 1113–1130; B. Senauer and L. Venturini, "The Globalization of Food Systems: A Concept Framework and Empirical Patterns," in *Food Agriculture and the Environment*, ed. by E. Defrancesco, L. Galletto, and M. Thiene (Milan, Italy: FrancoAngeli, 2005): 197–224; A. J. Oskam, G. B. C. Backus, J. Kinsey, and L. J. Frewer, "The New Food Economy," in *E.U. Policy for Agriculture, Food and Rural Area* (Wageningen, The Netherlands: Wageningen Academic Publishers, 2010): 297–306; J. Kinsey, "Expectations and Realities of the Food System," in *U.S. Programs Affecting Food and Agricultural Marketing*, ed. W. J. Armbruster and R. Knutson (New York: Springer, 2013): 11–42.

24. Robert Gottlieb and Anupama Joshi, *Food Justice* (Cambridge, MA: MIT Press, 2010), 5.

25. Ludwig von Bertalanffy, "An Outline of General System Theory," *British Journal for the Philosophy of Science* 1, no. 2 (1950): 134–165. See also Ludwig von Bertalanffy, *General System Theory: Foundations, Development, Applications* (New York: G. Braziller, 1969); and Donella Meadows and Diana Wright, *Thinking in Systems: A Primer* (White River Junction, VT: Chelsea Green, 2008).

26. Jay Goodman, "The Concept of 'System' in International Relations Theory," *Background* 8, no. 4 (February 1965): 257–268. See also Morton Kaplan, *System and Process in International Politics* (New York: John Wiley and Sons, 1957); and James N. Rosenau, ed., *International Politics and Foreign Policy* (New York: Free Press of Glencoe, 1961).

27. It is worth noting that what is considered food in such food systems is often unclear. When talking about food, the common image is of a thing that is the immediate result of hunting, fishing, gathering, or agriculture. But what is eaten as food, even in nonindustrial societies, often is the result of at least some level of preparation and processing. See Donald B. Thompson and Bryan McDonald, "What Food Is 'Good' for You? Toward a Pragmatic Consideration of Multiple Values Domains," *Journal of Agricultural and Environmental Ethics* 26, no. 1 (2013): 137–163.

28. Donald Worster, *Nature's Economy: A History of Ecological Ideas*, 2nd ed. (New York: Cambridge University Press, 1994), 293.

29. Worster, *Nature's Economy*, 291–301.

30. Manuel Castells, *The Rise of the Network Society*, 2nd ed. (Malden, MA; Oxford: Blackwell, 2000), 500.

31. Castells, *Rise of the Network Society*, 500–509; Albert-László Barabási, *Linked: How Everything Is Connected to Everything Else and What It Means for Business, Science, and Everyday Life* (New York: Plume, 2003); Duncan Watts, *Small Worlds: The Dynamics of Networks between Order and Randomness* (Princeton, NJ: Princeton University Press, 2004); Guido Caldarelli, *Scale-Free Networks: Complex Webs in Nature and Technology* (Oxford: Oxford University Press, 2007).

32. For more on these changes, see Adam Ward Rome, "American Farmers as Entrepreneurs, 1870-1900," *Agricultural History* 56 (1982): 37–49; Deborah Kay Fitzgerald, *Every Farm a Factory: The Industrial Ideal in American Agriculture* (New Haven, CT: Yale University Press, 2003); Harvey Levenstein, *Revolution at the Table: The Transformation of the American Diet* (Berkeley: University of California Press, 2003); James E. McWilliams, *A Revolution in Eating: How the Quest for Food Shaped America* (New York: Columbia University Press, 2005); Kristin Hoganson, "Stuff It: Domestic Consumption and the Americanization of the World Paradigm," *Diplomatic History* 30, no. 4 (2006): 571–594; Andrew F. Smith, *Eating History: Thirty Turning Points in the Making of American Cuisine* (New York: Columbia University Press, 2013).

33. National Intelligence Council, ed. *Global Trends 2030: Alternative Worlds* (Washington, DC: Central Intelligence Agency, 2013). See also Holger Hoff, *Understanding the Nexus* (Stockholm: Stockholm Environment Institute, 2011); and Food and Agriculture Organization of the United Nations, *The Water-Energy-Food Nexus: A New Approach in Support of Food Security and Sustainable Agriculture* (Rome: Food and Agriculture Organization, 2014).

34. On the great acceleration, see John Robert McNeill, *Something New under the Sun: An Environmental History of the Twentieth-Century World* (New York: Norton, 2000), 4; Robert Costanza, Lisa Graumlich, Will Steffen, Carole Crumley, et al. "Sustainability or Collapse: What Can We Learn from Integrating the History of Humans and the Rest of Nature?," *AMBIO: A Journal of the Human Environment* 36, no. 7 (2007): 522–527.

35. Jason W. Clay, *World Agriculture and the Environment: A Commodity-by-Commodity Guide to Impacts and Practices* (Washington, DC: Island Press, 2004); H. Charles J. Godfray, John R. Beddington, Ian R. Crute, Lawrence Haddad, David Lawrence, James F. Muir, Jules Pretty, Sherman Robinson, Sandy M. Thomas, and Camilla Toulmin, "Food Security: The Challenge of Feeding 9 Billion People," *Science* 327 (February 12, 2010): 812–818.

36. Edward Mead Earle, "American Military Policy and National Security," *Political Science Quarterly* 53, no. 1 (1938), 1–13.

37. David Ekbladh, "Present at the Creation: Edward Mead Earle and the Depression-Era Origins of Security Studies," *International Security* 36, no. 3 (2011/12): 107–141. On the establishment of the Department of Defense and the postwar American national security apparatus, see Douglas T. Stuart, *Creating the National Security State: A History of the Law That Transformed America* (Princeton, NJ: Princeton University Press, 2008).

38. Lawrence J. Vale, *The Limits of Civil Defence in the USA, Switzerland, Britain and the Soviet Union* (London: Macmillan, 1987), 59.

39. James Clapper, "Statement for the Record: Worldwide Threat Assessment of the US Intelligence Community," presented to the Senate Select Committee on Intelligence, January 29, 2014, accessed May 1, 2016, http://www.dni.gov/index.php/newsroom/testimonies/203-congressional-testimonies-2014/1005-statement-for-the-record-worldwide-threat-assessment-of-the-us-intelligence-community.

40. For an overview of contemporary threats to world food security, see Bryan McDonald, *Food Security* (Cambridge: Polity Press, 2010). On links between food and conflict, see Emmy Simmons, *Harvesting Peace: Food Security, Conflict, and Cooperation* (Washington, DC: Woodrow Wilson International Center for Scholars, 2013).

41. Nick Cullather, *The Hungry World* (Cambridge, MA: Harvard University Press, 2010); David Ekbladh, *The Great American Mission: Modernization and the Construction of an American World Order* (Princeton, NJ: Princeton University Press, 2010).

42. Warren Belasco, *Appetite for Change: How the Counterculture Took on the Food Industry* (Ithaca, NY: Cornell University Press, 2007).

CHAPTER 1

1. Catechetical Guild Educational Society, *Is This Tomorrow: America under Communism!* (St. Paul, MN: Catechetical Guild Educational Society, 1947).

2. "Grim Picture of Red Rule," *Abilene Reporter-News*, December 30, 1947, 18.

3. Catechetical Guild Educational Society, *Is This Tomorrow*, back cover.

4. John Foster, "The Slow Death of a Monochromatic World: The Social History of Australia as Seen through Its Children's Comic Books," *Journal of Popular Culture* 33, no. 1 (1999): 139–152; Emily Clark, "Of Catholics, Commies, and the Anti-Christ: Mapping American Social Borders through Cold War Comic Books," *Journal of Religion and Popular Culture* 21, no. 3 (2009), accessed May 1, 2016, http://www.usask.ca/relst/jrpc/art21%283%29-CatholicsCommies.html; Jean-Paul Gabilliet, *Of Comics and Men: A Cultural History of American Comic Books* (Jackson: University Press of Mississippi, 2010); Marc J. Selverstone, "A Literature So Immense: The Historiography of Anticommunism," *OAH Magazine of History* 24, no. 4 (2010): 7–11; Ben Sitz and Bill Geerhart, "Is This Tomorrow: America under Communism!" *CONELRAD Adjacent*, accessed May 1, 2016, http://www.conelrad.com/books/print.php?id=307_0_1_0. The prospect of a food crisis leading to a larger security crisis would continue to resonate throughout the Cold War, such as in the 1984 film *Red Dawn*, in which failures in Soviet agriculture provoke a communist invasion of the United States. See *Red Dawn*, DVD, directed by John Milius (Los Angeles: United Artists, 1984).

5. See Ruth Jachertz and Alexander Nützenadel, "Coping with Hunger? Visions of a Global Food System, 1930-1960," *Journal of Global History* 6, no. 1 (2011): 99–119; Lizzie Collingham, *Taste of War: World War II and the Battle for Food* (New York: Penguin, 2012); Jacob Darwin Hamblin, "The Vulnerability of Nations: Food Security in the Aftermath of World War II," *Global Environment* 10 (2012): 42–65.

204

6. Wilfred Malenbaum, *The World Wheat Economy, 1885-1939* (Cambridge, MA: Harvard University Press, 1953); Harriet Friedmann, "The Political Economy of Food: The Rise and Fall of the Postwar International Food Order," *American Journal of Sociology*, supplement 88 (1982): S248–S286.

7. Malenbaum, *World Wheat Economy*; Lawrence Goodwyn, *The Populist Moment: A Short History of the Agrarian Revolt in America* (New York: Oxford University Press, 1978); Adam Rome, "American Farmers as Entrepreneurs, 1870-1900," *Agricultural History*, 56, no. 1 (1982): 37–49; Denis S. Nordin and Roy V. Scott, *From Prairie Farmer to Entrepreneur: The Transformation of Midwestern Agriculture* (Bloomington: Indiana University Press, 2005).

8. International Harvester, *Every Farm Is a Factory: The Opportunity of the Town Lies in the Country* (Chicago, IL: International Harvester, 1916).

9. Deborah Fitzgerald, *Every Farm a Factory: The Industrial Ideal in American Agriculture* (New Haven, CT: Yale University Press, 2002); Malenbaum, *World Wheat Economy*; Friedmann, "Political Economy of Food."

10. League of Nations, *Nutrition: Final Report of the Mixed Committee of the League of Nations on the Relation of Nutrition to Health, Agriculture, and Economic Policy* (Geneva: League of Nations, 1937). See also Etienne Burnet and Wallace Ruddell Aykroyd, "Nutrition and Public Health," *League of Nations Quarterly Bulletin of the Health Organisation* 4, no. 2 (June 1935): 327–458.

11. "The Staff of Nations," *New York Times*, September 4, 1937, 14.

12. John D. Shaw, *World Food Security: A History since 1945* (New York: Palgrave Macmillan, 2007), 3–7; Nick Cullather, "The Foreign Policy of the Calorie," *American Historical Review* 112, no. 2 (2007): 360–362; Friedmann, "Political Economy of Food," S256–S260.

13. Cullather, "Foreign Policy of the Calorie," 357.

14. Collingham, *Taste of War*, 1–64; Timothy Snyder, *Black Earth: The Holocaust as History and Warning* (New York: Tim Duggan Books, 2015), 1–28.

15. Friedmann, "Political Economy of Food," S260–271; Shaw, *World Food Security*, 3–7; Cullather, "Foreign Policy of the Calorie," 360–364.

16. Harvey Levenstein, *Paradox of Plenty: A Social History of Eating in Modern America* (Berkeley: University of California Press, 2003), 65.

17. On food strategies during World War I, see Harvey Levenstein, *Revolution at the Table: The Transformation of the American Diet* (Berkeley: University of California Press, 2003), 137–146; Alesia Maltz, "'Plant a Victory Garden: Our Food Is Fighting': Lessons of Food Resilience from World War," *Journal of Environmental Studies and Sciences* 5, no. 3 (2015): 392–403.

18. Judith Russell and Renee Fantin, *Studies in Food Rationing* (report, Office of Price Administration, Historical Reports in War Administration General Publication no. 13, Washington, DC: Government Printing Office, 1948); George H. Gallup, *Public Opinion 1935-1971*, vol. 1 (New York: Random House, 1972), 506.

19. Gallup, *Public Opinion 1935-1971*, 426.

20. Levenstein, *Paradox of Plenty*, 80–87; Russell and Fantin, *Studies in Food Rationing*; Helen Marie Pundt, *AHEA: A History of Excellence* (Washington, DC: American Home Economics Association, 1980), 174–177.

21. Levenstein, *Paradox of Plenty*, 89.
22. T. Swann Harding, "Facts about Food for 1943," *New Leader*, March 20, 1943, 5.
23. Jean Drew, "Gal in the GI Kitchen," *Collier's Weekly*, July 26, 1952, 36–39; Irene Nehrling, "How America's Soldier Is Fed," *American Cookery*, March 1942, 342; Paul Dickson, *Chow: A Cook's Tour of Military Food* (New York: Plume, 1978), 47–63; Levenstein, *Paradox of Plenty*, 89–95.
24. Hershey Community Archives, "Ration D Bars," accessed May 1, 2016, http://www.hersheyarchives.org/essay/details.aspx?EssayId=26.
25. Dickson, *Chow*, 47–63; Levenstein, *Paradox of Plenty*, 89–95.
26. Franklin Delano Roosevelt, "Message to Congress 1941," January 6, 1941, 21, accessed May 1, 2016, http://www.fdrlibrary.marist.edu/pdfs/ffreadingcopy.pdf.
27. *Foreign Relations of the United States Diplomatic Papers*, 1941, vol. 1, general, the Soviet Union, eds. E. R. Perkins and Gustave A. Nuermberger (Washington, DC: Government Printing Office, 1958), 341–373, accessed May 1, 2016, http://digital.library.wisc.edu/1711.dl/FRUS.FRUS1941v01. See also, U.S. Department of State, Office of the Historian, "The Atlantic Conference and Charter, 1941," accessed May 1, 2016, https://history.state.gov/milestones/1937-1945/atlantic-conf.
28. Levenstein, *Paradox of Plenty*, 64–100; Norris E. Dodd, "The Food and Agriculture Organization of the United Nations: Its History, Organization and Objectives," *Agricultural History*, 23, no. 2 (1949): 83.
29. Collingham, *Taste of War*, 476–481; Hamblin, "Vulnerability of Nations," 42–65.
30. Collignham, *Taste of War*, 472.
31. Levenstein, *Paradox of Plenty*, 64–100; Dodd, "Food and Agriculture Organization."
32. "Text of Vice President Wallace's Address on this Nation's War Aims," *New York Times*, April 9, 1941, 18.
33. Dodd, "Food and Agriculture Organization," 85.
34. Friedmann, "Political Economy of Food," S260–S271; Shaw, *World Food Security*, 3–7; Cullather, "Foreign Policy of the Calorie," 360–364.
35. "Two Boards Set Up," *New York Times*, June 10, 1942, 1; S. McKee Rosen, *The Combined Boards of the Second World War: An Experiment in International Administration* (New York, Columbia University Press, 1951), 191–256.
36. Food and Agriculture Organization of the United Nations, *Proposals for a World Food Board* (Washington, DC: Food and Agriculture Organization, 1946).
37. "U.S. Position on World Food Proposals," *British Food Journal* 49, no. 3 (1947): 21–22.
38. Dodd, "Food and Agriculture Organization," 81–86.
39. For more on Orr's vision of a World Food Board, see Lord Boyd Orr, *As I Recall* (Garden City: Doubleday, 1967), 157–178; Amy L. S. Staples, "To Win the Peace: The Food and Agriculture Organization, Sir John Boyd Orr, and the World Food Board Proposals," *Peace and Change* 28, no. 4 (2003): 495–523; Amy Staples, *The Birth of Development: How the World Bank, Food and Agriculture Organization, and World Health Organization Changed the World, 1945-1965* (Kent, OH: Kent State University Press, 2006), 85–94; Shaw, *World Food Security*, 15–31; Jachertz and Nützenadel, "Coping with Hunger?," 99–119.

40. Allen W. Dulles, *The Marshall Plan* (Providence, RI: Berg, 1993), 63.

41. Food and Agriculture Organization of the United Nations, *World Food Appraisal for 1946-47* (Washington DC: Food and Agriculture Organization of the United Nations, 1946), 10.

42. William F. Sanford, *The Marshall Plan: Origins and Implementation* (Washington, DC: United Sates Department of State Bureau of Public Affairs, 1987), 3.

43. Michael Wala, *The Council on Foreign Relations and American Foreign Policy in the Early Cold War* (Providence, RI: Bergham Books, 1994), 103–104.

44. "Battle for Food" *New York Times*, February 10, 1946, 65.

45. Sanford, *Marshall Plan: Origins and Implementation*, 3; "World Famine Toll Seen Higher Than That of War," *New York Times*, February 18, 1946, 4; "Battle for Food," *New York Times*, February 10, 1946, 65; "Hoover Bids U.S. Save 500,000,000 in Famine Nations," *New York Times*, March 17, 1946, 1; "Foreign Food Production, Current Prospects for 1946–47" (report by United States Department of Agriculture, Office of Information, Washington DC, May 1946).

46. On wartime food relief efforts, see, for example, *Foreign Relations of the United States: Diplomatic Papers*, 1944, *General: Economic and Social Matters*, vol. 2, ed. E. Ralph Perkins, S. Everett Gleason, and Fredrick Aandahl (Washington, DC: Government Printing Office, 1963), docs. 194–228, accessed May 1, 2016, https://history.state.gov/historicaldocuments/frus1944v02.

47. On the formation of the UNRRA see, *Foreign Relations of the United States: Diplomatic Papers*, 1943, General, Vol. I, ed. William M. Franklin and E. R. Perkins (Washington, DC: Government Printing Office, 1963), docs. 762–863, accessed May 1, 2016, https://history.state.gov/historicaldocuments/frus1943v01.

48. Dulles, *Marshall Plan*, 63–64; Allen J. Matusow, *Farm Policies and Politics in the Truman Years* (Cambridge, MA: Harvard University Press, 1967), 35–36; Congressional Research Service, *Use of U.S. Food Resources*, 22–23; Michael J. Hogan, *The Marshall Plan: America, Britain, and the Reconstruction of Western Europe, 1947–1952* (New York: Cambridge University Press, 1987), 29.

49. Boyd Orr, *As I Recall*, 157–165; Shaw, *World Food Security*, 3–9; Staples, "To Win the Peace," 495–523; Cullather, "Foreign Policy of the Calorie," 362–363. Coverage of the conference is included in *Foreign Relations of the United States: Diplomatic Papers*, 1943, General, vol. I, ed. William M. Franklin and E. R. Perkins (Washington, DC: Government Printing Office, 1963), docs. 729–761, accessed May 1, 2016, https://history.state.gov/historicaldocuments/frus1943v01.

50. Coverage of the conference is included in *Foreign Relations of the United States: Diplomatic Papers*, 1944, General: Economic and Social Matters, vol. II, eds. E. Ralph Perkins, S. Everett Gleason, Fredrick Aandahl (Washington, DC: Government Printing Office, 1963), docs. 75–100, accessed May 1, 2016, https://history.state. gov/historicaldocuments/frus1943v01.

51. Dulles, *Marshall Plan*, 63–64; Hogan, *Marshall Plan: America, Britain*, 29. On Bretton Woods, see Alfred E. Eckes, *A Search for Solvency: Bretton Woods and the International Monetary System, 1941-1947* (Austin: University of Texas Press, 1975), 165–209; Georg Schild, *Bretton Woods and Dumbarton Oaks: American Economic and Political Postwar Planning in the Summer of 1944* (New York: St. Martin's Press,

1995); Michael D. Bordo and Barry Eichengreen, eds., *A Retrospective on the Bretton Woods System: Lessons for International Monetary Reform* (Chicago: University of Chicago Press, 1997).

52. On OXFAM see Maggie Black, *A Cause for Our Times: Oxfam the First 50 Years* (Oxford: Oxfam Professional, 1992). For the history of CARE, see Morris David, *A Gift from America: The First 50 Years of CARE* (Atlanta, GA: Longstreet Press, 1966).

53. Dulles, *Marshall Plan*, 63–65.

54. "Hoover Bids U.S. Save 500,000,000 in Famine Nations"; Jeremi Suri, *Liberty's Surest Guardian: Rebuilding Nations after War: From the Founders to Obama* (New York: Free Press, 2011), 139–141.

55. Henry Morgenthau Jr., *Germany Is Our Problem* (New York: Harper and Brothers, 1945), 46–48. For more on the Morgenthau Plan, see Hogan, *Marshall Plan: America, Britain*, 29; John Lewis Gaddis, *The United States and the Origins of the Cold War, 1941–1947* (New York: Columbia University Press, 2000), 117–120; John Morton Blum, *From the Morgenthau Diaries: Years of War, 1941-1945*, vol 3 (Boston: Houghton Mifflin, 1967), 356–378; "Morgenthau Plan Shelved," *New York Times*, September 28, 1944, 12; "Morgenthau Plan Discussed," *New York Times*, October 9, 1944, 22; State Department, "Fortnightly Survey of American Opinion on International Affairs, Survey No. 36," October 5, 1945. The plan also gained the attention of Nazi officials, who claimed it revealed the Allies' desire for revenge and retribution, see "Nazis Still Attack Morgenthau Project," *New York Times*, October 9, 1944, 3.

56. "1945 Directive to the Commander in Chief of U.S. Forces of Occupation (JCS 1067)," in United States Department of State, *Germany, 1947–1949: The Story in Documents* (Washington, DC: Government Printing Office, 1950), 21–32. See also *Foreign Relations of the United States: Diplomatic Papers*, 1945, European Advisory Commission, Austria, Germany, vol. III, ed. William Slany, John P. Glennon, Douglas W. Houston, N. O. Sappington, and George O. Kent (Washington, DC: Government Printing Office, 1968), docs. 308–375, accessed May 1, 2016, https://history.state.gov/historicaldocuments/frus1945v03/ch3.

57. Gaddis, *United States*, 122–131.

58. Herbert Hoover, "Report No. 3. The Necessary Steps for Promotion of German Exports, so as to Relieve American Taxpayers of the Burdens of Relief and for Economic Recovery of Europe," March 18, 1947, Papers of Harry S. Truman: Official Files, 12, accessed May 1, 2016, https://www.trumanlibrary.org/hoover/internaltemplate.php?tldate=1947-03-18&groupid=5170&collectionid=hoover.

59. "Text of the Hoover Mission's Findings on the Food Requirements of Germany," *New York Times*, February 28, 1947, 13.

60. Hoover's reports are reproduced in Herbert Hoover, *An American Epic: The Guns Cease Killing and Savings of Life from Famine Begins, 1939–1963*, vol. 4 (Chicago: Henry Regnery, 1964), 229–269. For more on their impact, see *Foreign Relations of the United States*, 1947, Council of Foreign Ministers; Germany and Austria, vol. II, ed. William Slany (Washington, DC: Government Printing Office, 1972), docs. 515–530, accessed May 1, 2016, https://history.state.gov/historical-documents/frus1947v02/ch12subch5.

61. "Text of the Hoover Mission's Findings."
62. "1947 Directive to the Commander in Chief of U.S. Forces of Occupation (JCS 1079)," in Department of State, *Germany 1947-1949*, 33–41.
63. Wala, *Council on Foreign Relations*, 103–105; Suri, *Liberty's Surest Guardian*, 141–151.
64. "Food Crises Rises, Aid Is Curtailed: Observers and Final Report of UNRRA Warn of World's Need this Winter," *New York Times*, November 3, 1946, 103; George Woodbridge, *UNRRA: The History of the United Nations Relief and Rehabilitation Administration* (New York: Columbia University Press, 1950).
65. George Kennan, "Excerpts from Telegraphic Message from Moscow of February 22, 1946," *Memoirs: 1925-1950* (Boston: Little, Brown, 1967), 559. See also *Foreign Relations of the United States*, 1946, Eastern Europe, the Soviet Union, vol. VI, eds Rogers P. Churchill and William Slany (Washington, DC: Government Printing Office, 1969), doc. 475, accessed May 1, 2016, https://history.state.gov/historical-documents/frus1946v06/d475.
66. John Lewis Gaddis, *The Cold War: A New History* (New York: Penguin, 2005), 27–30; Sanford, *Marshall Plan: Origins and Implementation*, 4–5.
67. "Text of President Truman's Speech on New Foreign Policy," *New York Times*, March 13, 1947, 2. Assessing the impact of the speech, the *Times* reported that Truman, once "rated timid, uncertain, and overpowered by events and responsibilities too big for him," had suddenly "emerged from comparative obscurity to the position of world leader." See Anne O'Hare McCormick, "The Emergence of President Truman as a World Leader," *New York Times*, March 15, 1947, 12.
68. Gaddis, *Cold War*, 28–31. For more on the Truman Doctrine, see *Foreign Relations of the United States*, 1948, Eastern Europe; the Soviet Union: vol. IV, ed. Rogers P. Churchill, William Slany, and Herbert A. Fine (Washington, DC: Government Printing Office, 1974), docs. 1–156, accessed May 1, 2016, https://history.state.gov/historicaldocuments/frus1948v04/ch1.
69. "Marshall's Civilian Dress His Right, Harvard Says," *New York Times*, June 6, 1947, 2.
70. "The News of the Week in Review: Plan for Europe," *New York Times*, June 15, 1947, sec. 4, 1.
71. "Marshall Sees Europe in Need of Vast New U.S. Aid; Urges Self-Help in Reconstruction," *Washington Post*, June 6, 1947, 1. The speech is also printed in *Foreign Relations of the United States*, 1947, Eastern Europe; the British Commonwealth; Europe, vol. III, ed. S. Everett Gleason and Frederick Aandahl (Washington, DC: Government Printing Office, 1972), doc. 140, accessed May 1, 2016, https://history.state.gov/historicaldocuments/frus1947v03/d140.
72. "Marshall Sees Europe in Need."
73. Kennan, "Excerpts from Telegraphic Message," 326.
74. Kennan, "Excerpts from Telegraphic Message," 311–343; Sanford, *Marshall Plan: Origins and Implementation*, 5–6.
75. Hogan, *Marshall Plan: America, Britain*, 26–40, 427; Gaddis, *United States*, 118–123; Sanford, *Marshall Plan: Origins and Implementation*, 6. For more on the origins of the Marshall Plan, see *Foreign Relations of the United States*, 1947, Eastern Europe;

the British Commonwealth; Europe, vol. III, ed. S. Everett Gleason and Frederick Aandahl (Washington, DC: Government Printing Office, 1972), docs. 128–143, accessed May 1, 2016, https://history.state.gov/historicaldocuments/frus1947v03/ch7subsubch1.

76. "Marshall Sees Europe in Need."

77. "Pas de Pagaille!," *Time*, July 28, 1947. For more on the conference, see Harry Bayard Price, *The Marshall Plan and Its Meaning* (Ithaca, NY: Cornell University Press, 1955), 29–39; *Foreign Relations of the United States*, 1947, Eastern Europe; The British Commonwealth; Europe, vol. III, eds. S. Everett Gleason and Frederick Aandahl (Washington, DC: Government Printing Office, 1972), docs. 144–257, accessed May 1, 2016, https://history.state.gov/historicaldocuments/frus1947v03/ch7subsubch2.

78. John Lewis Gaddis, *We Now Know: Rethinking Cold War History* (New York: Oxford University Press, 1997): 41–42. See also Scott D. Parrish, "The Turn Toward Confrontation: The Soviet Reaction to the Marshall Plan, 1947" (Cold War International History Project Working Paper No. 9, Washington, DC; Woodrow Wilson International Center for Scholars, 1994), 1–39; Mikhail M. Narinsky "The Soviet Union and the Marshall Plan," Cold War International History Project Working Paper No. 9 (Washington DC; Woodrow Wilson International Center for Scholars, 1994): 40–51.

79. Gaddis, *We Now Know*, 41–42; Parrish, "Turn Toward Confrontation"; Narinsky, "Soviet Union and the Marshall Plan."

80. Hogan, *Marshall Plan: America, Britain*, 51–53; Gaddis, *Cold War*, 32.

81. "Truman Calls Food Drive a 'Waste Less' Program," *New York Times*, September 26, 1947, 3.

82. "Texts of Truman's Food Plea and of the Cabinet Report," *New York Times*, September 26, 1947, 3.

83. Gallup, *Public Opinion 1935-1971*, 686.

84. Matusow, *Farm Policies and Politics*, 155–169.

85. Michael Wala, "Selling the Marshall Plan at Home: The Committee for the Marshall Plan to Aid European Recovery," *Diplomatic History* 10, no. 3 (1986): 247–265.

86. Quoted in Dulles, *Marshall Plan*, vii.

87. "CIO Overwhelmingly Supports Marshall and U.S. Foreign Policy," *The Kane Republican*, October 16, 1947, 1.

88. Gallup, *Public Opinion 1935-1971*, 683, 691; Matusow, *Farm Policies and Politics*, 157–160; Price, *The Marshall Plan and Its Meaning*, 39–60; Sanford, *Marshall Plan: Origins and Implementation*, 7–8.

89. Price, *The Marshall Plan and Its Meaning*, 39–70; Sanford, *Marshall Plan: Origins and Implementation*, 7–8; Matusow, *Farm Policies and Politics*, 157–160. For more on American responses to aid requests from Europe, see *Foreign Relations of the United States*, 1947, Eastern Europe; the British Commonwealth; Europe, vol. III, ed. S. Everett Gleason and Frederick Aandahl (Washington, DC: Government Printing Office, 1972), docs. 258–273, accessed May 1, 2016, https://history.state.gov/historicaldocuments/frus1947v03/ch7subsubch3.

90. Price, *The Marshall Plan and Its Meaning*, 49–70; Sanford, *Marshall Plan: Origins and Implementation*, 9–10.

91. Hearings before the Committee on Foreign Affairs on United States Foreign Policy for a Postwar Recovery Program, 80th Congress, 2d Session (1948), 940–941. In *Marshall Plan Volume*, accessed May 1, 2016, http://marshallfoundation. org/library/collection/marshall-plan-volume/#!/collection=335.

92. Hearings before the Committee on Foreign Affairs on United States Foreign Policy for a Postwar Recovery Program, 80th Congress, 2d Session (1948), 1122–1126. In *Marshall Plan Volume*, accessed May 1, 2016, http://marshallfoundation.org/ library/collection/marshall-plan-volume/#!/collection=335.

93. Price, *The Marshall Plan and Its Meaning*, 49–70; Sanford, *Marshall Plan: Origins and Implementation*, 9–10.

94. "Marshall Sees Europe in Need"; Gaddis, *Cold War*, 30–32; Sanford, *Marshall Plan: Origins and Implementation*, 5–6.

95. Dulles, *Marshall Plan*, 73.

96. U.S. Department of the Interior, *Natural Resources and Foreign Aid: Report of J. A. Krug, Secretary of the Interior, October 9, 1947* (Washington DC: Government Printing Office, 1947), 5–6.

97. Gaddis, *Cold War*, 30–32; Sanford, *Marshall Plan: Origins and Implementation*, 5–6.

98. U.S. Bureau of the Census, *Statistical Abstract of the United States: 1949* (70th ed.). (Washington, DC: Government Printing Office, 1949), 852.

99. U.S. Bureau of the Census, *Statistical Abstract of the United States: 1954* (75th anniv. ed.) (Washington, DC: Government Printing Office, 1954), 903.

100. Congressional Research Service, *Use of U.S. Food Resources*, 24.

101. Congressional Research Service, *Use of U.S. Food Resources*, 24.

102. Congressional Research Service, *Use of U.S. Food Resources*, 23–24, 76.

103. Henry R. Luce, "The American Century," *Life*, February 14, 1951, 61–65.

104. Kennan, "Excerpts from Telegraphic Message," 335.

105. Price, *The Marshall Plan and Its Meaning*, 394.

106. For discussions of the importance and impact of the Marshall Plan, see William Diebold Jr., "The Marshall Plan in Retrospect: A Review of Recent Scholarship," *Journal of International Affairs* 41 (Summer 1988): 421–35; Michael Cox and Caroline Kennedy-Pipe, "The Tragedy of American Diplomacy? Rethinking the Marshall Plan," *Journal of Cold War Studies* 7, no. 1 (2005): 97–134. For examples of invocations of the Marshall Plan, see Albert Gore, *Earth in the Balance: Ecology and the Human Spirit* (Boston: Houghton Mifflin, 1992); Dick Bell and Michael Renner, "A New Marshall Plan? Advancing Human Security and Controlling Terrorism," Worldwatch Institute, accessed May 1, 2016, http://www.worldwatch. org/new-marshall-plan-advancing-human-security-and-controlling-terrorism; and "Brown Calls for Africa Marshall Plan," *The Guardian*, June 3, 2005.

107. Gaddis, *Cold War*, 5–10.

108. Gaddis, *Cold War*, 34–40.

CHAPTER 2

1. "U.S. Gives Soviet Glittering Show: Fair Found Lavish in Color and Frills, but Lacking a Unifying Theme," *New York Times*, July 25, 1959, 2.

2. Monte Olmsted, "Nixon, Khrushchev and Betty Crocker at the 1959 'Kitchen Debate,'" *Taste of General Mills*, July 24, 2013, accessed May 1, 2016, http://blog. generalmills.com/2013/07/nixon-khrushchev-and-betty-crocker-at-the-1959-kitchen-debate/#sthash.1ntm5C9z.dpuf.

3. Olmsted, "Nixon, Khrushchev and Betty Crocker at the 1959 'Kitchen Debate;'" Carroll Pursell, *Technology in Postwar America: A History* (New York: Columbia University Press, 2013), 101–102; Harvey Levenstein, *Paradox of Plenty: A Social History of Eating in Modern America* (Berkeley: University of California Press, 2003), 114; Elaine Tyler May, *Homeward Bound: American Families in the Cold War Era* (New York: Basic Books, 2008), 19–38; Shane Hamilton and Sarah Phillips, *The Kitchen Debate and Cold War Consumer Politics: A Brief History with Documents* (Boston: Bedford St. Martins, 2014), 1–2. On the role of art in the American National Exhibition, see Marilyn S. Kushner. "Exhibiting Art at the American National Exhibition in Moscow, 1959: Domestic Politics and Cultural Diplomacy," *Journal of Cold War Studies* 4, no.1 (2002): 6–26.

4. Hamilton and Philips, 27–28; John Lewis Gaddis, *The Cold War: A New History* (New York: Penguin, 2005), 83–85.

5. On postwar consumption in America, see Gary S. Cross, *An All-Consuming Century: Why Commercialism Won in Modern America* (New York: Columbia University Press, 2000); Lizabeth Cohen, *A Consumer's Republic: The Politics of MA Consumption in Postwar America* (New York: Vintage Books, 2004); May, *Homeward Bound*.

6. See Ruth Jachertz and Alexander Nützenadel, "Coping with Hunger? Visions of a Global Food System, 1930-1960," *Journal of Global History* 6,, no. 1 (2011): 99–119; Lizzie Collingham, *Taste of War: World War II and the Battle for Food* (New York: Penguin, 2012); Jacob Darwin Hamblin, "The Vulnerability of Nations: Food Security in the Aftermath of World War II," *Global Environment* 10 (2012): 42–65.

7. "Revolution, Not Revolt," *Time* 67, no. 19 (1956), 31.

8. U.S. Bureau of the Census, *Statistical Abstract of the United States: 1959* (Eightieth ed.). (Washington, DC: Government Printing Office, 1959), 655.

9. U.S. Bureau of the Census, *Statistical Abstract of the United States: 1959*, 649.

10. Bruce L. Gardner, *American Agriculture in the Twentieth Century: How It Flourished and What It Cost* (Cambridge, MA: Harvard University Press, 2002), 28–47. Sally Clark suggests the productivity rate may have increased by as much as three percent between 1935 and the mid-1980s, see Sally H. Clark, *Regulation and the Revolution in United States Farm Productivity* (New York: Cambridge University Press, 2002), 3–6.

11. "The Pushbutton Cornucopia," *Time* 73, no. 10 (1959), 76.

12. Paul Conkin, *A Revolution Down on the Farm: The Transformation of American Agriculture since 1929* (Lexington, KY: University Press of Kentucky, 2008), 97–122.

13. "Congress Eyes your Market Bill: How Much Is Food, How Much Is Frills?" *Santa Cruz Sentinel*, May 29, 1957, 6.

14. "Farmer's Share of Food Dollar Is at New Postwar Low," *The Index-Journal*, October 2, 1953, 6.

15. "Loyalty Is Found for Brand Names: Grocery Convention Hears Results of Buyer Survey," *New York Times*, November 14, 1962, 53.

16. "The Fabulous Market for Food," *Fortune*, October 1953, 139.

17. Levenstein, *Paradox of Plenty*, 105.

18. Alfred Stefferud, "Preface" in *Food: The Yearbook of Agriculture 1959*, United States Department of Agriculture (Washington, DC: Government Printing Office, 1959), vii.

19. "Congress Eyes your Market Bill"; Levenstein, *Paradox of Plenty*, 101–118. On middle-class Americans use of servants and cooks, see Harvey Levenstein, *Revolution at the Table: The Transformation of the American Diet* (Berkeley, CA: University of California Press, 2003), 60–71.

20. "Fabulous Market for Food," 135.

21. "Fabulous Market for Food," 134.

22. "Fabulous Market for Food," 134–139, 271–274, 276, 278; Levenstein, *Paradox of Plenty*, 101–118; Conkin, *Revolution Down on the Farm*, 124.

23. "Congress Eyes your Market Bill."

24. "Congress Looks at Market Bill to Find Frills," *The Rhinelander Daily News*, May 16, 1957, 4.

25. "Congress Eyes your Market Bill."

26. "Congress Eyes your Market Bill."

27. Marguerite Burk, "Pounds and Percentages," in *Food: The Yearbook of Agriculture 1959*, United States Department of Agriculture (Washington, DC: Government Printing Office, 1959), 591–599.

28. "American Diet Is the Best, Most Expensive in History," *The Decatur Herald*, October 3, 1953, 8.

29. "Good Food Year Seen," *Delaware County Daily Times*, January 4, 1955, 37.

30. "Congress Eyes your Market Bill."

31. "The History of Mixes: Ten Year Success Story," *Practical Home Economics*, September 1958, 76.

32. "Fabulous Market for Food," 137.

33. Burk, 596.

34. Burk, 593.

35. "Fabulous Market for Food," 271.

36. "U.S. Diet Is Best Ever," *Anniston Star* (Alabama), September 29, 1953, 4.

37. R. D. McKirahan, J. C. Connell and S. J. Hotchner, "Application of Differentially Coated Tin Plate for Food Containers," *Food Technology* 13 (1959): 228–232; Robert L. Olson, "The Implications of Food Acceptability for Shelter Occupancy," in *Symposium on Human Problems in the Utilization of Fallout Shelters*, eds. George

W. Baker and John H. Rohrer (Washington, DC: National Academy of Sciences / National Research Council, 1960), 170.

38. Mildred Boggs and Clyde Rasmussen, "Modern Food Processing," in *Food: The Yearbook of Agriculture 1959*, United States Department of Agriculture (Washington DC, Government Printing Office, 1959), 420; Levenstein, *Paradox of Plenty*, 109.

39. "Fabulous Market for Food," 271.

40. "Cycla-matic at Walter Reed's," *Monroe Morning World* (Louisiana), March 30, 1952, 6; and "Refrigerator Is 'No Defrosting'" *Monroe Morning World* (Louisiana), March 30, 1952, 6. For more on the history of frozen foods, see Shane Hamilton, "The Economies and Conveniences of Modern-Day Living: Frozen Foods and MA Marketing, 1945–1965," *Business History Review* 77, no.1 (2003): 33–60; Smith, *Eating History*, 164–173.

41. "Fabulous Market for Food," 276.

42. "Fill Your Easter Basket with These IGA Savings," *Lewiston Daily Sun* (Maine), April 8, 1955, 9.

43. "Loyalty Is Found for Brand Names: Grocery Convention Hears Results of Buyer Survey," *New York Times*, November 14, 1962, 53.

44. On the importance of the rise of the trucking industry, see Shane Hamilton, *Trucking Country: The Road to America's Wal-Mart Economy* (Princeton, NJ: Princeton University Press, 2008).

45. Levenstein, *Revolution at the Table*, 30–43.

46. "Processors Deny U.S. Is Poorly Fed: Nation's Diet More Plentiful, Delicious and Nutritious, Spokesman Asserts Limit to Market Denied," *New York Times*, February 2, 1956, 35.

47. Krispy Automatic Ring-King Junior Doughnut Machine, National Museum of American History, ID Number: 1997.0179.01, accessed May 1, 2016, http://americanhistory.si.edu/collections/search/object/nmah_1215321; Bridget Madden, "July 1937: Krispy Kreme Opens in Winston-Salem," *This Month in North Carolina History*, July 2009, accessed May 1, 2016, http://www.learnnc.org/lp/editions/nchist-worldwar/5899.

48. Levenstein, *Paradox of Plenty*, 108.

49. Boggs and Rasmussen, "Modern Food Processing," 428; Levenstein, *Paradox of Plenty*, 109; Ann Vileisis, *Kitchen Literacy: How We Lost Knowledge of Where Food Comes From and Why We Need to Get It Back* (Washington, DC: Island Press, 2008), 185–196.

50. In-N-Out Burger, "In-N-Out Burger History," accessed May 1, 2016, http://shop.in-n-out.com/history.aspx; Nate Barksdale, "Fries with That? A Brief History of Drive-Thru Dining," History.com, May 16, 2014, accessed May 1, 2016, http://www.history.com/news/hungry-history/fries-with-that-a-brief-history-of-drive-thru-dining.

51. Ruth Noble, *A Guide to Distinctive Dining* (Cambridge, MA: Berkshire, 1954).

52. Duncan Hines, *Duncan Hines Food Odyssey* (New York: Crowell, 1955); "Hines Abroad," *New Yorker*, July 24, 1954: 15; Levenstein, *Paradox of Plenty*, 125–130.

53. John Love, *McDonald's: Behind the Arches* (New York: Bantam Books, 1995); John Vidal, *McLibel: Burger Culture on Trial* (New York: New Press, 1997); Ted Steinberg,

Down to Earth: Nature's Role in American History, 3rd ed. (New York: Oxford University Press, 2013), 195–196.

54. Levenstein, *Paradox of Plenty*, 127–130.

55. Levenstein, *Paradox of Plenty*, 117.

56. "Loyalty Is Found for Brand Names: Grocery Convention Hears Results of Buyer Survey," *New York Times*, November 14, 1962, 53.

57. Levenstein, *Paradox of Plenty*, 117–118.

58. Levenstein, *Paradox of Plenty*, 113–125; Smith, *Eating History*, 174–183.

59. For more on partnerships between home economics and the food industry, see Levenstein, *Revolution at the Table*, 72–97.

60. Centron Corporation, *Why Study Home Economics?*, film, Lawrence, Kansas, 1955, accessed May 1, 2016, https://archive.org/details/0130_Why_Study_Home_Economics_20_47_09_00.

61. Centron Corporation, *Buying Food*, film, Lawrence, Kansas, 1950, accessed May 1, 2016, https://archive.org/details/buying_food.

62. Centron, *Buying Food*; "Fabulous Market for Food," 274 and 276.

63. On the history of food labeling in the United States, see Institute of Medicine (IOM), *Examination of Front-of-Package Nutrition Rating Systems and Symbols: Phase I Report* (Washington, DC: National Academies Press, 2010), 19–36.

64. For more on the importance of films in civic education, see Arnold Ringstad, "The Evolution of American Civil Defense Film Rhetoric," *Journal of Cold War Studies* 14, no. 4 (Fall 2012): 93–121. On films and Home Economics, see Julia Barnard. "Home Economics and 'Housewifery' in 1950s America," in *The Role of Food in American Society*, KU Scholarworks, 2010, accessed May 1, 2016, http://kuscholarworks.ku.edu/handle/1808/6329.

65. The notion of the family as a bulwark against threats such as communism is discussed in May, *Homeward Bound*, and also in Sarah A. Lichtman, "Do-It-Yourself Security: Safety, Gender, and the Home Fallout Shelter in Cold War America," *Journal of Design History* 19, no. 1 (2006): 39–55.

66. Levenstein, *Revolution at the Table*, especially chapters 6 and 16.

67. Cullather, "Foreign Policy of the Calorie," 339.

68. Cullather, "Foreign Policy of the Calorie," 337–364. See also Amy Staples, *The Birth of Development: How the World Bank, Food and Agriculture Organization, and World Health Organization Changed the World, 1945-1965* (Kent, OH: Kent State University Press, 2006); Cullather, *Hungry World*.

69. Levenstein, *Revolution at the Table*, 45–47.

70. Wilbur O. Atwater, "The Chemistry of Foods and Nutrition: The Composition of Our Bodies and Our Food," *Century Magazine*, May 1887, 59–73; Wilbur O. Atwater, "The Pecuniary Economy of Food: The Chemistry of Foods and Nutrition," *Century Magazine*, January 1888, 437–445; Levenstein, *Revolution at the Table*, 45–46.

71. Levenstein, *Revolution at the Table*, 45–46.

72. Edward Atkinson, "The Art of Cooking," *Popular Science Monthly* 36 (November 1889); Levenstein, *Revolution at the Table*, 48.

73. Charlotte Smith Angstman, "College Women and the New Science," in *Appleton's Popular Science Monthly*, ed. William Jay Youmans, 53 (May–October 1898*): 674–690*; Caroline Louisa Hunt, *The Life of Ellen H. Richards, 1842-1911*, anniversary ed. (Washington, DC: American Home Economics Association, 1958); Levenstein, *Revolution at the Table*, 48–59.

74. James Hargrove, "History of the Calorie in Nutrition," *Journal of Nutrition* 136, no. 12 (2006): 2957–2961; Levenstein, *Revolution at the Table*, 72–74.

75. "The Wesleyan Calorimeter: Account of the Tests to Which A. W. Smith Was Subjected," *New York Times*, April 5, 1986, 5.

76. "Human Body and Food: Law Governing Its Consumption and Utilization Shown by the Respiration Calorimeter Experiment," *New York Times*, March 23, 1899, 3.

77. Cullather, "Foreign Policy of the Calorie," 339–340; "Armsby Calorimeter" History of the Department of Dairy and Animal Science, Penn State University, accessed May 1, 2016, http://animalscience.psu.edu/about/history/armsby-calorimeter.

78. Wilbur O. Atwater, "The Food Supply of the Future," *Century Magazine*, November 1891, 101–111.

79. Cullather, "Foreign Policy of the Calorie," 339–342.

80. A. P. Knight, "The Germ Theory of Disease," *Queen's Quarterly* 5 (July 1, 1897): 22–26.

81. Levenstein, *Revolution at the Table*, 147–153.

82. Levenstein, *Revolution at the Table*, 147–153.

83. "Experts Map Plan of Diet Education for Our Defense: Nation's Housewives Are to Be Enlisted in 'All-Out' Effort for Preparedness," *New York Times*, January 22, 1941, 1.

84. Levenstein, *Paradox of Plenty*, 9–23, 64–66.

85. Ezra Taft Benson, foreword to *Food: The Yearbook of Agriculture 1959*, United States Department of Agriculture (Washington, DC: Government Printing Office, 1959), v.

86. Hazel Sterling, "Food in Our Lives," in *Food: The Yearbook of Agriculture 1959*, United States Department of Agriculture (Washington, DC: Government Printing Office, 1959), 1.

87. National Research Council, *Recommended Dietary Allowances: Revised 1958* (Washington, DC: National Academy of Sciences, 1958).

88. Robert E. Shank, "The 1958 Revision of Recommended Dietary Allowances," *American Journal of Public Health* 49, no. 8 (August 1959): 1001.

89. Ruth Leverton, "Recommended Allowances," in *Food: The Yearbook of Agriculture 1959*, United States Department of Agriculture (Washington, DC: Government Printing Office, 1959), 227–230.

90. Ezra Taft Benson, foreword to *Food*, v.

91. Cullather, "Foreign Policy of the Calorie," 342.

92. See Herman Kahn, *Thinking about the Unthinkable* (New York: Horizon Press, 1962); and Jacob Darwin Hamblin, *Arming Mother Nature: The Birth of Catastrophic Environmentalism* (New York: Oxford University Press, 2013).

CHAPTER 3

1. "Minnesota Farm Disquiet Found Aiding Democrats," *New York Times*, October 19, 1958, 1.

2. Ezra Taft Benson, *Freedom to Farm* (Garden City, NY: Doubledayand, 1960), 12.

3. Benson, *Freedom to Farm*, 11–17; Edward L. Schapsmeier and Frederick H. Schapsmeier, "Eisenhower and Ezra Taft Benson: Farm Policy in the 1950s," *Agricultural History* 44, no. 4 (1970): 369–378.

4. Benson, *Freedom to Farm*, 11–17; Schapsmeier and Schapsmeier, "Eisenhower and Ezra Taft Benson." For concerns about the political impact of Benson's policies, see "Kerr Warns Benson Is Sowing Seeds of GOP Defeat in '54," *Winona Republican-Herald*, February 9, 1953, 1; "Demos Hope Benson Will Stick Around as Target," *Salina Journal* (Kansas), January 2, 1956, 7; "Benson Finds Trouble a Big Part of His Job," *New York Times*, February 5, 1956, 187; " 'Benson-Must-Go' Cry Now Louder in G.O.P.: President, Who Urged the Secretary to Stay, Is in Difficult Position," *New York Times*, November 24, 1957; "Friends Urged Benson to Fight," *New York Times*, December 14, 1957, 14.

5. "Minnesota Farm Disquiet Found Aiding Democrats."

6. "Minnesota Farm Disquiet Found Aiding Democrats." See also "Get Big or Get Out! Is That Formula for Farm Success?" *Wilmington News-Journal*, April 7, 1959, 21.

7. Schapsmeier and Schapsmeier, "Eisenhower and Ezra Taft Benson."

8. Nick Cullather, *The Hungry World* (Cambridge, MA: Harvard University Press, 2010), 142–146.

9. Raymond E. Owens, "An Overview of Agricultural Policy; . . . Past Present and Future," Federal Reserve Bank of Richmond, *Economic Review*, May/June 1987, 39–50; and Edward L. Schapsmeier and Frederick H. Schapsmeier, *Ezra Taft Benson and the Politics of Agriculture: The Eisenhower Years, 1953-1961* (Danville, IL: Interstate Printers and Publishers, 1975), 2. On the history of American agricultural policy, see Murray R. Benedict, *Farm Policies of the United States: 1790-1950* (New York: Octagon Books, 1966); John Schlebecker, *Whereby We Thrive: A History of American Farming, 1607-1972* (Ames: Iowa State University Press, 1975); Willard W. Cochrane and Mary E. Ryan, *American Farm Policy, 1948-1973* (Minneapolis: University of Minnesota Press, 1976); Gilbert Fite, *American Farmers: The New Minority* (Bloomington: Indiana University Press, 1981); Don Paarlberg and Philip Paarlberg, *The Agricultural Revolution of the 20th Century* (Ames: Iowa State University Press, 2000); Bruce L. Gardner, *American Agriculture in the Twentieth Century: How It Flourished and What It Cost* (Cambridge, MA: Harvard University Press, 2002); Deborah Kay Fitzgerald, *Every Farm a Factory: The Industrial Ideal in American Agriculture* (New Haven, CT: Yale University Press, 2003); Conkin, *Revolution Down on the Farm*; and Shane Hamilton, "Agribusiness, the Family Farm, and the Politics of Technological Determinism in the Post–World War II United States," *Technology and Culture* 55, no. 3 (2014): 560–590.

10. Owens, "Overview of Agricultural Policy," 39–40. Schapsmeier and Schapsmeier, *Ezra Taft Benson and the Politics of Agriculture*, 2; Martin Fausold, "President

Hoover's Farm Policies 1929-1933," *Agricultural History* 51, no. 2 (April 1977): 362–377.

11. On parity, see E. W. Grove, *The Concept of Income Parity for Agriculture, Studies in Income and Wealth*, vol. 6 (New York: National Bureau of Economic Research, 1937); Gilbert C. Fite, *George N. Peek and the Fight for Farm Parity* (Norman: University of Oklahoma Press, 1954); United States Department of Agriculture, National Agricultural Statistics Service, "Parity Prices, Parity Ratio, and Feed Price Ratios" in United States Department of Agriculture, National Agricultural Statistics Service, Price Program: History, Concepts, Methodology, Analysis, Estimates and Dissemination (2001), 4-1-4-17, accessed May 1, 2016, http://www.nass.usda.gov/Surveys/Guide_to_NASS_Surveys/Prices/Price_Program_Methodology_v11_03092015.pdf.

12. Owens, "Overview of Agricultural Policy," 48; Conkin, *Revolution Down on the Farm*, 51–76.

13. Owens, "Overview of Agricultural Policy," 39–50; Schapsmeier and Schapsmeier, *Ezra Taft Benson and the Politics of Agriculture*, 2; Virgil W. Dean, *An Opportunity Lost: The Truman Administration and the Farm Policy Debate* (Columbia: University of Missouri Press, 2006), 78–109.

14. Harry S. Truman, "Statement by the President upon Signing the Agricultural Act," July 3, 1948. Gerhard Peters and John T. Woolley, *The American Presidency Project*, website, accessed May 1, 2016, http://www.presidency.ucsb.edu/ws/?pid=12956.

15. Harry S. Truman, "Statement by the President upon Signing the Agricultural Act."

16. Owens, "Overview of Agricultural Policy," 39–50. Schapsmeier and Schapsmeier, *Ezra Taft Benson and the Politics of Agriculture*, 2; Dean, *Opportunity Lost*, 78–109.

17. Quoted in R. Douglas Hurt, *Problems of Plenty: The American Farmer in the Twentieth Century* (Chicago: Ivan R. Dee, 2002), 107.

18. Hurt, *Problems of Plenty*, 107–108; Dean, *Opportunity Lost*, 110–200; Conkin, *Revolution Down on the Farm*, 126–130.

19. Conkin, *Revolution Down on the Farm*, 123–124; Dean, *Opportunity Lost*, 201–241.

20. "Prosperity Issue Again Key to the Farm Vote: Observers Feel That a Lot May Depend On the Price Picture in November," *New York Times*, August 17, 1952, E10; Schapsmeier and Schapsmeier, *Ezra Taft Benson and the Politics of Agriculture*, 4–7; Conkin, *Revolution Down on the Farm*, 123–124; Dean, *Opportunity Lost*, 201–241.

21. "Debate Is Held on Price Support," *Maryville Daily Forum*, October 12, 1948, 1; "Farm Price Jitters Ebb in the Midwest," *New York Times*, September 5, 1949, 14; "Ike Pledges to Support Present Farm Prices," *Edwardsville Intelligencer*, September 6, 1952, 1.

22. Schapsmeier and Schapsmeier, *Ezra Taft Benson and the Politics of Agriculture*, 6–7; "Prosperity Issue Again Key to the Farm Vote: Observers Feel That a Lot May Depend on the Price Picture in November," *New York Times*, August 17, 1952, E10.

23. "Text of Address by Eisenhower Pledging Aid for Agriculture," *New York Times*, September 7, 1952, 70.

24. On the grain storage hoax, see "A Truman Hoax," *Pittsburgh Press*, August 14, 1952, 18; Allen J. Matusow, *Farm Policies and Politics in the Truman Years* (Cambridge, MA: Harvard University Press, 1967), 170–190.

25. "Text of Address by Eisenhower Pledging Aid for Agriculture."

26. "Text of Address by Eisenhower Pledging Aid for Agriculture."

27. "Politics: Eisenhower," *Traverse City Record-Eagle*, September 6, 1952, p. 1; "Ike Ends Blazing Dixie Tour: No 'Breadlines, Depression' Are General's Promises in Memphis Talk," *Beckley Post-Herald*, October 16, 1952, 1.

28. Schapsmeier and Schapsmeier, *Ezra Taft Benson and the Politics of Agriculture*, 8.

29. "Truman Sees Theft of Farm Policies: In Iowa He Accuses General of 'Baldest Attempt to Steal' Democratic Party Record," *New York Times*, October 9, 1952, 1.

30. Schapsmeier and Schapsmeier, *Ezra Taft Benson and the Politics of Agriculture*, 6–11.

31. Ezra Taft Benson, *Crossfire: The Eight Years with Eisenhower* (Garden City: NY, 1962), 3–12; Schapsmeier and Schapsmeier, *Ezra Taft Benson and the Politics of Agriculture*, 12–16; "Ezra Taft Benson: Thirteenth President of the Church," in *Presidents of the Church Student Manual*, 2012, 216–236, accessed May 1, 2016, https://www.lds.org/manual/presidents-of-the-church-student-manual/ezra-taft-benson-thirteenth-president-of-the-church?lang=eng. A further sign of the esteem in which Eisenhower held his secretary of agriculture was his selecting Benson as the administrator designate of the Emergency Food Agency, a secret group that became known as the Eisenhower Ten, created by Eisenhower in 1958 to serve in the event of a national emergency such as a nuclear war. Bill Geerhart, "The Eisenhower Ten: Ezra Taft Benson." *Conelrad*, accessed May 1, 2016, http://conelrad.com/atomicsecrets/secrets.php?secrets=e02.

32. Benson, *Crossfire*, 51.

33. "Behind the Committee Doors: The Senate Questions Ike's Cabinet," *New Republic*, February 2, 1953, 1–2.

34. Benson, *Crossfire*, 61.

35. "General Statement on Agricultural Policy," reproduced in Benson, *Crossfire*, 602–605.

36. Benson, *Crossfire*, 61.

37. Benson, *Crossfire*, 51–63; Schapsmeier and Schapsmeier, *Ezra Taft Benson and the Politics of Agriculture*, 34–39; Denis S. Nordin and Roy V. Scott, *From Prairie Farmer to Entrepreneur: The Transformation of Midwestern Agriculture* (Bloomington: Indiana University Press, 2005), 165–166.

38. "Benson Outlines Long-Term Policy: Backs Price Props Primarily as Disaster Bar—Self-Help, Not Federal Aid, Stressed," *New York Times*, February 6, 1953, 13.

39. "General Statement on Agricultural Policy," 603.

40. Benson, *Crossfire*, 63.

41. Benson, *Crossfire*, 51–63; Schapsmeier and Schapsmeier, *Ezra Taft Benson and the Politics of Agriculture*, 34–39.

42. Benson, *Crossfire*, 58.

43. Benson, *Crossfire*, 51–63; Schapsmeier and Schapsmeier, *Ezra Taft Benson and the Politics of Agriculture*, 34–39.

44. "General Statement on Agricultural Policy," 602.

45. Benson, *Crossfire*, 58.

46. Quoted in "Revolution, Not Revolt," 31.

47. Ezra Taft Benson as Told to Carlisle Bargeron, *Farmers at the Crossroads* (New York: Devin-Adair Company, 1956), especially chapters 1 and 3.

48. Benson, *Crossfire*, 58.

49. Benson, *Crossfire*, 58.

50. "Benson Plans Trip to 'Sell' His Views," *New York Times*, March 1, 1953, 55.

51. Benson, *Crossfire*, 204; Schapsmeier and Schapsmeier, *Ezra Taft Benson and the Politics of Agriculture*, 59–80.

52. "Price Support Is Advocated by Benson Here," *Kossauth County Advance*, October 14, 1954, 1.

53. Quoted in Schapsmeier and Schapsmeier, *Ezra Taft Benson and the Politics of Agriculture*, 75.

54. Benson, *Crossfire*, 204; Schapsmeier and Schapsmeier, *Ezra Taft Benson and the Politics of Agriculture*, 59–80.

55. Quoted in Schapsmeier and Schapsmeier, *Ezra Taft Benson and the Politics of Agriculture*, 82.

56. "Ike Pleads for Political Unity behind Program," *San Bernardino County Sun*, June 11, 1954, 1.

57. Benson, *Crossfire*, 204; Schapsmeier and Schapsmeier, *Ezra Taft Benson and the Politics of Agriculture*, 80–82.

58. Dwight D. Eisenhower, "Statement by the President upon Signing the Agricultural Act of 1954," August 28, 1954. Gerhard Peters and John T. Woolley, *The American Presidency Project* website, accessed May 1, 2016, http://www.presidency.ucsb.edu/ws/?pid=10010.

59. On the history of school lunch programs in the United States, see Janet Poppendieck, *Free for All: Fixing School Food in America* (Berkeley: University of California Press, 2010), especially chapter 2.

60. "Farm Bill Will Count in Election: Farm Leaders Credit Benson with Victory in Bill Passage," *Sedalia Democrat* (Missouri), August 15, 1954, 1; "Gratifying Victory," *San Bernardino County Sun*, August 11, 1954, 24.

61. Quoted in Benson, *Crossfire*, 211.

62. Schapsmeier and Schapsmeier, *Ezra Taft Benson and the Politics of Agriculture*, 82–91, Eisenhower, "Statement by the President"; Benson, *Crossfire*, 204–211.

63. Schapsmeier and Schapsmeier, *Ezra Taft Benson and the Politics of Agriculture*, 125–154; Conkin, *Revolution Down on the Farm*, 129.

64. Quoted in Schapsmeier and Schapsmeier, *Ezra Taft Benson and the Politics of Agriculture*, 151.

65. Schapsmeier and Schapsmeier, *Ezra Taft Benson and the Politics of Agriculture*, 125–154; Schlebecker, *Whereby We Thrive*, 278.

66. Quoted in "Revolution, Not Revolt."

67. Quoted in Schapsmeier and Schapsmeier, *Ezra Taft Benson and the Politics of Agriculture*, 160.

68. Dwight D. Eisenhower, "Veto of the Farm Bill," April 16, 1956. Gerhard Peters and John T. Woolley, *The American Presidency Project*, website, accessed May 1, 2016, http://www.presidency.ucsb.edu/ws/?pid=10781.

69. Schapsmeier and Schapsmeier, *Ezra Taft Benson and the Politics of Agriculture*, 154–165; "Revolution, Not Revolt."

70. J. Douglas Helms, "Brief History of the USDA Soil Bank Program." *Historical Insights* no. 1 (January 1985) USDA Natural Resources Conservation Service, 1–3; Conkin, *Revolution Down on the Farm*, 129–130; Schapsmeier and Schapsmeier, *Ezra Taft Benson and the Politics of Agriculture*, 165–170.

71. Helms, "Brief History," 1–3; Conkin, *Revolution Down on the Farm*, 129–130; Schapsmeier and Schapsmeier, *Ezra Taft Benson and the Politics of Agriculture*, 165–170; Cochrane and Ryan, *American Farm Policy*, 77–78.

72. Harriet Friedmann, "The Political Economy of Food: The Rise and Fall of the Postwar International Food Order," *American Journal of Sociology*, supplement 88 (1982): S261 and Earl O. Heady, Edwin O. Haroldsen, Leo V. Mayer, and Luther G. Tweeten, *The Roots of the Farm Problem* (Ames: Iowa State University Press, 1965), 1–44.

73. Schapsmeier and Schapsmeier, *Ezra Taft Benson and the Politics of Agriculture*, 74–76.

74. "Revolution, Not Revolt,"

75. Congressional Research Service, *Use of U.S. Food Resources*, 24.

76. Congressional Research Service, *Use of U.S. Food Resources*, 24–29; Schapsmeier and Schapsmeier, *Ezra Taft Benson and the Politics of Agriculture*, 97–99; Vernon W. Ruttan, "The Politics of U.S. Food Aid Policy: A Historical Review," in *Why Food Aid?*, ed. Vernon W. Ruttan (Baltimore: Johns Hopkins University Press, 1993), 2–36.

77. Agricultural Trade Development and Assistance Act of 1954 (Public Law 480), 83rd Cong., 2nd sess., January 6, 1954, accessed May 1, 2016, http://www.gpo.gov/fdsys/pkg/STATUTE-68/pdf/STATUTE-68-Pg454-2.pdf.

78. Congressional Research Service, *Use of U.S. Food Resources*, 26–28; Ruttan, "Politics of U.S. Food Aid Policy," 2–36.

79. Emma Rothschild, "Is It Time to End Food for Peace?," *New York Times*, March 13, 1977, 208; Schapsmeier and Schapsmeier, *Ezra Taft Benson and the Politics of Agriculture*, 97–106; Ruttan, "Politics of U.S. Food Aid Policy," 7–9.

80. "Benson in Venezuela," *Corpus Christi Caller-Times*, February 27, 1955, 12; "Secretary Benson Says Latins Happy with U.S. Cattle," *Abilene Reporter-News*, March 10, 1955, 10–A.

81. Schapsmeier and Schapsmeier, *Ezra Taft Benson and the Politics of Agriculture*, 100–104.

82. "Wide Farm Task: Benson Appeals for Global Cooperation in Adjusting the Production," *Kansas City Times*, September 9, 1955, 20.

83. "Revolution, Not Revolt."

84. Schapsmeier and Schapsmeier, *Ezra Taft Benson and the Politics of Agriculture*, 100–104.

85. Schapsmeier and Schapsmeier, *Ezra Taft Benson and the Politics of Agriculture*, 101.

86. Schapsmeier and Schapsmeier, *Ezra Taft Benson and the Politics of Agriculture*, 104–110.

87. Owens, "Overview of Agricultural Policy," 41; Schapsmeier and Schapsmeier, *Ezra Taft Benson and the Politics of Agriculture*, 109–124.

88. Owens, "Overview of Agricultural Policy," 41; Schapsmeier and Schapsmeier, *Ezra Taft Benson and the Politics of Agriculture*, 109–124.

89. Benson, *Crossfire*, 67.

90. Benson, *Crossfire*, 67.

91. Quoted in Benson, *Crossfire*, 67.

92. Benson, *Crossfire*, 70.

93. "Revolution, Not Revolt." This episode is also recounted in Benson, *Crossfire*, 203.

94. "Revolution, Not Revolt"; Benson, *Crossfire*, 65–70, 201–212; Schapsmeier and Schapsmeier, *Ezra Taft Benson and the Politics of Agriculture*, 38–40.

95. See Wendell Berry, "Nation's Destructive Farm Policy Is Everyone's Concern," *Herald-Leader*, July 11, 1999; Paul Roberts, *The End of Food* (Boston: Houghton Mifflin, 2008), 120. On the attribution of this advice to Butz rather than Benson, see "Farmers May Lose Subsidies: Fewer Government Controls Needed," *Baytown Sun*, September 25, 1985, 26.

96. Tom Philpott, "The USDA's Sustainable Food Champion Steps Down" *Mother Jones* March 18, 2013, accessed May 1, 2016, http://www.motherjones.com/tom-philpott/2013/03/usdas-sustainable-food-champion-steps-down.

97. Schapsmeier and Schapsmeier, *Ezra Taft Benson and the Politics of Agriculture*, 174.

CHAPTER 4

1. Duke Behnke, "Wis. Family's Fallout Shelter Becomes Historical Exhibit," *USA Today*, May 1, 2013, accessed May 1, 2016, http://www.usatoday.com/story/travel/destinations/2013/05/01/wisconsin-fallout-shelter-now-exhibit/2126687/; Meg Jones, "Backyard Fallout Shelter Inspires Historical Exhibit in Neenah," *Milwaukee Wisconsin Journal Sentinel*, May 4, 2013, accessed May 1, 2016, http://www.jsonline.com/news/wisconsin/backyard-fallout-shelter-inspires-historical-exhibit-in-neenah-uj9qdch-206115631.html; Derek Paulus, "UWO Faculty, Students Collaborate on Neenah Historical Society Bomb Shelter Exhibit," *UW Oshkosh Today*, April 29, 2013, accessed May 1, 2016, http://www.uwosh.edu/today/26948/uwo-faculty-students-collaborate-on-neenah-historical-society-exhibit/.

2. On civil defense planning in the United States, see Thomas J. Kerr, *Civil Defense in the U.S.: Bandaid for a Holocaust?* (Boudler, CO: Westview Press, 1983); B. Wayne Blanchard, "American Civil Defense 1945–1984: The Evolution of Programs and Policies," *Federal Emergency Management Agency Monograph Series* 2, no. 2, July 1986; Lawrence J. Vale, *The Limits of Civil Defense in the USA, Switzerland, Britain and the Soviet Union* (London: Macmillan, 1987); Laura McEnaney, *Civil Defense Begins at Home: Militarization Meets Everyday Life in the Fifties* (Princeton, NJ: Princeton University Press 2000); Kenneth D. Rose, *One Nation Underground: The Fallout Shelter in American Culture* (New York: New York University Press, 2004); David F. Krugler, *This Is Only a Test: How Washington DC Prepared for Nuclear War* (New York: Palgrave MacMillan, 2006); Sarah A. Lichtman, "Do-It-Yourself Security: Safety, Gender, and the Home Fallout Shelter in Cold War America," *Journal of Design History* 19, no. 1 (2006): 39–55; U.S. Department of Homeland Security, *Civil Defense and Homeland Security: A Short History of National Preparedness Efforts*, 2006, accessed May 1, 2016, https://training.fema.gov/hiedu/docs/dhs%20civil%20defense-hs%20-%20short%20history.

pdf; Elaine Tyler May, *Homeward Bound: American Families in the Cold War Era*, rev. ed. (New York: Basic Books, 2008).

3. See, for example, the five plans contained in Office of Civil and Defense Mobilization, *The Family Fallout Shelter* (Washington, DC: Government Printing Office, 1959).

4. Jacob Darwin Hamblin, *Arming Mother Nature: The Birth of Catastrophic Environmentalism* (New York: Oxford University Press, 2013), 5.

5. Hamblin, *Arming Mother Nature*, chapter 1.

6. Vale, *Limits of Civil Defense*, 59.

7. On the informational and educational challenges of civil defense, see Arnold Ringstad, "The Evolution of American Civil Defense Film Rhetoric," *Journal of Cold War Studies* 14, no. 4 (Fall 2012), 93–121.

8. Kerr, *Civil Defense in the U.S.*, 43.

9. Kerr, *Civil Defense in the U.S.*, 27–28.

10. Rose, *One Nation Underground*, 14–38; Lichtman "Do-It-Yourself Security."

11. U.S. Department of Homeland Security, *Civil Defense and Homeland Security*.

12. Kerr, *Civil Defense in the U.S.*, 60.

13. Blanchard, "American Civil Defense 1945-19844-6"; Rose, *One Nation Underground*, 22–27.

14. Security Resources Panel of the Science Advisory Committee, *Deterrence and Survival in the Nuclear Age* (Washington, DC: The White House, 1957), 7–8.

15. Rand Corporation, *Report on a Study of Non-Military Defense, Report R-322-RC* (Santa Monica, CA: Rand Corporation, 1958), 5–8.

16. Rand Corporation, *Report on a Study of Non-Military Defense*, 7.

17. See, for example, Panel on the Human Effects of Nuclear Weapons Development, *The Human Effects of Nuclear Weapons Development: A Report to the President and the National Security Council* (Washington, DC: The White House, 1956); John H. Rohrer, "Implications for Fallout Shelter Living from Studies of Submarine Habitability and Adjustment to Polar Isolation," in *Symposium on Human Problems in the Utilization of Fallout Shelters*, ed. George W. Baker and John H. Rohrer (Washington, DC: National Academy of Sciences / National Research Council, 1960), 21–30.

18. Edward J. Murray, "Adjustment to Environmental Stress in Fallout Shelters," in Baker and Rohrer, *Symposium on Human Problems*, 67–78; and Hermann Leutz, "A Shelter Occupancy Experiment near Bonn, Germany," in Baker and Rohrer, *Symposium on Human Problems*, 95–100; U.S. Department of Homeland Security, *Civil Defense and Homeland Security*.

19. Samuel L. Guskin, "English World War II Bombshelter Experiences and Their Application to U.S. Civil Defense Problems," in Baker and Rohrer, *Symposium on Human Problems*, 79–88; Vale, *Limits of Civil Defense*,123–151.

20. Asa Brand-Persson, "The Shelter Program and Shelter Occupancy Experiments in Sweden," in Baker and Rohrer, *Symposium on Human Problems*, 89–94; and "Sweden: The Cavemen," *Time*, June 23, 1958, 22.

21. See for example, Edward Geist, "Was There a Real "Mineshaft Gap"? Bomb Shelters in the USSR, 1945-1962," *Journal of Cold War Studies* 14, no. 2 (Spring 2012): 3–28.

22. U.S. Department of State, "Telegram," DEPTEL 733, January 8, 1958 (incomplete), Document Number: CK3100416274. *Declassified Documents Reference System.* Farmington Hills, MI: Gale, 2015.

23. Other participants in the meeting raised questions about this assessment and the level of protection offered by the shelters that had been constructed, see Marion W. Boggs, "Memorandum of Discussion at the 359th Meeting of the National Security Council," March 20, 1958, 2–4, in Eisenhower Papers 1953–1961, Ann Whitman File, Dwight D. Eisenhower Presidential Library (incomplete), Document Number: CK3100502026, *Declassified Documents Reference System.* Farmington Hills, MI: Gale, 2015.

24. Leon Goure, "Soviet Civil Defense," in Baker and Rohrer, *Symposium on Human Problems*, 100–102. See also Leon Gouré, *Civil Defense in the Soviet Union* (Berkeley: University of California Press, 1962); and Vale, *Limits of Civil Defense*, 152–191.

25. For an overview of known United States government shelters and estimated construction costs (in 1998 dollars), see Stephen I. Schwartz, ed., *Atomic Audit: The Costs and Consequences of US Nuclear Weapons since 1940* (Washington, DC: Brookings Institution Press, 1998).

26. Krugler, *This Is Only a Test*, 168.

27. Ted Gup, "The Ultimate Congressional Hideaway," *Washington Post Magazine*, May 31, 1992, 10–15, 24–27; Tom Curley, "Inside Look at Cold War Secret," *USA Today*, November 7, 1995, 10A; Ted Gup, "Civil Defense Doomsday Hideaway," *Time*, June 21, 2001, accessed May 1, 2016, http://content.time.com/time/magazine/article/0,9171,156041,00.html; Jon Wiener, *How We Forgot the Cold War: A Historical Journey across America* (Berkeley: University of California Press, 2012), 183–192.

28. Rand Corporation, *Report on a Study of Non-Military Defense*, 36.

29. Blanchard, "American Civil Defense 1945-1984," 5.

30. OCDM, *Annual Report of the Office of Civil and Defense Mobilization for Fiscal Year 1959* (Washington, DC: Government Printing Office, 1960), 1–8.

31. Gerald R. Gallagher, "Introduction to the Symposium," in Baker and Rohrer, *Symposium on Human of Problems*, 4.

32. "Operation YOU," *National Business Woman*, November 1958, 10. See also, Federal Civil Defense Administration, "Administrator Hoegh calls for 'Operation you' to Strengthen National Preparedness," January 21, 1958 (Battle Creek, MI: Federal Civil Defense Administration, 1958). On links between civil defense and postwar do-it-yourself, see Lichtman, "Do-It-Yourself Security," 42–44.

33. OCDM, *Family Fallout Shelter.*

34. May, *Homeward Bound*, 1.

35. "Survival: Are Shelters the Answer?," *Newsweek*, November, 6 1961, 19.

36. "The Walker House," Penn State University Libraries, accessed May 1, 2016, http://www.libraries.psu.edu/psul/digital/hallock/residential/walker.html.

37. Rose, *One Nation Underground*, 37.

38. Rand Corporation, *Report on a Study of Non-Military Defense*, 36.

39. Rose, *One Nation Underground*, 1–37.

40. OCDM, *Family Fallout Shelter*, 2.

41. Lichtman, "Do-It-Yourself Security," 47.

42. On leisure activities, see Rohrer, "Implications for Fallout Shelter Living," 23–24.

43. See for example, Rand Corporation, *Report on a Study of Non-Military Defense*, 24–25; Joseph Carrier, "Food Problems," in Herman Kahn, *Research Memorandum: Some Specific Suggestions for Achieving Early Non-Military Defense Capabilities and Initiating Long-Range Programs* (Santa Monica, CA: Rand Corporation, 1958), 99–100; Robert L. Olson, "The Implications of Food Acceptability for Shelter Occupancy," in *Symposium on Human Problems in the Utilization of Fallout Shelters*, ed. Baker and Rohrer, 167–179; U.S. Department of Defense (DoD), Office of Civil Defense, *Shelter Management Textbook* (Washington, DC: Government Printing Office, 1967), 67–69.

44. Olson, "Implications of Food Acceptability," 167.

45. Robert W. Smith and Mary Ann Lasky, *Planning Guides for Dual-Purpose Shelters*, AD 412342 (Pittsburgh, PA: American Institute for Research, 1963), 59.

46. Olson, "Implications of Food Acceptability"; Carrier, "Food Problems."

47. Olson, "Implications of Food Acceptability," 167. See also Robert L. Olson, Robert E. Ferrel, Marcel E. Juilly, Vern F. Kaufman, and Eleanor C. Taylor, "Food Supply for Fallout Shelters," Appendix 10 in House Committee on Government Operations, *Hearings Before a Subcommittee of the Committee on Government Operations, Civil Defense*, 87th Cong., 1st sess., 1–9 August, 1961, 401–500.

48. Smith and Lasky, *Planning Guides for Dual-Purpose Shelters*, 62–63.

49. Smith and Lasky, *Planning Guides for Dual-Purpose Shelters*, 65–66. On links between cooking and ventilation, see also Asa Brand-Persson, "Experiments on Air Conditioning in Sealed Rock Shelters," in *Proceedings of the Meeting on Environmental Engineering in Protective Shelters* (Washington, DC: National Academy of Sciences / National Research Council, 1960), 147–170.

50. Olson, "Implications of Food Acceptability," 170.

51. Olson, "Implications of Food Acceptability," 170–171.

52. Smith and Lasky, *Planning Guides for Dual-Purpose Shelters*, 61–63; DoD, *Shelter Management Textbook*, 67–69.

53. Executive Office of the President (EOP), National Security Resources Board, Civil Defense Office, *Survival under Atomic Attack: The Official U.S. Government Booklet*, NSDB Doc. 130 (Washington, DC: Government Printing Office, 1950), 12, 14, 19.

54. EOP, *Survival under Atomic Attack*, 28.

55. EOP, 18, 27–28; Olson, "Implications of Food Acceptability," 176; Smith and Lasky, *Planning Guides for Dual-Purpose Shelters*, 62.

56. Federal Civil Defense Administration, *Grandma's Pantry Was Ready—Is Your Pantry Ready in Event of Emergency?* (Washington, DC: Government Printing Office, 1955).

57. Rose, *One Nation Underground*, 142; May, *Homeward Bound*, 104–106; Lichtman, "Do-It-Yourself Security," 49.

58. Lucy Reeves, "Speaking of Foods: Grandma's Pantry Is for Emergency Only," *Mason City Globe-Gazette* (Iowa), April 29, 1955, 6.

59. Reeves, "Speaking of Foods," 6.

60. Alice Keegan, "Is Your "Pantry" Ready in Event of Emergency?" *Post-Standard* (Syracuse, NY), March 24, 1955, 8.

61. Reeves, "Speaking of Foods," 6.
62. "Mrs. Ray Altmire Discusses Civil Defense at CMCHS," *Daily Register* (Harrisburg, IL), March 28, 1958, 6.
63. Norman Indall, "Grandma's Pantry Vital in Disaster," *Santa Cruz Sentinel* (CA), August 24, 1958, 5.
64. For discussions of gender and civil defense efforts, see May, *Homeward Bound*; McEnaney, *Civil Defense Begins at Home*; Lichtman, "Do-It-Yourself Security."
65. "Fill Your Easter Basket with These IGA Savings," *Lewiston Daily Sun* (Maine), April 8, 1955, 9.
66. A. I. Meyer and M. V. Klicka, *Operational Rations: Current and Future of the Department of Defense*, Technical Report NATICK/TR-82/031 (Natick, MA: United States Army Natick Research and Development Laboratories, 1982), 6.
67. Carrier, "Food Problems," 99.
68. Meyer and Klicka, *Operational Rations*, 10.
69. Olson, "Implications of Food Acceptability," 174.
70. Bill Geerhart, "The Life Cycle of the Civil Defense Survival Biscuit," *Conelrad Adjacent*, August 13, 2010, accessed May 1, 2016, http://conelrad.blogspot.com/2010/08/life-cycle-of-civil-defense-suvival.html.
71. Nebraska State Historical Society, "A Biscuit Named for Nebraska Was Stockpiled in Case of Nuclear Attack?," January 1962, accessed May 1, 2016, http://nebraska-history.org/sites/mnh/weird_nebraska/biscuit_named.htm.
72. "Cool Things—Civil Defense Food Kit," *Kansapedia*, accessed May 1, 2016, http://www.kshs.org/kansapedia/cool-things-civil-defense-food-kit/10155; William Shurtleff and Akiko Aoyagi, "The Meals for Millions Foundation and Multi-Purpose Food: Work with Soyfoods," unpublished manuscript, 2011, accessed May 1, 2016, http://www.soyinfocenter.com/HSS/meals_for_millions.php.
73. DoD, *Shelter Management Textbook*, 124.
74. DoD, *Shelter Management Textbook*, 68. On relationship between diet and water needs, see Smith and Lasky, *Planning Guides for Dual-Purpose Shelters*, 59.
75. House Committee on Government Operations, *Hearings Before a Subcommittee of the Committee on Government Operations, Civil Defense*, 86th Cong., 2nd sess., March, 1960, 115–116.
76. Hershey Community Archives, "Ration D Bars," accessed May 1, 2016, http://www.hersheyarchives.org/essay/details.aspx?EssayId=26.
77. Olson, "Implications of Food Acceptability," 168.
78. Smith and Lasky, *Planning Guides for Dual-Purpose Shelters*, 59.
79. DoD, *Shelter Management Textbook*, 67.
80. House Committee on Government Operations, *Hearings*, 55.
81. Defense Civil Preparedness Agency, *Guidance for Development of an Emergency Fallout Shelter Stocking Plan*, CPG 1–19 (Washington, DC: DoD / Defense Civil Preparedness Agency, 1978), 1.
82. Congress ceased appropriating funds for shelter stocking in 1969. In 1976, based on laboratory tests of stored foods, the Defense Civil Preparedness Agency recommended disposing of all stockpiled foods, see Defense Civil Preparedness Agency, *Guidance for Development of an Emergency Fallout Shelter Stocking Plan*, 1.

83. Office of Civil Defense, *Personal and Family Survival: Civil Defense Adult Education Course Student Manual*, SM-3-11 (Washington, DC: DoD / Office of Civil Defense, 1966), 117.

84. USDA, *Defense against Radioactive Fallout on the Farm*, Farmers' Bulletin No. 2107 (Washington, DC: United States Department of Agriculture, 1958), 14–15. See also United States Federal Extension Service, United States, Office of Civil Defense, *Your Family Survival Plan* (Washington, DC: Government Printing Office, 1963).

85. Gretchen Heefner, *The Missile Next Door: The Minuteman in the American Heartland* (Cambridge, MA: Harvard University Press, 2012).

86. The potential impact of nuclear war on rural areas was further heighted by use of counterforce strategies and tactics, such as hardening nuclear weapons silos. See Rose, *One Nation Underground*, 152–168. On civil defense efforts in rural areas, see Jenny Barker-Devine. "'Mightier than Missiles:' The Rhetoric of Civil Defense for Rural American Families, 1950-1970," *Agricultural History* 80, no. 4 (2006), 415–435.

87. Gup, "Ultimate Congressional Hideaway."

88. USDA, *Defense against Radioactive Fallout*, 2.

89. USDA, *Defense against Radioactive Fallout*, 2.

90. USDA, "Bunker-type Fallout Shelter . . . for Beef Cattle," Miscellaneous Publication no. 947 (Washington, DC: United States Department of Agriculture, 1964).

91. See, for example, Cooperative Extension Work in Agricultural and Home Economics, State of Mississippi, Mississippi State University, "Bunker Type Fallout Shelter for Beef Cattle, Ex. 5950," 1963, accessed May 1, 2016, http://msucares. com/pubs/plans/5950.pdf.

92. USDA, *Defense against Radioactive Fallout*, 10.

93. USDA, *Guide to Civil Defense Management in the Food Industry*, Agricultural Handbook no. 254 (Washington, DC: United States Department of Agriculture, 1963), i.

94. USDA, *Guide to Civil Defense Management*.

95. USDA, *Guide to Civil Defense Management*.

96. Rand Corporation, *Report on a Study of Non-Military Defense*, 24.

97. Carrier, "Food Problems," 100.

98. Cited in Lichtman, "Do-It-Yourself Security," 50.

99. Linda Lyons, "The Gallup Brain: Facing Fear in America," March 4, 2003, accessed May 1, 2016, http://www.gallup.com/poll/7903/gallup-brain-facing-fear-america. aspx.

100. "Gun Thy Neighbor?," *Time*, August 18, 1961, 60.

101. Rose, *One Nation Underground*, chapter 3; May, *Homeward Bound*, 1–38.

102. See, for example, Joint Committee on Atomic Energy, U.S. Congress, *Biological and Environmental Effects of Nuclear War: Summary Analysis of Hearings, June 22–26, 1959* (Washington, DC: Government Printing Office, 1959); Saul Aronow, Frank R. Ervin, and Victor W. Sidel, eds., *The Fallen Sky: Medical Consequences of Thermonuclear War* (New York: Hill and Wang, 1963); Paul Boyer, "Physicians

Confront the Apocalypse: The American Medical Profession and the Threat of Nuclear War," *JAMA* 254, no. 5 (1985): 633–643.

103. Department of Homeland Security, *Civil Defense and Homeland Security*, 7–8.

CHAPTER 5

1. "Excerpts from Kennedy's Address Outlining His Farm Program," *New York Times*, September 23, 1960, 22.

2. "Nixon Discloses 4-Year Crop Plan to Trim Surpluses," *New York Times*, September 17, 1960; "Operation Consume," *Time*, September 26, 1970, 20.

3. "Excerpts from Nixon Farm Policy Talk," *New York Times*, September 24, 1960, 14.

4. "Kennedy Offers a Farm Program of Income Parity," *New York Times*, September 23, 1960, 1. See also "Henry Wallace Assays Candidates' Farm Plans," *New York Times*, October 27, 1960, 25; "Nixon Says Kennedy's Program Would End a Million Farm Jobs," *New York Times*, October 29, 1960, 15.

5. "Nixon Farm Plan Hailed," *New York Times*, September 25, 1960, 56.

6. "Candidates Farm Plans Compared," *New York Times*, September 25, 1960, E10.

7. John F. Kennedy, "The New Frontier" (speech at the 1960 Democratic National Convention, July 15, 1960) accessed May 1, 2016, http://www.jfklibrary.org/Asset-Viewer/AS08q5oYz0SFUZg9uOi4iw.aspx.

8. Warren Belasco, *Appetite for Change: How the Counterculture Took on the Food Industry* (Ithaca, NY: Cornell University Press, 2007).

9. "Kennedy's Victory Won by Close Margin," *New York Times*, November 10, 1960, 1.

10. Harriet Friedmann, "The Political Economy of Food: The Rise and Fall of the Postwar International Food Order," *American Journal of Sociology*, supplement, 88 (1982): S261.

11. Gilbert Fite, *American Farmers: The New Minority* (Bloomington: Indiana University Press, 1981), 150–174; James N. Giglio, "New Frontier Agricultural Policy: The Commodity Side, 1961-1963," *Agricultural History* 61, no. 3 (Summer 1987): 53–59.

12. "The Dismemberment of Orville Freeman," *Time*, July 7, 1961, 15; Fite, *American Farmers*, 169–170; Giglio, "New Frontier Agricultural Policy," 59–65.

13. "Dismemberment of Orville Freeman"; Fite, *American Farmers*, 169–170; Giglio, "New Frontier Agricultural Policy," 59–65.

14. Giglio, "New Frontier Agricultural Policy," 66–68; Conkin, *A Revolution Down on the Farm: The Transformation of American Agriculture since 1929* (Lexington: University Press of Kentucky, 2008), 130–132.

15. Fite, *American Farmers*, 170–171; Patti S. Landers, "The Food Stamp Program: History, Nutrition Education and Impact," *Journal of the American Dietetic Association* 107, no. 11 (2007): 1945–1951; US Department of Agriculture (USDA), Food and Nutrition Service, "A Short History of SNAP," accessed May 1, 2016, http://www.fns.usda.gov/snap/short-history-snap.

16. Fite, *American Farmers*, 170–171; Landers, "Food Stamp Program"; USDA, "Short History of SNAP."

17. John F. Kennedy, "Executive Order 10914—Providing for an Expanded Program of Food Distribution to Needy Families," January 21, 1961, Gerhard Peters and John T. Woolley, *The American Presidency Project*, website, accessed May 1, 2016, http://www.presidency.ucsb.edu/ws/?pid=58853.

18. Fite, *American Farmers*, 170–171; Landers, "Food Stamp Program"; USDA, "Short History of SNAP."

19. Fite, *American Farmers*, 171–172; Landers, "Food Stamp Program"; USDA, "Short History of SNAP."

20. Fite, *American Farmers*, 171–172; Landers, "Food Stamp Program"; USDA, "Short History of SNAP." On the history of school lunch programs in America, see Janet Poppendieck, *Free for All: Fixing School Food in America* (Berkeley: University of California Press, 2010), especially chapter 2.

21. Lyndon B. Johnson, "Presidential Policy Paper No. 4: Farm Policy," November 1, 1964, in *Public Papers of the Presidents of the United States: Lyndon B. Johnson, 1963–64*, vol. 2 (Washington, DC: Government Printing Office, 1965), 1568–1569.

22. Fite, *American Farmers*, 172–174; Kristin L. Ahlberg, *Transplanting the Great Society: Lyndon Johnson and Food for Peace* (Columbia: University of Missouri Press, 2008), 56.

23. "Remarks of Senator John F. Kennedy at Corn Palace, Mitchell, South Dakota," John F. Kennedy Library, September 22, 1960, accessed May 1, 2016, http://www.jfklibrary.org/Research/Research-Aids/JFK-Speeches/Mitchell-SD_19600922.aspx.

24. "Excerpts from Kennedy's Address Outlining His Farm Program," *New York Times*, September 23, 1960, 22.

25. John D. Shaw, *World Food Security: A History since 1945* (New York: Palgrave Macmillan, 2007), 85–90. On the World Food Program, see John D. Shaw, *The UN World Food Programme and the Development of Food Aid* (New York: Palgrave, 2001); Vernon W. Ruttan, *United States Development Assistance Policy: The Domestic Politics of Foreign Economic Aid* (Baltimore: Johns Hopkins University Press, 1996), 163–165.

26. Shaw, *World Food Security*, 85–86.

27. Hubert Humphrey, *Food and Fiber as a Force for Freedom: Report to the Committee on Agriculture and Forestry, United States Senate*, 85th Cong., 2nd sess. (Washington, DC: Government Printing Office, 1958).

28. Humphrey, *Food and Fiber*, 1.

29. Humphrey, *Food and Fiber*; Vernon W. Ruttan, "The Politics of U.S. Food Aid Policy: A Historical Review," in *Why Food Aid?*, ed. Vernon W. Ruttan (Baltimore: Johns Hopkins University Press, 1993), 9–12; Ahlberg, *Transplanting the Great Society*, 11–31.

30. Dwight D. Eisenhower, "Special Message to the Congress on Agriculture," January 29, 1959, Gerhard Peters and John T. Woolley, *American Presidency Project*, website, accessed May 1, 2016, http://www.presidency.ucsb.edu/ws/?pid=11523.

31. Public Law 86-341. Passed by Congress to extend the Agricultural Trade Development and Assistance Act of 1954, and for other purposes. September 21,

1959 [H.R. 8609] 73 Stat. 606. 86th Cong., 1st sess., accessed May 1, 2016, http://www.gpo.gov/fdsys/pkg/STATUTE-73/pdf/STATUTE-73-Pg606.pdf.

32. "Five Wheat Nations Plan to Feed Needy Areas and Aid Economies," *New York Times*, May 7, 1959, 8; Shaw, *World Food Security*, 85–86.

33. Ruttan, "Politics of U.S. Food Aid Policy," 9–12; Ahlberg, *Transplanting the Great Society*, 11–31.

34. John F. Kennedy, "Statement by Senator John F. Kennedy, Washington, DC," October 31, 1960. Gerhard Peters and John T. Woolley, *The American Presidency Project*, website, accessed May 1, 2016, http://www.presidency.ucsb.edu/ws/?pid=74308.

35. Kennedy, "Statement by Senator John F. Kennedy."

36. "The Food for Peace Program: A Report of the Food for Peace Committee Appointed by Senator Kennedy, October 31, 1960, submitted by the Committee to the President-elect, January 19, 1961," cited in Ahlberg, *Transplanting the Great Society*, 31.

37. "Council to Advise on Food for Peace: Kennedy Names Citizen Unit for Attack on Hunger," *New York Times*, May 7, 1961, 50; "Three Negroes on American Food for Peace Council," *Jet Magazine*, May 25, 1961, 5.

38. Ahlberg, *Transplanting the Great Society*, 30–49.

39. John F. Kennedy, "Executive Order 10915—Amending Prior Executive Orders to Provide for the Responsibilities of the Director of the Food-for-Peace Program," January 24, 1961, Gerhard Peters and John T. Woolley, *American Presidency Project*, website, accessed May 1, 2016, http://www.presidency.ucsb.edu/ws/?pid=58939.

40. John F. Kennedy, "Annual Message to the Congress on the State of the Union, January 30, 1961," *Public Papers of the Presidents of the United States: John F. Kennedy* (Washington, DC: Government Printing Office, 1962), 19–28.

41. Ruttan, "Politics of U.S. Food Aid Policy," 18–21; Ahlberg, *Transplanting the Great Society*, 29–41; Shaw, *World Food Security*, 94–95.

42. John F. Kennedy, "Special Message to the Congress on Agriculture," March 16, 1961. Gerhard Peters and John T. Woolley, *The American Presidency Project*, website, accessed May 1, 2016, http://www.presidency.ucsb.edu/ws/?pid=8539.

43. Shaw, *World Food Security*, 94–95.

44. *Foreign Relations of the United States*, 1961–1963, vol. IX, *Foreign Economic Policy*, ed. Evans Gerakas, David S. Patterson, William F. Sanford Jr., Carolyn B. Yee (Washington, DC: Government Printing Office, 1995), doc. 87, accessed May 1, 2016, https://history.state.gov/historicaldocuments/frus1961-63v09/d87.

45. George S. McGovern, "Memorandum for the President: Food for Peace Mission—Argentina and Brazil, February 14–20, 1961," February 27, 1961, Papers of John F. Kennedy, Presidential Papers, President's Office Files, Departments and Agencies, Food for Peace Program, 1961: January–March, accessed May 1, 2016, http://www.jfklibrary.org/Asset-Viewer/Archives/JFKPOF-078-026.aspx.

46. George S. McGovern, *War against Want: America's Food for Peace Program* (New York: Walker, 1964), 70. See also *Foreign Relations of the United States*, 1961–1963, vol. VII, *Arms Control*; vol. VIII, *National Security*; vol. IX, *Foreign Economic Policy*, microfiche supplement, ed. Evans Gerakas, David W. Mabon, David

S. Patterson, William F. Sanford Jr., Carolyn B. Yee (Washington, DC: Government Printing Office, 1997), doc. 402, accessed May 1, 2016, https://history.state.gov/historicaldocuments/frus1961-63v07-09mSupp/d402.

47. "Key Role Urged for Food as Part of Foreign Policy: Food Use Is Urged in Foreign Policy," *New York Times*, March 31, 1961, 1.

48. Shaw, *World Food Security*, 96–101; Ahlberg, *Transplanting the Great Society*, 36.

49. John F. Kennedy, "Executive Order 10973—Administration of Foreign Assistance and Related Functions," November 3, 1961, Gerhard Peters and John T. Woolley, *American Presidency Project*, website, accessed May 1, 2016, http://www.presidency.ucsb.edu/ws/?pid=58911.

50. US Government, *Feed the Future Guide*, May 2010, accessed May 1, 2016, http://feedthefuture.gov/sites/default/files/resource/files/FTF_Guide.pdf.

51. Shaw, *World Food Security*, 96–101; Ahlberg, *Transplanting the Great Society*, 36–37.

52. Lazar Volin, *A Century of Russian Agriculture: From Alexander II to Khrushchev* (Cambridge, MA: Harvard University Press, 1970), 484–496.

53. John Lewis Gaddis, *The Cold War: A New History* (New York: Penguin, 2005), 83–85.

54. Quoted in Lazar Volin, "Khrushchev and the Soviet Agricultural Scene," in *Soviet and East European Agriculture*, ed. Jerzy F. Karcz (Berkeley: University of California Press, 1967), 6.

55. Shane Hamilton and Sarah Phillips, *The Kitchen Debate and Cold War Consumer Politics* (New York: Bedford / St. Martins, 2014), 27–28; Volin, "Khrushchev and the Soviet Agricultural Scene," 1–21.

56. Hamilton and Phillips, *Kitchen Debate*, 27–28; Volin, "Khrushchev and the Soviet Agricultural Scene," 1–21.

57. "Memorandum for McGeorge Bundy on Setbacks in Soviet Agriculture," CIA, no. 1703, January 10, 1963, Document Number: CK3100433768, Declassified Documents Reference System. Farmington Hills, MI: Gale, 2015.

58. Orville Freeman, "Memo to the President re Tour of the Soviet Union," in Hamilton and Philips, *Kitchen Debate*, 146–148.

59. Hamilton and Philips, *Kitchen Debate*, 27–28; Volin, "Khrushchev and the Soviet Agricultural Scene," 1–21.

60. "USSR Contracts for Huge Purchases of Canadian Wheat," Office of Research and Reports Current Support Brief, CIA/RR CB 63-76, Sept. 17, 1963, Document Number: CK3100390245, Declassified Documents Reference System, Farmington Hills, MI: Gale, 2015.

61. *Foreign Relations of the United States*, 1961–1963, vol. V, *Soviet Union*, ed. Charles S. Sampson and John Michael Joyce (Washington, DC: Government Printing Office), doc. 359, accessed May 1, 2016, https://history.state.gov/historicaldocuments/frus1961-63v05/d359.

62. "Russia Broaches Wheat Purchase," *New York Times*, October 8, 1963, 1.

63. John F. Kennedy, "The President's News Conference," October 9, 1963, Gerhard Peters and John T. Woolley, *American Presidency Project*, website, accessed May 1, 2016, http://www.presidency.ucsb.edu/ws/index.php?pid=9460; "Aid to Peace

Seen: President Also Calls Deal Beneficial to U.S. Economy," *New York Times*, October 10, 1963, 1.

64. "Soviet Grain Crisis Assayed by Freeman," *New York Times*, October 14, 1963, 5.

65. "Soviet Grain Sale Is Snagged Again on Shipping Rates," *New York Times*, November, 30 1963, 1; "Wheat for Russia: How It Began in North Dakota," *New York Times*, January 23, 1964, 4.

66. "First Sale of Rice to Soviet Is Made," *New York Times*, January 16, 1964, 12; "U.S. Wheat Sales to Soviet Ended," *New York Times*, March 3, 1964, 5.

67. Hamilton and Phillips, *Kitchen Debate*, 27–28.

68. "President Urges New Federalism to 'Enrich' Life," *New York Times*, May 23, 1964, 1. On the presidency of Lyndon Johnson, see Randall B. Woods, ed., *Vietnam and the American Political Tradition: The Politics of Dissent* (Cambridge: Cambridge University Press, 2003); Mitchell B. Lerner, ed., *Looking Back at LBJ: White House Politics in a New Light* (Lawrence: University Press of Kansas, 2005); Thomas Alan Schwartz, *Lyndon Johnson and Europe in the Shadow of Vietnam* (Cambridge, MA: Harvard University Press, 2003).

69. Lyndon B. Johnson, *The Vantage Point: Perspectives on the Presidency, 1963–1969* (New York: Holt, Rinehart and Winston, 1971), 222–231; Ruttan, "Politics of U.S. Food Aid Policy," 19.

70. Johnson, *Vantage Point*, 223.

71. Lyndon B. Johnson, "Presidential Policy Paper No. 4: Farm Policy," November 1, 1964, in *Public Papers of the Presidents of the United States: Lyndon B. Johnson, 1963–64*, vol. 2 (Washington, DC: Government Printing Office, 1965), 1568–1569.

72. Kristen L. Ahlberg, "'Machiavelli with a Heart:' The Johnson Administration's Food for Peace Program in India, 1965-1966," *Diplomatic History* 31, no. 4 (2007): 665–701.

73. Lyndon B. Johnson, "Special Message to the Congress: Food for Freedom," February 10, 1966, Gerhard Peters and John T. Woolley, *American Presidency Project*, website, accessed May 1, 2016, http://www.presidency.ucsb.edu/ws/?pid=28038.

74. Johnson, "Special Message to the Congress"; Ruttan, "Politics of U.S. Food Aid Policy," 15. For an excellent discussion of Johnson's changing ideas on the Food for Peace program, see Ahlberg, *Transplanting the Great Society*, especially chapter 3.

75. Lyndon B. Johnson, "Statement by the President upon Signing the Food for Peace Act of 1966," November 12, 1966. Gerhard Peters and John T. Woolley, *American Presidency Project*, website, accessed May 1, 2016, http://www.presidency.ucsb.edu/ws/?pid=28025.

76. Ruttan, "Politics of U.S. Food Aid Policy," 15.

77. Johnson, "Statement by the President upon Signing the Food for Peace Act of 1966."

78. "Food for Peace Act of 1966 (PL 98-808)," 1536, accessed May 1, 2016, http://www.gpo.gov/fdsys/pkg/STATUTE-80/pdf/STATUTE-80-Pg1526.pdf.

79. "Food for Peace Act of 1966"; Ruttan, "Politics of U.S. Food Aid Policy," 15–16.

80. Johnson, *Vantage Point*, 222–231. See also Robert L. Paarlberg, *Food Trade and Foreign Policy: India, the Soviet Union, and the United States* (Ithaca, NY: Cornell University Press, 1985), 143–169; Carolyn Castore, "The United States and India:

The Use of Food to Apply Economic Pressure," in *Economic Coercion and U.S. Foreign Policy*, ed. Sidney Weintraub (Boulder, CO: Westview, 1982), 129–153.

81. Ahlberg, "Machiavelli with a Heart," 666.
82. Ahlberg, "Machiavelli with a Heart," 665–701; Nick Cullather, *The Hungry World* (Cambridge, MA: Harvard University Press, 2010), 205–231; Ruttan, "Politics of U.S. Food Aid Policy," 18–21.
83. J. R. McNeill, *Something New under the Sun: An Environmental History of the Twentieth-Century World* (New York: Norton, 2000), 223; Paul Conkin, *Revolution Down on the Farm*, 97–122.
84. Conkin, *Revolution Down on the Farm*, 121–122; McNeill, *Something New under the Sun*, 192–227.
85. For more on the Rockefeller Foundation, see John Ensor Harr and Peter J. Johnson, *The Rockefeller Century* (New York: Charles Scriber's Sons, 1988).
86. Conkin, *Revolution Down on the Farm*, 121–122; McNeill, *Something New under the Sun*, 192–227.
87. Conkin, *Revolution Down on the Farm*, 121–122; McNeill, *Something New under the Sun*, 192–227.
88. Deborah Fitzgerald, "Exporting American Agriculture: The Rockefeller Foundation in Mexico, 1943–53," *Social Studies of Science* 16, no. 3 (August 1986), 457–483.
89. John H. Perkins, "The Rockefeller Foundation and the Green Revolution, 1941–1956," *Agriculture and Human Values* 7, no. 3–4 (1990): 7–9; Fitzgerald, "Exporting American Agriculture," 457–464.
90. Perkins, "Rockefeller Foundation," 7–9; Fitzgerald, "Exporting American Agriculture," 457–464.
91. " 'Know-How' Urged to Help Feed All," *New York Times*, August 27, 1946, 30.
92. Harry S. Truman, "Inaugural Address of the President," *Department of State Bulletin* 33 (January 30, 1949): 125.
93. Cullather, *Hungry World*, 34–42; David Ekbladh, *The Great American Mission: Modernization and the Construction of an American World Order* (Princeton, NJ: Princeton University Press, 2010), 77–113; Ruttan, *United States Development Assistance Policy*, 49–114.
94. "U.S. Agronomist Gets Nobel Peace Prize," *New York Times*, October 22, 1970, 1.
95. William S. Gaud, "The Green Revolution: Accomplishments and Apprehensions," Address to the Society for International Development, Shoreham Hotel, Washington, DC, March 8, 1968, accessed May 1, 2016, http://www.agbioworld.org/biotech-info/topics/borlaug/borlaug-green.html.
96. McNeill, *Something New under the Sun*, 219.
97. Gaud, "Green Revolution."
98. Gaud, "Green Revolution;" "The Green Revolution" *New York Times*, May 21, 1968, 46.
99. Gaud, "Green Revolution." For more on the role of American support in the Green Revolution, see Ruttan, *United States Development Assistance Policy*, 69–145. See also Daniel Immerwahr, *Thinking Small: The United States and the Lure of Community Development* (Cambridge, MA: Harvard University Press, 2015).

100. Perkins, "Rockefeller Foundation," 6; Fitzgerald, "Exporting American Agriculture," 457–459.
101. "Little Iowa Town Pours Out in Cold to Fete Its Nobel Laureate," *New York Times*, December 20, 1970, 40.
102. Perkins, "Rockefeller Foundation," 6; Fitzgerald, "Exporting American Agriculture," 457–459. For additional assessments of the impacts of the Green Revolution, see Kenneth A. Dahlberg, *Beyond the Green Revolution* (New York: Plenum Press, 1979); Vandana Shiva, *Violence of the Green Revolution: Ecological Degradation and Political Conflict in Punjab* (Dehra Dun, India: Research Foundation for Science and Ecology, 1989); John H. Perkins, *Geopolitics and the Green Revolution: Wheat, Genes, and the Cold War* (New York: Oxford University Press, 1997). For contemporary calls for new green revolutions, see, for example, Monkombu Sambasivan Swaminathan, "An Evergreen Revolution," *Crop Science* 46, no. 5 (2006): 2293–2303; Justin Gills, "A Warming Planet Struggles to Feed Itself," *New York Times*, June 5, 2011; "Alliance for a Green Revolution in Africa," Bill and Melinda Gates Foundation, accessed May 1, 2016, http://www.gatesfoundation.org/How-We-Work/Resources/Grantee-Profiles/Grantee-Profile-Alliance-for-a-Green-Revolution-in-Africa-AGRA.
103. On soft power, see Joseph Nye, *Bound to Lead: The Changing Nature of American Power* (New York: Basic, 1990).

CHAPTER 6

1. "The World Food Crisis," *Time*, November 11, 1974, 94.
2. This shift would also prompt efforts to correct the focus of American efforts by Senator Hubert Humphrey in 1975. See Vernon W. Ruttan, "The Politics of U.S. Food Aid Policy: A Historical Review," in *Why Food Aid?*, ed. Vernon W. Ruttan (Baltimore: Johns Hopkins University Press, 1993), 26–32. See also Mitchel B. Wallerstein, *Food for War–Food for Peace: United States Food Aid in a Global Context* (Cambridge, MA: MIT Press, 1980), 180–225.
3. D. Gale Johnson, "World Agriculture, Commodity Policy and Price Variability," *American Journal of Agricultural Economics* 57, no. 5 (1975): 823–828; Derek Heady and Shenggen Fen, *Reflections on the Global Food Crisis: How Did It Happen? How Has It Hurt? And How Can We Prevent the Next One?* (Washington, DC: International Food Policy Research Institute, 2010), 81–88.
4. Heady and Fen, *Reflections on the Global Food Crisis*, 82–88.
5. "Moscow Agrees to Buy U.S. Grain for $750-Million," *New York Times*, July 9, 1972, 1.
6. "Soviet Purchase of Grain from U.S. May Total Billion," *New York Times*, August 10, 1972, 1.
7. Clifton B. Luttrell, "The Russian Wheat Deal: Hindsight vs. Foresight Federal Reserve," *Bank of St. Louis Review*, October 1973, 2–9; "Chaff in the Great Grain Deal," *Time*, August 6, 1973, 63–64; Heady and Fen, *Reflections on the Global Food Crisis*, 82–84.
8. Cable to Secretary of Agriculture Earl Butz from National Security Adviser Henry Kissinger, the White House, April 12, 1972, document number: CK3100673320,

Declassified Documents Reference System, Farmington Hills, MI: Gale, 2015. For more on the Moscow Summit, see *Foreign Relations of the United States*, 1969–1976, vol. XIV, *Soviet Union*, October 1971–May 1972, ed. David C. Geyer, Nina D. Howland, and Kent Sieg (Washington, DC: Government Printing Office, 2006), doc. 125–302, accessed on May 1, 2016, https://history.state.gov/historicaldocuments/frus1969-76v14.

9. Memorandum to the President from Peter Flanigan, the White House, April 26, 1972, document number: CK3100554994, Declassified Documents Reference System. Farmington Hills, MI: Gale, 2015.

10. They also discussed a forthcoming visit to the United States, at which Kissinger informed Dobrynin that he had been able to set up a tour for him of Universal Studios that included lunch with Alfred Hitchcock. See telephone conversation between Henry Kissinger and Soviet Ambassador Dobrynin, the White House, July 6, 1972, document number: CK3100554996, Declassified Documents Reference System. Farmington Hills, MI: Gale, 2015.

11. Central Intelligence Agency, USSR Branch, Office of Economic Research, Soviet Grain: Purchases and Prospects, September 29, 1972, document number: CK3100381828. Declassified Documents Reference System, Farmington Hills, MI: Gale, 2015.

12. Central Intelligence Agency, "Intelligence Memorandum: Some Implications of the Poor Soviet Grain Harvest," August 11, 1972, document number: CK3100381795, Declassified Documents Reference System, Farmington Hills, MI: Gale, 2015.

13. "Lesson in Soviet Grain Deal," *Evening Standard*, October 11, 1972, 4.

14. "Slowing Down Arms Race," *Standard-Speaker*, December 1, 1972, 14.

15. The waiver was issued as "National Security Decision Memorandum 179," see *Foreign Relations of the United States*, 1969–1976, vol. XV, Soviet Union, June 1972–August 1974, ed. Douglas E. Selvage and Melissa Jane Taylor (Washington, DC: Government Printing Office, 2011), doc., accessed May 1, 2016, https://history.state.gov/historicaldocuments/frus1969-76v15/d11. See also *Foreign Relations of the United States*, 1969–1976, vol. XV, Soviet Union, June 1972–August 1974, ed. Douglas E. Selvage and Melissa Jane Taylor (Washington, DC: Government Printing Office, 2011), doc. 9, accessed May 1, 2016, https://history.state.gov/historicaldocuments/frus1969-76v15/d9. The waiver was to National Security Action Memorandum 220 of February 1963, which stipulated that shipments of goods financed by the United States government could not be carried on ships that stopped in Cuba, see *Foreign Relations of the United States*, 1961–1963, vol. XI, Cuban Missile Crisis and Aftermath, ed. Edward C. Keefer, Charles S. Sampson, and Louis J. Smith (Washington, DC: Government Printing Office, 1996), doc. 277, accessed May 1, 2016, https://history.state.gov/historicaldocuments/frus1961-63v11/d277.

16. "Telephone conversation, National Security Advisor Henry Kissinger and Secretary of Commerce Peter Peterson," July 6, 1972, document number: CK3100724373. Declassified Documents Reference System. Farmington Hills, MI: Gale, 2015.

17. "Telephone conversation, National Security Advisor Henry Kissinger."

18. "Memorandum for Pat Buchanan from Charles Colson," the White House, September 8, 1972, document number: CK3100690548, Declassified Documents Reference System. Farmington Hills, MI: Gale, 2015.

19. I. M. Destler, "United States Food Policy 1972–1976: Reconciling Domestic and International Objectives," *International Organization* 32, no. 3 (1978): 617–653; Luttrell, "Russian Wheat Deal," 2–9; Heady and Fen, *Reflections on the Global Food Crisis*, 84–86.

20. "Lesson in Soviet Grain Deal."

21. "Chaff in the Great Grain Deal."

22. Comptroller General of the United States, *Russian Wheat Sale and Weakness in Agriculture's Management of Wheat Export Subsidy Program* (Washington, DC: United States General Accounting Office, 1973); Luttrell, "Russian Wheat Deal," 2–9; Heady and Fen, *Reflections on the Global Food Crisis*, 84–86.

23. Comptroller General, *Russian Wheat Sale*, 3.

24. Comptroller General, *Russian Wheat Sale*, 25–39; Luttrel, "Russian Wheat Deal," 2–9.

25. "Bread Prices to Rise 1C to 4C a Loaf as Wheat Soars," *New York Times*, August 9, 1973, 1.

26. "Shultz Finds U.S. 'Burned' on Grain," *New York Times*, September 8, 1973, 1.

27. "Grain for Moscow," *New York Times*, July 11, 1972, 34.

28. "Only the Taxpayers Suffered a Loss," *New York Times*, July 29, 197, E2.

29. "Chaff in the Great Grain Deal."

30. "Some Deal: The Full Story of how Amepnka [*sic*] got burned and the Russians got Bread," *New York Times*, November 25, 1973, 306. On allegations of corruption, see Attorney General Richard Kleindienst to Counsel to the President John Dean, "Memorandum: United States-Soviet Union Grain Sale Agreement," January 22, 1973, document number: CK3100691620. Declassified Documents Reference System. Farmington Hills, MI: Gale, 2015.

31. "Soviet Sets Loan of Grain to India," *New York Times*, September 29, 1973.

32. "U.S. Food Power: Ultimate Weapon in World Politics," *BusinessWeek*, December 15, 1975, 54–60.

33. "Canada and China in Big Wheat Deal," *New York Times*, October 6, 1973, 1.

34. "Some Deal," *New York Times*, November 25, 1973, 306.

35. Luttrell, "Russian Wheat Deal," 5; Heady and Fen, *Reflections on the Global Food Crisis*, 84–85.

36. John D. Shaw. *World Food Security: A History since 1945* (New York: Palgrave Macmillan, 2007), 115–116.

37. Luttrell, "Russian Wheat Deal," 5; Heady and Fen, *Reflections on the Global Food Crisis*, 84–85.

38. Malthus, Thomas (1826). *An Essay on the Principle of Population: A View of its Past and Present Effects on Human Happiness; With an Inquiry into Our Prospects Respecting the Future Removal or Mitigation of the Evils which It Occasions*, 6th ed. London: John Murray, accessed May 1, 2016, www.econlib.org/library/Malthus/malPlong.html.

39. "World Food Crisis"; Heady and Fen, *Reflections on the Global Food Crisis*, 85–87; Shaw, *World Food Security*, 115.

40. "World Food Crisis."

41. "World Food Crisis."

42. For more on discussion of population issues, see Betsy Hartmann, "Rethinking the Role of Population in Human Security," in *Global Environmental Change and Human Security*, ed. Richard A. Matthew, Jon Barnett, Bryan McDonald, and Karen L. O'Brien, (Cambridge, MA: MIT Press), 193–214; Paul Harrison, *The Third Revolution: Population, Environment and a Sustainable World* (London: Penguin Books, 1992); Thomas Robertson, *The Malthusian Moment: Global Population Growth and the Birth of American Environmentalism* (New Brunswick, NJ: Rutgers University Press, 2012).

43. Paul Ehrlich, *The Population Bomb* (New York: Ballantine, 1968); Harry Harrison, *Make Room! Make Room!* (Garden City, NY: Doubleday, 1966); Richard Fleischer, dir., *Soylent Green*, DVD (Burbank, CA: Warner Entertainment, 2003).

44. "World Food Crisis"; Shaw, *World Food Security*, 115; Heady and Fen, *Reflections on the Global Food Crisis*, 85–87.

45. B. Ward, "The Fat Years and the Lean: A Special Report on the UN World Food Conference," *The Economist*, November 2 1974, 19.

46. "World Food Crisis."

47. "World Food Crisis."

48. Concerns about the environmental impacts of the chemical insecticides and pesticides used in agriculture were popularized by Rachel Carson's book, *Silent Spring* (Boston: Houghton Mifflin, 1962). For a discussion of the origins of consumer trends in natural and organic food, see Harvey Levenstein, *Paradox of Plenty: A Social History of Eating in Modern America* (Berkeley: University of California Press, 2003), 160–177. See also Frances Moore Lappé, *Diet for a Small Planet* (New York: Ballantine, 1971); and Warren Belasco, *Appetite for Change: How the Counterculture Took on the Food Industry* (Ithaca, NY: Cornell University Press, 2007).

49. "World Food Crisis;" Shaw, *World Food Security*, 115; Heady and Fen, *Reflections on the Global Food Crisis*, 86–87.

50. Daniel Yergin and Joseph Stanislaw, *The Commanding Heights: The Battle between Government and the Marketplace That Is Remaking the Modern World* (New York: Simon and Schuster, 1999), 60–64; Roger Lowenstein, "The Nixon Shock," *BusinessWeek*, August 8, 2011, 1.

51. Richard Nixon, "Executive Order 11615—Providing for Stabilization of Prices, Rents, Wages, and Salaries," August 15, 1971. Gerhard Peters and John T. Woolley, *American Presidency Project*, website, accessed May 1, 2016, http://www.presidency.ucsb.edu/ws/?pid=60492.

52. "Raw Food Exempted from the Price Freeze," *New York Times*, August 18, 1971, 22.

53. "Severs Link between Dollar and Gold: A World Effect—Unilateral Move Means Others Face Parity Decisions," *New York Times*, August 16, 1971, 1.

54. The address did, however, force CBS to cancel *Comedy Playhouse*, so that the hour-long *Sonny and Cher Comedy Hour* could run in its entirety. "Talk Causes Networks Only Minor Difficulties," *New York Times*, August 16, 1971, 15.

55. Richard Nixon, "Address to the Nation Outlining a New Economic Policy: 'The Challenge of Peace,'" August 15, 1971, Gerhard Peters and John T. Woolley, *American Presidency Project*, website, accessed May 1, 2016, http://www.presidency.ucsb.edu/ws/?pid=3115.

56. "Pressure by Speculators Forced Action on Dollar," *New York Times*, August 16, 1971, 15; Heady and Fen, *Reflections on the Global Food Crisis*, 87; Yergin and Stanislaw, *Commanding Heights*; Lowenstein, "Nixon Shock," 1.

57. "The New Economic Policy," *New York Times*, August 17, 1971, 34.

58. D. G. Johnson, "World Agriculture, Commodity Policy and Price Variability," 823–828; Yergin and Stanislaw, *Commanding* Heights, 60–64; Lowenstein, "Nixon Shock," 1; Heady and Fen, *Reflections on the Global Food Crisis*, 87.

59. "Oil as an Arab Weapon," *New York Times*, October 18, 1971, 97.

60. "President Asks Congress for Energy-Crisis Action; Insists He'll Stay on the Job," *New York Times*, November 8, 1973; Richard Nixon, "Address to the Nation about Policies to Deal with the Energy Shortages," November 7, 1973, Gerhard Peters and John T. Woolley, *American Presidency Project*, website, accessed May 1, 2016, http://www.presidency.ucsb.edu/ws/?pid=4034; Richard Nixon, "Statement on Signing the Emergency Daylight Saving Time Energy Conservation Act of 1973," December 15, 1973, Gerhard Peters and John T. Woolley, *American Presidency Project*, website, accessed May 1, 2016, http://www.presidency.ucsb.edu/ws/?pid=4073; Richard Nixon, "Statement on Signing the Emergency Highway Energy Conservation Act," January 2, 1974, Gerhard Peters and John T. Woolley, *American Presidency Project*, website, accessed May 1, 2016, http://www.presidency.ucsb.edu/ws/?pid=4332.

61. "Arabs Term Their Oil Embargo More Severe Than Forseen," *New York Times*, November 5, 1973, 62; "The Oil Weapon," *New York Times*, November 6, 1973, 37; Heady and Fen, *Reflections on the Global Food Crisis*, 87.

62. "World Food Crisis."

63. Heady and Fen, *Reflections on the Global Food Crisis*, 87–88.

64. "Butz Hints U.S. Weighed Food Embargo on Arabs," *New York Times*, November 14, 1973.

65. "World Food Crisis"; Heady and Fen, *Reflections on the Global Food Crisis*, 88.

66. United Nations, *United Nations World Food Conference: Assessment of the World Food Situation, Present and Future* (New York: United Nations, 1974), 55.

67. *Malnutrition* is a set of concerns related to inadequate diets, in contrast to *undernutrition*, when a person does not receive adequate energy, typically measured in calories, from his or her diet to lead an active and healthy life. Malnutrition involves micronutrient deficiencies, that is, insufficient amounts of vitamins and minerals, a problem that is especially critical for women and children, as well as *overnutrition*, often discussed as overweight and obesity, which stems in part from diets that provide too many calories and is linked to such problems as type-2 diabetes

and heart disease. See Bryan McDonald, *Food Security* (Cambridge: Polity Press, 2010), 77–97.

68. United Nations, *United Nations World Food Conference*; Shaw, *World Food Security*, 118.

69. United Nations, *United Nations World Food Conference*; Shaw, *World Food Security*, 118–119.

70. Henry Kissinger, "A Just Consensus, A Stable Order, A Durable Peace," *Department of State Bulletin*, October 15, 1973, 469–473. See also *Foreign Relations of the United States, 1969–1976*, vol. E–14, part 1, *Documents on the United Nations, 1973–1976*, ed. William B. McAllister (Washington, DC: Government Printing Office, 2008), doc. 145, accessed on May 1, 2016, https://history.state.gov/historicaldocuments/frus1969-76ve14p1/d145.

71. Ruttan, "Politics of U.S. Food Aid Policy, 23–26; Shaw, *World Food Security*, 121–123.

72. Ruttan, "Politics of U.S. Food Aid Policy, 23–26; Shaw, *World Food Security*, 126–127. For more on the World Food Conference, see *Foreign Relations of the United States, 1969–1976*, vol. E–14, part 1, *Documents on the United Nations, 1973–1976*, ed. William B. McAllister (Washington, DC: Government Printing Office, 2008), docs. 128–164, accessed on May 1, 2016, https://history.state.gov/historicaldocuments/frus1969-76ve14p1/ch4.

73. United Nations, "Universal Declaration on the Eradication of Hunger and Malnutrition," adopted on November 16, 1974, by the World Food Conference convened under General Assembly resolution 3180 (XXVIII) of December 17, 1973; and endorsed by General Assembly resolution 3348 (XXIX) of December 17, 1974, accessed May 1, 2016, http://www.ohchr.org/EN/ProfessionalInterest/Pages/EradicationOfHungerAndMalnutrition.aspx.

74. Shaw, *World Food Security*, 139–149; Heady and Fen, *Reflections on the Global Food Crisis*, 92.

75. "World Food Crisis."

76. Congressional Research Service, *International Food Reserves: Background and Current Proposals* (Washington, DC: Government Printing Office, 1974); United Nations Food and Agriculture Organization, *Food Reserves Policies for World Food Security: A Consultant Study of Alternative Approaches* (Rome: United Nations Food and Agriculture Organization, 1975); D. G. Johnson, "World Agriculture, Commodity Policy and Price Variability," 827–828; Ruttan, "Politics of U.S. Food Aid Policy, 23–25. For an assessment of the problem faced by the United States in 1974, see Foreign Relations of the United States, 1969–1976, vol. XXXI, *Foreign Economic Policy, 1973–1976*, ed. Kathleen B. Rasmussen (Washington, DC: Government Printing Office, 2009), doc. 277, https://history.state.gov/historicaldocuments/frus1969-76v31/d277.

77. "Ford Urges Worldwide Food Reserve Program," *Beaver County Times*, September 19, 1974, 1.

78. Congressional Research Service, *International Food Reserves*, 18–19; *Foreign Relations of the United States*, 1969–1976, vol. XXXI, *Foreign Economic Policy, 1973–1976*, ed. Kathleen B. Rasmussen (Washington, DC: Government Printing

Office, 2009), doc. 262, accessed May 1, 2016, https://history.state.gov/historical-documents/frus1969-76v31.

79. Steve Wiggins and Sharada Keats, "Grain Stocks and Price Spikes," in *Grain Reserves and the Food Price Crisis: Selected Writings from 2008-2012*, ed. Ben Lilliston and Andrew Ranallo (Minneapolis, MN: Institute for Agriculture and Trade Policy, 2012), 21–23.

80. Sophia Murphy, "Grain Reserves: A Smart Climate Adaptation Policy," in *Grain Reserves and the Food Price Crisis: Selected Writings from 2008-2012*, ed. Ben Lilliston and Andrew Ranallo (Minneapolis, MN: Institute for Agriculture and Trade Policy, 2012), 17–19.

81. In his address to the World Food Conference, FAO Director-General Addeke Boerma drew an explicit connection between the world food problems in the 1940s and in the 1970s, see Shaw, *World Food Security*, 135.

82. Shaw, *World Food Security*, 155–158.

83. Kissinger, *Just Consensus*, 473.

84. "U.S. Food Power," *BusinessWeek*, December 15, 1975, 54–60; "Power in US Food Harvests," *The Guardian*, January 7, 1976, 2.

85. "Butz Hints U.S. Weighed Food Embargo on Arabs."

86. "U.S. Food Power."

87. "Iranian Food Embargo Has Support in Illinois," *The Pantagraph*, December 29, 1979, 11.

88. Ibid; Paul B. Thompson, "The Food Weapon and the Strategic Concept of Food Policy," in *The Ethics of Aid and Trade: U.S Food Policy, Foreign Competition and the Social Contract* (Cambridge: Cambridge University Press, 1992), 20–40.

89. Harriet Friedmann, "The Political Economy of Food: A Global Crisis," *New Left Review*, 197 (January–February 1993): 31.

CONCLUSION

1. On transnational threats, see Richard A. Matthew and George E. Shambaugh, "Sex, Drugs and Heavy Metal: Transnational Threats and National Vulnerabilities," *Security Dialogue* 29, no. 22 (1998): 163–175.

2. David Ekbladh, "Present at the Creation: Edward Mead Earle and the Depression-Era Origins of Security Studies," *International Security* 36, no. 3 (Winter 2011/12): 107–141. On the establishment of the Department of Defense and the postwar American national security apparatus, see Douglas T. Stuart, *Creating the National Security State: A History of the Law that Transformed America* (Princeton, NJ: Princeton University Press, 2008).

3. Edward Mead Earle, "American Military Policy and National Security," *Political Science Quarterly* 53, no. 1 (March 1938), 1–13.

4. On soft power, see Joseph Nye, *Bound to Lead: The Changing Nature of American Power* (New York: Basic, 1990).

5. For a discussion on the role of core American values on foreign policy, see Anne-Marie Slaughter, *The Idea That Is America: Keeping Faith with Our Values in a Dangerous World* (New York: Basic, 2007).

6. Dan Charles, "A Political War Brews over 'Food for Peace' Aid Program," National Public Radio, April 4, 2013, accessed May 1, 2016, http://www.npr.org/sections/thesalt/2013/04/04/176154775/a-political-war-brews-over-food-for-peace-aid-program. For an overview of recent changes to American food-aid programs, see Congressional Research Service, *U.S. International Food Aid Programs: Background and Issues*, by Randy Schnepf, April 1, 2015, accessed May 1, 2016, https://www.fas.org/sgp/crs/misc/R41072.pdf.
7. US Government, *Feed the Future Guide*, May 2010, accessed May 1, 2016, http://feedthefuture.gov/sites/default/files/resource/files/FTF_Guide.pdf.
8. "U.S. Food Power: Ultimate Weapon in World Politics," *BusinessWeek*, December 15, 1975, 54–60.
9. For an excellent discussion of efforts to apply industrial ideals to agricultural production, see Deborah Kay Fitzgerald, *Every Farm a Factory: The Industrial Ideal in American Agriculture* (New Haven, CT: Yale University Press, 2003).
10. Derek Heady and Shenggen Fen, *Reflections on the Global Food Crisis: How Did It Happen? How Has It Hurt? And How Can We Prevent the Next One?* (Washington, DC: International Food Policy Research Institute, 2010).
11. On the history of forecasting, see Matthew Connelly, Matt Fay, Giulia Ferrini, Micki Kaufman, Will Leonard, Harrison Monsky, Ryan Musto, Taunton Paine, Nicholas Standish, and Lydia Walker, "'General, I Have Fought Just as Many Nuclear Wars as You Have': Forecasts, Future Scenarios, and the Politics of Armageddon," *American Historical Review* 117, no. 5 (2012): 1431–1460. For forecasts of the possible impacts of climate change on agriculture and food production, see IPCC, *Climate Change 2014: Impacts, Adaptation, and Vulnerability*, part A: Global and Sectoral Aspects. Contribution of Working Group II to the Fifth Assessment Report of the Intergovernmental Panel on Climate Change [Field, C. B., V. R. Barros, D. J. Dokken, K. J. Mach, M. D. Mastrandrea, T. E. Bilir, M. Chatterjee, K. L. Ebi, Y. O. Estrada, R. C. Genova, B. Girma, E. S. Kissel, A. N. Levy, S. MacCracken, P. R. Mastrandrea, and L. L.White (eds.)] (New York: Cambridge University Press, 2014); Risky Business Project, *Risky Business: The Economic Risks of Climate Change in the United States*, June 2014, accessed May 1, 2016, http://riskybusiness.org/index.php?p=reports/national-report/executive-summary; Jerry M. Melillo, Terese Richmond and Gary W. Yohe, eds., *Climate Change Impacts in the United States: The Third National Climate Assessment* (Washington, DC: Government Printing Office, 2014). For a discussion of the difficulty of establishing causal links between climate change, food, and conflict and insecurity, see "Global Warming Linked to Syrian Refugee Crisis," *Living on Earth*, September 11, 2015, accessed May 1, 2016, http://loe.org/shows/segments.html?programID=15-P13-00037andsegmentID=3.
12. Ben Lilliston and Andrew Ranallo, eds., *Grain Reserves and the Food Price Crisis: Selected Writings from 2008-2012* (Minneapolis, MN: Institute for Agriculture and Trade Policy, 2012).
13. Rod O'Conner, "These Suburban Preppers Are Ready for Anything," *Chicago*, April 27, 2015, accessed May 1, 2016, http://www.chicagomag.com/Chicago-Magazine/May-2015/Suburban-Survivalists/.
14. Ready.gov. "Build a Kit," accessed May 1, 2016, http://www.ready.gov/.

15. Emmy Simmons, *Harvesting Peace: Food Security, Conflict, and Cooperation* (Washington, DC: Woodrow Wilson International Center for Scholars, 2013).

16. Paul Thompson makes a similar point about the value of understanding concepts such as sustainability as contested concepts that resist permanent definition. See Paul Thompson, "Agricultural Sustainability: What It Is and What It Is Not," *International Journal of Agricultural Sustainability* 5, no. 1 (2007): 5–16.

shelters, bomb or fallout, 5, 13;
community, 107, 117, 121, 129;
Eisenhower administration's policies
on, 108–109, 111–112, 115; enthusiasm
wanes for, 14; family or private,
105–107, 109, 112–117, 119–120, 122;
food stored in (*see* shelter provisioning);
government, 106, 111, 223n25;
government advice about, 107, 112–113,
122; Kennedy administration's policies
on, 113; length of time in, 109, 115, 120,
124; other uses for, 106, 114; reluctance
to build, 106, 129; responsibility for,
106–109, 111, 114, 129
Soil Bank, 92–95. *See also* acreage reserve
programs
sorghum, 52, 138, 168
Soviet Union, 20, 36, 45–46, 51–52, 143,
161, 186–187; agriculture in, 100,
133, 136, 148–150, 166–167, 180, 193,
203n4; American National Exhibition
in, 48–49; civil defense in, 110–111;
containment of influence of, 5, 12–13,
45–46, 158, 190; Eastern European
countries and, 35, 38–39, 42, 44, 100,
150; food or grain sales to, 6, 14, 97,
100, 135, 136, 150–151, 164–172, 175,
189, 192, 193; in global food network,
189, 191; India and, 171, 193; as nuclear
power, 46, 73, 107–108, 150
Stalin, Joseph, 38, 46, 187
standards of living, 2, 4, 52, 142, 148, 175
statistics: on agricultural production, 50,
139, 155, 156, 158, 163, 181; on farm
income, 133; on food consumption,
54–56, 158; on food costs, 1, 50, 51,
53, 169, 170; on food exports, 44; on
food stamps, 140–141; Gallup polls, 26,
39–40, 129; on hunger, malnutrition,
etc., 25, 162, 182; on imported food
in US, 7; on Marshall Plan, 12, 39–40;
on military vs. civilian diet, 26–27; on
postwar Europe, 31, 32, 43; on shelters,
129; on Victory Gardens, 26; on wheat
production, 23, 42, 44, 50

Stevenson, Adlai, 83, 85
sugar, 1, 25, 27–28, 33, 98, 148
supply management, 76, 133, 135–137, 146
surpluses, 33, 50, 52, 174; Benson on,
76–77, 85, 87, 89–90, 92, 95, 102, 104;
Canada, Australia, and/or Argentina
as source of, 4–5, 23; elimination or
reduction of, 6, 13–15, 77, 80–81, 89,
91–92, 94–95, 100–101, 102, 104, 128,
135, 138–139, 152, 161–164, 166, 171,
173, 184–185; food aid's use of, 44–46,
89, 91, 96–102, 104, 133, 135, 139,
141–148, 152, 161, 163; food power's use
of, 2, 4, 45–46, 85, 180; food system and,
29, 49, 161, 163, 190, 193–194; Kennedy
on, 132–133, 135, 138, 143, 146, 147,
151; Nixon on, 132–133; policymakers
on (*see under* policymakers); as problem
or opportunity, 2, 14, 72, 151, 160, 181,
190; Soil Bank and, 94–95; storage of,
2, 5, 13, 50, 81, 83–84, 90, 95, 97–98,
101, 133, 138–139, 147, 163–164, 166,
196; strategic or foreign policy uses of,
21–22, 45, 89, 96–97, 132, 135, 145, 146,
151–152, 190. *See also* corn; meat;
wheat
sustainability, 7, 103, 164, 241n16

tobacco, 42, 80, 94
transportation, 9–10, 21, 23, 31, 54, 57,
158, 164, 169, 179, 192; in US-only
vessels, 97–98, 150, 165, 168
Truman Doctrine, 20, 36, 38, 208n68
Truman, Harry S., 36, 44, 77, 154, 208n67;
administration or advisers of, 33, 39,
42, 75, 78, 80–81, 115, 145, 157–158;
agricultural or farm policies of, 75,
80–83, 85; Economic Cooperation Act
(ECA) and, 42; Marshall Plan or postwar
food crisis and, 28, 33, 42, 45, 158
Turkey, 20, 36, 158

Union of Soviet Socialist Republics. *See*
Soviet Union
United Kingdom, 6, 178